Gift of

MPL Star & Tribune

April 1977

His Majesty the American

His Majesty the American

The Cinema of Douglas Fairbanks, Sr.

by
John C. Tibbetts
James M. Welsh

South Brunswick and New York: A. S. Barnes and Company
London:Thomas Yoseloff Ltd

A. S. Barnes and Co., Inc.
Cranbury, New Jersey 08512

Thomas Yoseloff Ltd
Magdalen House
136-148 Tooley Street
London SE1 2TT, England

Library of Congress Cataloging in Publication Data

Tibbetts, John C 1946-
His majesty the American.

Bibliography: p.
Includes index.
1. Fairbanks, Douglas, 1883-1939. I. Welsh,
James M., joint author. II. Title.
PN2287.F3T5   1976   791.43′028′0924 [B]   75-20606
ISBN 0-498-01607-2

PN
2287
F3
T5
1977

PRINTED IN THE UNITED STATES OF AMERICA

Contents

Acknowledgments 7

Introduction: Shadows from the Past 9

PART I: *Early Works*

1 Fairbanks Comes to Hollywood 19
2 Gamboling First Steps: *The Lamb* and *Double Trouble* 28
3 Gymnastic Evangelist and *The Habit of Happiness* 37
4 The Social Climber 53
5 Elastic Soil—Fairbanks and the Western Tradition 63
6 The Satire of Anita Loos and Douglas Fairbanks 83
7 The Founding of United Artists 102
8 On an Odd Note—*The Nut* and *When the Clouds Roll By* 110

PART II: *The Costume Films and Beyond*

9   *Zorro* and *Don Q:* The Mark of Greatness 119
10 *Robin Hood:* A Dance of Free Men in a Forest 132
11 Architecture in Motion: *The Thief of Bagdad* 139
12 A Painted Ship on a Painted Ocean: *The Black Pirate* 145
13 The Fall from Grace in *The Gaucho:* Douglas Fairbanks and the Byronic Hero 155
14 *The Three Musketeers* and *The Iron Mask:* Farewell to All That! 163
15 Love and Marriage: *The Taming of the Shrew* 175
16 Turning the Corner: The Final Bow 185

Epilogue 207
Appendix: A Fairbanks Filmography 210
Postscript on Available Prints of the Fairbanks Films 216
Bibliography 217
Index 219

Acknowledgments

The authors are especially grateful for the assistance, cooperation, and encouragement that a number of people gave us. We particularly wish to thank Mary Corliss, *Stills Archivist* at the Museum of Modern Art in New York, who was very helpful in selecting the stills that accompany our text. Thanks, also, in this regard to Patrick Montgomery of Killiam Shows, Inc., and to Herman Weinberg for his advice. Several film archivists gave us full cooperation in enabling us to see a number of the rare early films, in particular, William K. Everson of New York University, Patrick Sheehan of the Film Division at the Library of Congress, Robert R. Gitt and Anthony Slide of the American Film Institute in Washington, and Don Malkames of Tuckahoo, New York, a former Hollywood cameraman, for showing original tinted nitrate prints of some of the early works. All of these people generously donated their time to arrange screenings. Without their aid, the book could not have been adequately researched.

We are grateful to Douglas Fairbanks, Jr. for sharing his observations about his father's last projects. Matty Kemp of the Mary Pickford Company was helpful in providing information about the sound version of *The Taming of the Shrew,* as was Robert Hamilton Ball, Professor Emeritus of Queens College of the City University of New York. Our chapter concerning *The Taming of the Shrew* first appeared in *English Journal* and is reprinted by permission of the National Council of Teachers of English, Copyright © 1973. Steven Kramer's translation of the Jean Epstein poem first appeared in *Literature/Film Quarterly* and is reprinted here by permission of the editors. Finally, we wish to thank Richard Dyer MacCann, formerly of the University of Kansas and presently at the University of Iowa, for his interest, advice, and encouragement.

Introduction: Shadows from the Past

Natural exuberance, unlimited energy, a seemingly naive faith in those old American values that seem to have all but evaporated over the last half-century—these were the qualities that defined his character and sustained his popularity as one of the first-rate motion-picture personalities of his era. Douglas Fairbanks was everyman's hero, undaunted by precipitous feats and perilous foes alike, always ready to laugh in the face of danger. He reveled in his super-flamboyant style, yet always retained a mock-ironic stance, demonstrating that he certainly understood the excesses of his screen *persona.*

In September of 1974, for the first time in this country a major retrospective was launched by the American Film Institute in Washington, D.C., to honor the accomplishments of his career. *The Black Pirate,* directed by Albert Parker in 1926, opened this retrospective, playing to a full house of thirteen hundred enthusiastic people in the Eisenhower Theater in the Kennedy Center. Arthur Kleiner, perhaps the foremost authority on the music of the "silent" cinema, came to Washington from Minnesota to play the accompaniment. Douglas Fairbanks, Jr., the famous son of the famous father, was also there to make introductory comments about his father's career. The sophisticated Washington audience was charmed and tremendously pleased by the film. The notion that is facetiously expressed by Gilbert and Sullivan in *The Pirates of Penzance,* Fairbanks knew all along: "it is, *it is* a glorious thing to be a pirate king!"

The silent films of Douglas Fairbanks hold up remarkably well, and these, of course, far outnumber the few sound films produced at the latter end of his career. As Fairbanks, Jr. remarked at the opening of the AFI Retrospective, his father and Charlie Chaplin, "who had been his close partner and friend from the start, both felt . . . that the silent screen was their proper medium. They could express themselves in mime and tell the story in action, a purely visual medium. . . . They told their story in movement and in visual effect."

The trick was to translate raw energy and imagination into action, and few screen actors have done so better. Fairbanks, Jr. stated that his father did all of his own stuntwork; in fact, he did most of it, even though, as is not commonly known, he was afraid of heights. In *The Black Pirate,* for example, we see him perform almost impossible feats of derring-do, capturing a merchantman singlehandedly, taking the wind out of its sails by sliding down each one of them on his knife,* fencing off an entire pirate crew, and, finally, rescuing a virginal princess from a fate, presumably (in those days, at least), worse than death. His features are dominated by an almost constant, sunny smile, regardless of the odds against him. Such supreme confidence cannot be vanquished.

---

* According to William K. Everson (*Films in Review,* Oct. 1955, p. 398), this stunt was not performed by Fairbanks himself, but by Richard Talmadge, a member of the Metzetti Brothers acrobatic team.

The character develops: Doug in an exotic dilemma in
Bound in Morocco *(1918) cannot be upset.*

*Doug translates raw energy into action in the pre-costume
period.*

Surprisingly enough, relatively little has been written about Douglas Fairbanks, Sr. This is not to say that Doug was not appreciated by his own generation. He was, and was rewarded by it as well. In his own time he was noticed, analyzed and celebrated by Vachel Lindsay in this country, and by Jean Epstein and René Clair—among others—abroad. As his book, *Cinema, Yesterday and Today*, makes clear, René Clair had a special fondness for both Charlie Chaplin and Douglas Fairbanks, and it is no accident that the bridegroom of Clair's farcical masterpiece, *The Italian Straw Hat* (made in 1927, when Fairbanks was at the peak of his career), looks—and often moves—like the Fairbanks of the early comedies. In this case, one suspects that the man who invented the *auteur* concept was paying *hommage* to an American actor whose work he admired. Fairbanks surely had helped Clair to see delight!

Fairbanks' importance to Hollywood during the years spanning 1915 to 1934 can hardly be underestimated. On all levels his activities in the movie industry were influential. Not only was he one of the top-ranking stars for almost twenty years, but his influence upon the business and artistic aspects of moviemaking was considerable. To date, there has been only one biography that pretends to be all-inclusive—Ralph Hancock's *Douglas Fairbanks: The Fourth Musketeer*. Other pertinent works include Alistair Cooke's *Douglas Fairbanks: The Making of a Screen Character*, Richard Schickel's *His Picture in the Papers*, and Brian Connell's biography of Douglas, Jr., *Knight Errant*.

The Hancock book is more concerned with Fairbanks' personal life than with his screen work. Consequently, it is a mine of anecdotes and incidental information of a personal nature. Its drawbacks stem from an excessive use of dialogue, as if the author were somehow present with a tape recorder at crucial moments in Fairbanks' career, something scarcely creditable as an authoritative technique. It is also regrettably cursory in its treatment of the films. Its chief value would seem to be its opening and closing chapters, which deal in some detail with Fairbanks' early and late years. Particularly, the research involving Fairbanks' stage work before coming to Hollywood is of great value.

Alistair Cooke's *Douglas Fairbanks: The Making of a Screen Character* was the first and is still the best attempt to discuss Fairbanks' work in a sociocultural context. Any subsequent book that attempts to develop this kind of approach will necessarily owe a great debt to it. Cooke dealt most perceptively with the pre-1920 films; his delineation of the "popular philosopher" and "gymnastic evangelist" aspects of the Fairbanks personality at this time are further considered in our book.

The most recent reconsideration of Douglas Fairbanks is presented in Richard Schickel's *His Picture in the Papers*. Schickel's main concern is suggested by his subtitle: "A Speculation on Celebrity in America, Based on the Life of Douglas Fairbanks, Sr." This book contributes nothing towards any kind of fresh evaluation of the films themselves; moreover, it reveals little about Fairbanks' personality that had not already been revealed by the work of Cooke and Hancock. What it does do is to place Fairbanks within a kind of social context, and to examine his function as a public figure.

Brian Connell's biography of Douglas, Jr., *Knight Errant*, contains many fascinating glimpses of Douglas, Sr.'s last years, providing insights into the strained relationship Fairbanks had with his son. Again, the emphasis is not upon the films, but upon the man's personal life.

Obviously, there is a great gap in scholarship as far as the films themselves are concerned. It is the purpose of this book to concentrate upon these films, some forty-three works spanning the years 1915 to 1934. One of the interesting distinctions of Fairbanks' career is that his screen personality and his personal life are very closely linked. An attempt to delve into the one will inevitably lead to a revelation of the other. Thus, this book attempts to do more than list the casts and credits of the films; it seeks to trace the emerging Fairbanks personality as reflected in his screen work. It is a biography reflected through cinema, as the artist is revealed through his work. The foregoing biographies cited above certainly have value, but we believe it is now time to look back to the films themselves. To do so, we shall have to attempt a long jump from our own context back to the boom-town years of Hollywood in 1915. But, then, no one could hope to keep up with Fairbanks unless he were willing to stretch his legs, and, perhaps, his imagination.

First, however, the years before 1915 need to be summarized. Douglas Fairbanks' youth was marked early by the various dichotomies that would affect all of his subsequent screen work. Although he grew up in the goldfields of Denver, Colorado, he yearned for the society and legitimacy of the East, particularly New York. If he inherited an almost irresponsible restlessness from his father, his father also provided his first exposure to Shakespeare and to the glamor of the stage. From his mother he learned the values and

The mature Fairbanks, as he appeared out of costume at the peak of his career.

distinctions of society and the importance of money.

He came with a kick into the world on 23 May 1883. He was born into the boom-town milieu of Denver, Colorado, an appropriate beginning for one who was later to thrive in the boom-town milieu of Hollywood, California. Lured by the recent gold and silver strikes, Ella Fairbanks Ulman and her husband, the prominent New York attorney H. Charles Ulman, set up housekeeping and cast about for their fortune. Douglas was the last of three children: Robert was born a year earlier; Jack came from Ella's first marriage with John Fairbanks some years before.

The Ulmans grew up in a world of primitive conditions. Doug's father invested heavily in a series of mining operations and much of the time was spent by the family in the rough mining camps. When Doug was five years old, something happened that would profoundly affect the rest of his life—the desertion of the family by his father. Apparently, there has never been an adequate explanation for the desertion. But its legacy for Douglas was to be a yearning drive toward social acceptance and legitimacy that would increase in its intensity in later years. At any rate, Ella obtained a divorce on the grounds of desertion and resumed the name of Fairbanks. The fragmented family moved and began taking in boarders.

Doug, however, had a more positive legacy from his father—a sensitivity towards the theater. Charles Ulman had been acquainted with Edwin Booth and has been considered an ardent Shakespearean scholar. After Ulman's desertion, Ella continued to take the boys to the theater, and soon Doug was expressing an avid interest in theatrical matters. When he was sixteen, he met the itinerant Shakespearean actor Frederick Warde on one of his tours through Denver. From that moment Doug's attention was focused upon the bright lights of Broadway, and he chafed at having to remain in the goldfields of Denver. Finally, in 1900 he and his mother moved to New York.

Fairbanks' Broadway career was marked by a singularly erratic course. By the time he was, at last, a "name" juvenile lead in 1914, he had experienced quite a number of ups and downs, all marked by that great restlessness that was to remain with him throughout his life. He went from bit parts in Frederick Warde's company to the lead roles in plays like *He Comes Up Smiling* and *The Show Shop*. Not all of these years were spent on the stage. For a scant few months he was enrolled at Harvard. Later, he embarked on

Doug in a moment of restlessness, about to demonstrate "gymnastic calisthenics" on board an ocean liner in Reaching for the Moon.

the first of his extensive travels abroad—in this case, to Europe via cattleboat. He even was a stockbroker for a time.

During one of his sporadic returns to the stage he met Beth Sully, daughter of the wealthy businessman Daniel J. "Cotton King" Sully. His **marriage to Beth Sully in 1907** may have indirectly contributed to many of the plots of his later films. The marriage was sanctioned, it has been claimed, only on the condition that Doug give up the stage and set himself up in a business given him by his father-in-law. Consequently, Doug found himself chained to a desk at the Buchan Soap Corporation. There can be no doubt that this marriage brought the socially conscious Doug advantageous introductions into the world of society and money. It was only the first of many moves that would demonstrate his striving ever harder for recognition in social circles.

13

Fortunately for Doug, the business failed, and he was soon back on Broadway—a success by the year 1914. When Douglas, Jr. was born in 1909, it seemed that a family and a future were solid and assured. But one thing would disrupt the rosy picture of a comfortable future, the very thing that would mark the only constant in his life. It ushers us into this book and will mark its conclusion as well.

He was restless.

His Majesty the American

Agile
like the baton of a conductor over an ocean
    of flats
The windows are the only doors
and the gutters
tender paths to take his betrothed for a walk

the roofs converge
horses tumble
and in the frenzy of a film
where one earns $200,000 by laughing
and making a joke of blows
the villain spends a pretty nasty quarter hour

Resuscitate
the heavy dust of nuggets
among the wind of fine mirages
the female curve of a beach
Nymphs! the automobile barque
carries your civilized laughs
A burnous
A palm tree
sand
The motorcycle bursts the desert like a paper
    hoop
Camels stand aside because a horn belches

and suddenly
a smile bursts
yawns sweetly
winks and twinkles
under the light of 15 arc lamps which violate
    a face.

Douglas Fairbanks

—Jean Epstein*

* Originally published in Jean Epstein's *Cinéma* (Paris: Editions de la Sirène, 1921), pp. 88–89. Translated by Steven Philip Kramer.

Part I: *Early Works*

The Popular Philosopher

1
Fairbanks Comes to Hollywood

In the autumn of 1914 Adam Kessel and Charlie Bauman approached Douglas Fairbanks in the Knickerbocker Hotel in New York to sign a contract to make films for Triangle Film Corporation. He was only one of many such stars eagerly sought out by Triangle. By this time, Fairbanks' position as one of Broadway's brightest light talents was secure. His last three plays, in particular, were singled out by the critics and public as worthy successes. In 1913 he had traveled extensively with *The New Henrietta*. In 1914 he appeared in what many believe to have been his best Broadway play, *He Comes Up Smiling*, wherein he played a young vagabond attempting to escape a stuffy and monotonous rut and find adventure. On New Year's Eve, 1914, he opened in James Forbes' *The Show Shop,* a comedy satirizing theatrical conventions. It, too, was a resounding success; it was also his last Broadway appearance. He had made his decision by then. He would go to Hollywood to make movies.

Fairbanks represents the stage in several ways in 1915. For one thing, he was riding high on a crest of success; the theater, too, seemed for 1914–1915 to be enjoying prosperity: "More brilliant names starred in more outstanding roles than ever before and no other season in the history of the theater equaled its popularity . . ."[1] The motion picture spelled a turning point,

wherein the challenge of great sums of money and increased public exposure both threatened the stage star's "legitimate" status and lured them to the movies. Fairbanks shared the theater's disdain for the "galloping tintypes," as movies were called. It was a form of snobbishness, however, that could not withstand the monetary lures that the movies held out to him.

While he was making his decision to come to Hollywood, the entertainment scene saw a beleaguered Broadway and a burgeoning and awkward film industry. For film, at least, the pot seemed to be either boiling or going dry. The clumsy bulk of the movies and more elegant body of the stage grunted and scrabbled about, turning handsprings past the open doorways of public acceptance. Christmas Eve of that year was likely to see either of them springing from the sooty fireplaces of that public. The success of either was a valuable commodity; the potency of the fission of the star-system was spreading fallout; New Vanity Fair was hauling up and tearing down its silken tents.

And Fairbanks stood within it all, palms itching like those of the Thief of Bagdad in the bazaars. Certainly he had precedents for whatever decision he made. If he opted to go to the movies he had only to remember how John Barrymore let Daniel Frohman present him in Famous Players'

19

From stage to screen: Doug is shown here in a scene from
Say! Young Fellow *(1918).*

American Citizen; how Ethel Barrymore was paid $10,000 by All Star Film Corporation to appear in a film version of her *Captain Jinks of the Horse Marines;* that Elsie Janis and Cyril Maude each had made feature films; that films had made a greater star of Mary Pickford than she had been on the stage.

On the other hand, he was aware of the objections to such a move. By 1915 the theater's General Booking Office had become alarmed at the proportion of stage stars "defecting" to the movies. They warned high-salaried actors—especially in vaudeville—to ignore the movies' siren song, lest their celluloid performances depreciate their value as live stage performers. They pointed out the undeniable fact that a star like Elsie Janis found herself playing against her own shadows on the screen.[2] The film colony itself balked against this trend in importing stage stars. Many of the film stars bristled at the humiliation of appearing in their own medium playing second fiddle to a stage star. Francis X. Bushman and Lottie Briscoe quit the screen in 1915 for this very reason. The film, after all, was a different medium from the stage. It called for a great deal of adjustment. It required a more subtle range of gestures as opposed to the broad vocabulary of movements the stage star was used to. And what if the stage star failed to conform to these new demands? Among legitimate producers Charles Frohman put a clause in all his contracts to the effect that there would be no welcome for any stage actor returning to the stage after experience before the cameras.[3]

As for Fairbanks, he had already considered leaving the stage at least once before. It is a little-known fact that in 1911 *Variety* reported he was getting ready to leave the legitimate stage—but not for the movies. He was asking $2,000 a week for his debut in vaudeville. A move to vaudeville was only a shade better than a move to the movies—representing still another threat to the legitimate stage. Still, his decision to come to Hollywood must have revealed some insight into the greater glories available to him there. Certainly the movies were not in the crude state that the legitimate stage supposed them to be in. In many ways like a boom-town, Hollywood was nevertheless a going *business* territory; its celluloid product, at least in the hands of people like Griffith, was far from crude.

Money, of course, was a decisive factor. Harry E. Aitken, Kessel and Bauman, first approached him in 1914 with an offer of two thousand a week for Triangle. At that time Fairbanks was receiving a salary in proportion to the success and length of run of his current play. Frank Case, the owner of the Algonquin Hotel, advised him that two thousand dollars was considerably more than he could possibly hope to earn in the theater. Moreover, the employment and salary would probably be for fifty-two weeks a year, not for the indefinite season customary in the theater and vaudeville.

Actually, Fairbanks' proposed salary was one of the smaller of those proposed to a great number of stage stars. Many of these other offers seem so large that they might be set down as the fevered imaginings of press agents. Sir Herbert Beerbohm Tree, for instance, made $100,000 in six months! Benjamin Hampton reports that

> [These] actors, accustomed to receiving $250 to $500 a week on the stage for thirty or forty weeks a year when their plays were successful and much less . . . when unsuccessful, were so fearful that screen appearance would injure their stage prestige that Aitken had had to double, treble, and quadruple their salaries and give them contracts for a year or more.[4]

It was the Triangle way, and the stage stars came to heel in droves.

Fairbanks was by no means unexposed to the possibilities of the movie. For instance, when Griffith's *Birth of a Nation* opened in New York in April of 1915, Fairbanks was invited to attend. That viewing confirmed some of his earlier impressions of the moving picture:

> Oftimes the question of "why I deserted the

speaking stage for the films" had been hurled at me. Because of the possibilities and the outdoor life. Three years ago when I played with W. H. Crane in *The New Henrietta* we often spent our time between shows seeking vivid melodramatic pictures, especially Western subjects. We were amused by the primitive emotions and active life in the west . . .[5]

He noted at the time that an actor's process of elimination rather than elaboration is of paramount importance in the movies. This allows for greater range of expression. An actor's scope is unlimited in the film profession and offered more dramatic opportunities than the theater. He goes on:

> . . . almost everyone at the Lamb's Club talked of nothing but the wonderful Griffith production, *Birth of a Nation*. My curiosity was naturally aroused and I attended a matinee. I was dumbfounded after sitting through three hours of motion pictures at the strides made since the ordinary melodramatic days.[6]

Fairbanks' biographer, Ralph Hancock, recalls a more high-flown reaction, crediting Douglas with the vision of a seer in imagining the great potential in movies. He states:

> Nothing in the field of entertainment had ever stirred his emotions quite so much. Profoundly moved by the great story itself, he was even more impressed by the apparently unlimited possibilities of motion picture photography . . . He returned again and again to view the picture and left the theater each time more enthusiastic than the time before.[7]

This sounds both elevated and admirable but it should be noted that one of the great myths surrounding Fairbanks is that he was not a businessman. Nothing could be further from the truth. He was sharp and had plenty of business acumen and would soon prove it. But if an outfit like Triangle Film Corporation could command and hold a two dollar admission price (a fact that will be noted at length later), it could command his attention as well. This last phenomenon must have seemed to him like the pot of gold at the end of the rainbow.

The motion picture in 1915 was the necessary arena of expansion for the restless, fast-moving Fairbanks. In the grill of the Knickerbocker Hotel in New York he signed a contract to make films for Triangle Film Corporation.

He joined the great number of Broadway stars

bound for Hollywood, many of them to Triangle. With him were Sir Herbert Beerbohm Tree, Weber and Fields, DeWolf Hopper, Billie Burke, Texas Guinan, Dustin Farnum, Raymond Hitchcock, William Desmond—nearly sixty in all. Of this stellar list of Broadway stars only a handful secured any kind of lasting screen success. One was Marie Dressler; another, William S. Hart. But Dressler's fame was already at its height before she ever got to pictures; Hart had arrived at Ince's studios a full year earlier than any of the aforementioned stars. It was Fairbanks, and Fairbanks only, that achieved the greatest success *after* coming to Hollywood in 1915.

Doug caught in a rare pensive moment: His initial reception was not warm.

Doug and his brother, Jack, who served as treasurer of the Douglas Fairbanks Pictures Corporation.

Fairbanks' initial reception in Hollywood at the Fine Arts studios reveals many things typical of the Broadway star in the film colony. His confrontation with D. W. Griffith is revelatory of the personalities and aims of both.

Fine Arts (and the other two Triangle studios as well) stood in the tradition of a newer, more intimate kind of filmmaking. Griffith had brought his studio closer to a prestigious reputation than any other studio had hitherto enjoyed. An increased literacy had been achieved in the Majestic-Reliance/Fine Arts product through adaptations of classic works and the incorporation of effective and pungent subtitles. More efficient systems of scenario and studio production were an effective factor in the movies' drive for commercial success.

Fairbanks' reception in the middle of all this was, according to all reports, a cold one. Considering the mood at Fine Arts, this is not in the least surprising. This reception had to do in part with the man's personality. The Fairbanks manner was expansive and rambunctious. The character of the man remains even today somewhat unique. He had a quick, swaggering way of meeting people, dodging about them while he spoke in a slightly high-pitched voice so fast as to be sometimes almost inarticulate, with a tendency to lisping, born of carelessness.*

Moreover, Fairbanks' personal manner was punctuated with a very physical emphasis. He was a restless person, constantly in motion, constantly active. Biographer Ralph Hancock points this up in describing the months just prior to Fairbanks' decision to come to Hollywood:

> That old affliction restlessness was acting up again. For several years now he had stuck to the grind, applied himself conscientiously to his work, and kept his restlessness under wraps. Frequent visits to the gymnasium in the neighborhood of Times Square had helped him to work off some of his surplus energy, but for several months now he had been yearning for new worlds to conquer.[8]

Fairbanks was forever in motion, like a clock.

---

* For those curious about the natural manner of the man we recommend two films near the end of his career: *Reaching for the Moon* and *Around the World in 80 Minutes*. The opening scene in the first: the camera dollies in with Fairbanks as he enters a business meeting. "Bring me some cornflakes and milk—warm," he shouts in a voice a bit hoarse and strident. He munches away and talks about six things at once to six different people, like a machine gun spitting out round after round. "One must impede this explosive urge," says a stuffed-shirt, leaving indignantly. In *Around the World* he talks and jokes with his camera in the same way, most likely, that he would have done in 1915 with his camera crew. The effect, if the viewer is not sufficiently prepared, is rather appalling.

Even standing still he positively ticked and pulsed with energy. This was not a quality unique to just his films. It was not unique for him at all. On stage, screen, or off he was continually like an engine in motion. In a way, he was the living embodiment of the principle of the persistence of vision, that physical phenomenon upon which the motion picture is based. If frames of film pass through the projector gate at fewer than twelve frames per second, the viewer is conscious of a kind of *flickering* movement, that is, the frames of film flicking past the eyes. Watch a perfectly stationary object on the screen at about twelve frames per second and it fairly quivers with movement. Fairbanks was like this—even when relatively motionless, he seemed to twitch and yearn toward movement. Additionally, the range of his moods was eccentric, to say the least, and often the polar moods of the classic manic-depressive held sway in rapid succession. He could throw himself into a depression just as actively as he could throw himself over a high wall in one of his films.

This quality of movement in the man could and would be infectious to others. He could get people to follow him in rounds of physical activity who otherwise would not consider walking around the block. Numerous occasions would find European royalty meekly, and sometimes enthusiastically, following Fairbanks through his physical appointments while visiting his home at Pickfair. But in 1915 the reaction he had on the film colony was at first a largely negative one. Griffith, for one, was not pleased with his new star's athletic tendencies:

> Fairbanks seemed to have a notion that in a motion picture one had to keep eternally in motion, and he frequently jumped the fence or climbed a church at unexpected moments not prescribed by the script. Griffith advised him to go into Keystone comedies.[9]

Parenthetically, that Griffith's judgment was a hasty one is clearly borne out in that highly interesting, but disastrous attempt at Keystone farce that Fairbanks made in 1916, *The Mystery of the Leaping Fish*. Nor was Griffith pleased at Fairbanks' sometimes ebullient sense of humor:

> While he [Fairbanks] recognized Griffith as a great artist, he always preferred greatness tempered with humor. He found it difficult to adjust himself to this pioneer movie visionary in whose august presence everyone spoke in hushed and awed tones, and it was impossible for him to work without an outlet for laughs and practical jokes. He got off on the wrong

foot with D. W. on their first encounter.[10]

Griffith's confrontation with Fairbanks probably amounted to trying to catch quicksilver in a sieve. Sure, Griffith could pour action across the screen in great cataracts, yet, his greatness lay in focussing the action in the big scenes upon the little details. He was engrossed with the apparently limitless range of the camera and its power to delay the tempo of conventional acting and to focus casual facial expressions into meaningful detail. Moreover, a real sense of humor is relatively rare in Griffith. When it appears in the rustic comedy scenes of *Way Down East,* for instance, it seems forced. Obsessed with inner action and development of cinematic grammar, he perhaps could be likened to a kind of cinematic Henry James, whose humor was only occasionally gratifying. As will be seen, it was left to others like Frank Woods and Harry Aitken to assess accurately Fairbanks' potential before the camera.

But there was more to Fairbanks' reception than just a personality and aesthetic clash with D. W. Griffith. 1915 Hollywood was still a rough and ready kind of proving ground, distrustful of "strangers." Its newly acquired vestiges of prestige incorporated into it a kind of sturdy pride that brooked no outsiders—especially from Broadway. Broadway represented many things to the film colony. It was Establishment, it was a standard of success, it was even a bit decadent. Moreover, theater people seemed quite snobbish regarding movies and treated them with disdain until the price was right. The Broadway stars that began arriving in Hollywood around 1915 represented both a threat and a means for greater success to the film colony. These stars could lend to the movies their prestige and drawing power; however, their presence also threatened the position of the film stars.

Fairbanks represented all of these things. His collision with Griffith was perhaps more of an aesthetic difference than anything else. But consider the effect he must have had upon the film crews themselves. It was with these people, Griffith's "lieutenants" as they have been called, that he worked daily. The motion picture for many of them was predominantly a livelihood, not just an aesthetic consideration. It is likely that he, like many of the Broadway stars, was looked upon at first as effete, an image of the swishy, silk-hatted, foppish Broadway stereotype. Certainly Fairbanks' snobbishness must have been immediately apparent. He *was* a snob, in a way, all his life. He always felt the exclusive pull of some

kind of aristocracy, of acceptance in social circles. Concepts of royalty and lineage were virtually obsessions with him, both in his films and in his private life. It can be seen later in all three of his marriages and in his way of life at Pickfair after 1920. Fairbanks, like the stage, remained geographically oriented to the East Coast. Such characteristics must have rubbed the sensibilities of the Fine Arts unit a bit raw.

The question remains as to the extent that Griffith was involved in Fairbanks' first few films. If the premise is accepted that Griffith's influence on the aforementioned supervised films was nominal, then it must be extended to include the Fairbanks films as well. The researcher is hard put to unearth any indication of a close-working rapport between them. With the possible exception of certain scenes in Fairbanks' first two films, *The Lamb,* and *Double Trouble,* the films and ambitions of both were very different. After *Double Trouble* Fairbanks made many of his films on the East Coast, well away from the Griffith touch. His directors, like Allan Dwan, acknowledged their debt to The Master, but were individuals and went their own way. Certainly Fairbanks' acrobatic comedy style finds no parallels in Griffith's work. Regarding such disparities, it is to be remembered that Griffith was earlier quoted as advising Fairbanks to go to Keystone. Yet, in another quotation attributed to him, his attitude toward the Broadway star was quite different. Immediately after the premiere of the first Triangle film, Fairbanks' *The Lamb,* Griffith apparently had this to say:

It is an interesting question whether "legitimate" stars or so-called "stock stars" of film organizations will prove the more serviceable in making the highest quality pictures. The legitimate star brings to the studio not only the well-deserved reputation of a great name in old-line theatricals, but also usually an enormous amount of material in the way of scripts, characters and business. . . . Douglas Fairbanks has already proven himself of such great worth in the pictures that we have engaged him for an exclusive three-year contract and he has definitely abandoned his old associations for that time at least.[11]

Although this comment would seem to explode many of the ideas that Fairbanks and Griffith had never had any artistic rapport, it is also possible that the whole quotation is simply gush from a studio spokesman in Griffith's name. If Griffith was willing to attach his name above the titles of pictures he had had nothing to do with, then it is

D.W. GRIFFITH

is that Griffith has given no further attention to any Fairbanks release and never looked at one of the Fairbanks films before release excepting the first, when Griffith remained one day at the studio.[12]

The irony is that Griffith and Fairbanks found themselves later in 1919 as business associates in the formation of United Artists. At that time, it was Fairbanks' star that was on the ascendent and Griffith's that was beginning to wane.

There remains one addendum to the whole issue of Fairbanks' involvement with Griffith and, more generally, his position as a Broadway star in the still-fledgling film colony. If animosity existed between the studio crews and the Broadway stars, there would be ample opportunities for "sabotage." According to Alistair Cooke, Fairbanks himself soon found himself on the short end of such a plot:

> The crew that worked with Griffith was a busy unit, jealous of its habits and, as small contented staffs are apt to be, unwilling to change its routine. They took a dislike to Fairbanks not as a person but as a symbol. There had been much speculation over the move to recruit theater stars, and by the time Fairbanks arrived the crew had come to the conclusion that they were against it. Fairbanks' hearty good nature defeated their expectations but they were not so easily denied a little resentment. According to G. W. Bitzer . . . they saw to it that Fairbanks was given a wrong and rather ghastly make-up . . . The combined effect of acrobatic levity in comedy scenes with strenuous hamming was enough to convince Griffith that there was little hope for Fairbanks in Triangle's ambitious program.[13]

Close examination of the film reveals no glaring examples of this, yet there are several shots where close-ups of Fairbanks' face reveal features that seem claylike and a bit ashen in color. The effect is only subtly disturbing and may stem from the rather uncharacteristic seriousness of the Fairbanks facial expression. If Cooke's story is true, it adds another almost bizarre touch to an already interesting confrontation between the stage stars and the film colony.

FAIRBANKS' DEPARTURE

By late December of 1916 Fairbanks had become one of Triangle's most successful stars. He had been making pictures for eighteen months—thirteen films that had taken him from

possible that statements like this could appear that he had never actually said. It is also doubtful if Triangle felt that Fairbanks was of "great worth" at that time. According to Anita Loos, it was not until his third picture, *His Picture in the Papers,* that Fairbanks found the style and formula that made him a ranking popular star and a valuable asset to Triangle.

No, it is very doubtful if Griffith had any significant influence on Fairbanks when he first came to Fine Arts in 1915. The clincher to that argument comes when Fairbanks was getting ready to leave Triangle in 1917 to join the newly formed Artcraft company, a producing company under the aegis of Paramount Pictures. Fairbanks, at that time, was one of the most popular movie stars in the country. He had made thirteen films in eighteen months. Along the way his salary had more than doubled. His attempts to leave were blocked by a contract that still had a year to run. In January of 1917 Fairbanks and his attorney Dennis F. O'Brien prepared a statement that outlined several violations in Fairbanks' original contract with Triangle. One of those violations relates directly with his association with Griffith:

> Fairbanks is reported dissatisfied with [the contract] through Griffith having failed to give the Fairbanks feature productions the personal attention promised by that director. One story

the status of Broadway juvenile to the top star at Triangle. His salary had doubled along the way, and his position among the ranking stars industry-wide was becoming more solidly assured with each film. Yet he was dissatisfied. Just as he was typical of the many stars who had left Broadway for Triangle, so now he was representative of those new stars who sought greater profits and independence. He chafed at his three-year contract with Fine Arts. "Actually, I'm working for nothing," Fairbanks is reported to have said.

> I'm only making about $500,000 a year. My pictures have been netting the studio more than a million a year each and when you multiply that by a dozen pictures, you can see I really am, comparatively, working for nothing.[14]

By his figures, organizing his own company would bring him an income of well over a million dollars a year, depending only upon his ability to turn out films. He set to work. A private enterprise, to be successful in Hollywood, has always had to have something more than enthusiasm and screen talent, qualities already abundant in Fairbanks. It also needed hard-headed business acumen of people who greatly respected the art work on United States currency. Douglas brought his brother Jack to Hollywood. He had always been a sort of checkrein to balance Doug's enthusiasm and grandiose visions—he was needed now. Jack decided that things looked favorable for the organizing of the Douglas Fairbanks Pictures Corporation and left for New York to consult Dennis F. O'Brien, Doug's personal friend and lawyer (Mary Pickford's lawyer also).

By December of 1916 Fairbanks began to demand a greater salary from Triangle: $15,000 weekly for one year or more, reaching a gross annual salary of $780,000. This would be one of

Doug in a 1917 attempt to persuade his public that he was, after all, a bookish man. In fact, Doug's book Laugh and Live *was published in 1917, followed in 1918 by* Making Life Worthwhile.

the highest salaries ever paid to a film star. Many proposals were made him by filmmakers, but the highest amount reached by bidders reached $10,000 weekly for two years. Not enough. Fairbanks played his ace. He offered the alternative, that he would organize his own company and produce eight features within a year, himself as a star, each feature to be purchased for $200,000 or $1,600,000 in all. In effect, he proposed to break his still binding contract to Triangle-Fine Arts. Attorney O'Brien, with partners Malevinsky and Driscoll, went to work on finding loopholes in the contract. Soon, in January of 1917, a statement was made regarding "violations" in Fairbank's present contract. One reason, the lack of supervision by Griffith, has been quoted earlier. Another violation, reportedly, was that actresses were billed in Fairbanks films to establish their names for value by association with his name. And a loophole was described in this way:

> One clause of the Fairbanks-Majestic contract not divulged so far is said to give Fairbanks the right upon 30 days notice to take six months leave from picture work. In this way the Fairbanks people are said to believe that by giving another similar notice when the first six months expire, his leave could be indefinitely postponed and in such a situation the courts would not be called upon.[15]

Injunctions were issued against Fairbanks and John Emerson (a Fine Arts director Fairbanks wanted to retain for his own company) from working anywhere else. By March of 1917, however, O'Brien settled things: a sum of money was paid to Fine Arts, and the injunctions were vacated. The Douglas Fairbanks Pictures Corporation was on its way. Fairbanks was president; his wife, Beth, his vice-president; his brother and **general manager, Jack, was treasurer; and** Dennis F. O'Brien was secretary. Headquarters would be in New York. Negotiations were completed with Artcraft for distribution. Fairbanks would get $200,000 upon delivery of each picture, the agreement calling for eight annually. He would produce them himself. Beside the advance sum upon delivery, he would thereafter receive seventy-three percent of the gross receipts, Artcraft withholding twenty-seven percent for distribution services. The estimated income for the ensuing years was placed at between $500,000 and $1,000,000.[16] Financially, then, Fairbanks was on his way to success.

NOTES

1. Ralph Hancock and Letitia Fairbanks, *Douglas Fairbanks: The Fourth Musketeer* (New York: Henry Holt, 1953), p. 99.

2. Abel Green and Joe Laurie, Jr., *Variety, from Vaude to Video* (New York: Henry Holt, 1951), p. 145.

3. *Ibid.,* p. 62.

4. Benjamin B. Hampton, *History of the American Film Industry, from Its Beginnings to 1931* (New York: Dover Publications, Inc., 1970), p. 144.

5. Quoted from a collection of clippings held by the New York Public Library, Lincoln Center.

6. *Ibid.*

7. Hancock, *Fourth Musketeer,* p. 111.

8. *Ibid.,* p. 104.

9. Terry Ramsaye, *A Million and One Nights* (New York: Simon and Schuster, 1964), p. 721.

10. Hancock, *Fourth Musketeer,* p. 120.

11. *Variety* (24 September 1915), p. 17.

12. *Variety* (12 January 1917), p. 3.

13. Alistair Cooke, *Douglas Fairbanks: The Making of a Screen Character* (New York: Museum of Modern Art, 1940), p. 14.

14. Hancock, *Fourth Musketeer,* p. 140.

15. *Variety* (12 January 1917), p. 3.

16. *New York Times* (7 February 1917), p. 11.

2
Gamboling First Steps: *The Lamb* and *Double Trouble*

The genesis of Douglas Fairbanks' first film, *The Lamb*, is a puzzling one, particularly in the light of a remark made by Ralph Hancock in his biography: "The role of Bertie, 'the lamb,' which Douglas Fairbanks had played in *The New Henrietta* on Broadway, was adapted and expanded into his first screen play and entitled *The Lamb*." [1] This remark is supported by Doug Jr.'s biographer. When one goes back to the play, however, it is difficult to trace any parallel between it and the subsequent film. Indeed, Buster Keaton's first feature film, *The Saphead* (1920), is a much closer link to the play in that, the Wall Street background is retained.

Bronson Howard's tragicomedy, *The Henrietta*, was first produced in 1887. According to *The Bookman* of February 1914 (pp. 611–12):

> *The Henrietta* was the earliest attempt to exhibit the dramatic elements in American businesslife; and to this day remains a better drama than any of the host of plays which have been devised in imitation of it.

In it, the evils of Wall Street can be seen extending to the household. The narrative mixes elements of tragedy within a comic format. The main characters were Nicholas van Alstyne and his son Bertie.

On 22 December 1913, a new version of *The Henrietta* opened on Broadway. It was a play in four acts adapted by Winchell Smith and Victor Mapes and called *The New Henrietta*. It starred William H. Crane as Nicholas van Alstyne and Douglas Fairbanks as his son Bertie.

The modern version differed from the original in several respects. The plot and characters were altered, the soliloquies and asides of the earlier text were cut out, and a contemporary setting including telephones and motorcars was incorporated. A new character, Mark Turner, van Alstyne's son-in-law, became the villain, while Bertie was relegated to the status of hero.

Van Alstyne is smitten by the widow Updike. He has a rival, a clergyman, the Reverend Murray Hilton. To get her away from him he takes her for a cruise on his yacht. Meanwhile, the son-in-law, Turner, tampers with the *Henrietta* stock. Bertie, who had earlier been given a million dollars and been turned loose to sink or swim, finds himself in an important position when his father's stock is all

The Fairbanks character introduced in The Lamb *(1915)*
establishes a pattern for the pre-costume films. Here we see him
in Say! Young Fellow *(1918)*.

but declared worthless. Bertie proves himself a man and gives his father a check for all the money he has left. Van Alstyne saves the day and Bertie makes a pile.[2]

That Bertie's new character was a good thing for Fairbanks' portrayal is evident in the February 1914 *Theater Magazine's* comment (p. 62):

> Fairbanks is whimsical and unctiously humorous. As the son who is equal to the emergency . . . he is so entertaining that criticism must be silenced . . . with all his overcharged vacuity he has the saving grace of infinite comedy.

The jump from this role to that of Gerald in *The Lamb* is nothing less than a long broad jump. About the only parallel is that Gerald, like Bertie, is a rich young idler who never had to earn a living—a situation that changes when he is confronted with a challenge and subsequently proves himself a man. In short, *The Lamb* does not seem to be founded to any great extent upon the

Broadway play, at least not any more than any of Fairbanks' other films are based on his plays. For a better example of how Douglas adapted one of his plays for the screen one should turn to the 1918 *He Comes Up Smiling*.

Viewing *The Lamb* today is an interesting experience to say the least. One recalls Paul Rotha's words to the effect that *The Lamb* is with *The Matrimaniac* and *A Modern Musketeer* (1917 and 1918), one of the best presentations of an essentially lawless and dashing character. How long had it been since Rotha had seen any of them one wonders? *The Lamb* is merely a foothold in Fairbanks' screen career. Certainly it is not in the same class with the other two. We will examine it as an apprentice film, with all the seeds of later greatness already implanted.

In gaining an adequate understanding of *The Lamb*, one must first admit that it is something of a curiosity piece—and stop just short of saying "museum piece." It is an unquestionable delight for students of early American cinema, but

Doug with Marjorie Daw on the brink of the Grand Canyon in A Modern Musketeer *(1918).*

therein lies the problem—it needs a good deal of perspective. The opening title, for instance, bears repeating:

> *This is the story of a Lovesick Lamb, whose Dad, an Old War Horse, had died. Clinching his Teeth in a Wall Street Bear, leaving the Lamb to gambol around on the Long Green.*

We smile in amusement at the bad grammar and the false tone. Yet, there is a good deal of information here in this title. Note the capitalized words. Although an accepted convention in the German language, the English language does not permit capitalization of all nouns. The title is, instead, an awkward method to establish an exaggerated comedy atmosphere. More importantly, it is representative of a method at the time of naming characters. D. W. Griffith was particularly guilty of this sort of thing. "Lovesick Lamb," "Old War Horse," "Wall Street Bear" are similar to titles he employed in his own films such as "Brown Eyes," "Princess Beloved," or simply "The Girl." Characters at this time (1915) were often "typed" for greater ease of audience identification. Their physical characteristics, their vocations, their part in the action to follow would account for these curious appellations. In this respect, the Griffith presence in *The Lamb* is strongly felt (the film's opening title says that it is "supervised by D. W. Griffith").

Besides the character constantly referred to as "The Lamb," we have his girl friend, called simply "Mary." This sort of thing, the reference to the nursery rhyme, grows wearing after a very short while. In the credits the characters are enumerated as follows:

> **The American Girl** *(Seena Owen)*
> Son of the Idle Rich
> Her Model Type of Man *(Alfred Paget)*
> The Wealthy Mine *(Monroe Salisbury)*
> His Mother *(Kate Toncray)*
> His Valet *(Edward Warren)*
> Eagle Eye *(Himself)*

Later, "Her Model Type of Man" is referred to as "Cactus-Fed Goat from Arizona." An aviator is introduced as "the Birdman"; the half-caste Mexicans are called at various times "Giddy Huns" and "those unpleasant Mexicans." This reckless flinging about of stereotypes and labels plagues the film throughout, even during some of the action scenes at the end. Even the machine gun at this point is referred to as "the Death Pumper!"

Briefly, the plot concerns a rich idler (Fairbanks) and his love for Mary. Despite his effeminate ways she has decided to accept his proposal. One day at the beach a cry of help is heard from the surf. While Gerald stares on paralyzed, his rival, Bill Cactus, a rancher from Arizona rushes in to save the drowning man. Now aware of himself as a coward he decides to build himself up as a man by boxing and jujitsu lessons while Mary is away with friends at a party at Cactus' ranch. When he tries to rejoin the group in Arizona he is waylaid by two crooks and knocked out. A tribe of Yaqui Indians on the rampage captures him, while Mary falls into their clutches only a little later when she is separated from the party. While Bill Cactus and the others rush back to the U. S. Barracks on the American side of the border for help, Gerald and Mary face certain death at the hands of the Indians. In desperation, Gerald breaks loose and manhandles a number of cutthroats and finally rejoins Mary. Together they defend themselves with a machine gun the Indians had previously captured from the Mexican army. As they use the last of their ammunition the American troops gallop to the rescue. The Griffith-style last minute rescue is accomplished and Gerald has proved himself a man at last.

In effect we see two Geralds. The Gerald we meet in the opening scenes is not the Gerald at the end. These two characters within one skin represent polar opposites—how the distance from one to the other is traversed constitutes the chief interest in Fairbanks' acting. To the credit of *The Lamb* this journey is much more credible than the one in *The Mollycoddle* four years later in 1919. In both films, the foppish character finds his strength in the fastnesses of the Arizona desert. In the latter the change is sudden and arbitrary, whereas in the former it is more reasonable and natural. It is, nonetheless, an astonishing one in both. In *The Lamb,* however, we are given hints of it from the very beginning and we can follow the process with doubled interest. There is the title, for instance, that preceeds his initial effort to woo Mary: *Mamma wanted to show him off but he longed to jump the Hedge.* Having negotiated the hedge we can get an idea of Gerald's nature. The fact that the feat is essayed by a man wearing a morning suit with top hat and cane imparts a slightly mad and jaunty air to the whole thing. This is the sort of touch that marked many of his best early pictures.

Gerald's athletic potential is also indicated in a scene a short time later. This time it is Gerald's inclination toward, rather than the achievement of, the virile characteristics of manhood that keys the scene. Cactus Bill has just arrived and been introduced. His handshake has disrupted both Mary and Gerald and his swaggering Arizona ways eclipse Gerald's mild manner, to say the least. At a party that night it is not Bill that seems out of place, it is Gerald. Mary is highly impressed with Bill and cannot understand why Gerald is not like him. So, scorning him, she attends to Bill while Gerald, now curious, stalks about behind the broad, oblivious back of Bill, coughing, bulging his cheeks prizefighter fashion, squaring his shoulders, and otherwise aping his style. Fairbanks balances opposing traits with some convincing pantomime. It is also a welcome indication of his mute obsequiousness changing to a more aggressive stance.

Gerald's arrival in Arizona is to be echoed later in many films. As the embodiment of the American West it served as the Fairbanksian proving ground for the athletic virtues. It is fitting that Fairbanks' arrival in *The Lamb* is a slightly mad affair—after all, we shall find in this, and in later films, that anything can happen there—for him it is the Land of Oz. Gerald shows up in the desert country wearing nothing less than alpine togs, with an accompanying title: *Geography meant nothing to Gerald.* But it meant everything to Fairbanks, and as he disembarks there, the whole film begins to move like a heavy machine finally overcoming its inertia. Not only does the action pick up, as we shall see later, but the comedy element improves. There is a beautiful little routine with an automobile that has arrived to pick him up. Seating himself in the car he props his cane at a racy angle upon the fender, gripping

its stock as if it were a gear shift; the cane moves forward the car drives off.

He misses his train and in a long sequence gets taken in by some Indian bead sellers. He tries to proffer the Indians a huge wad of bills to buy their blanket and a piece of fool's gold. Nearby, two crooks just happen to see this exchange and sensing a wealthy target, offer to drive him to the train. These rough, tobacco-chewing scoundrels knock him out and find nothing but the piece of fool's gold. They leave him lying in the dust of the desert.

So at last Gerald is alone in the desert. The situation that has long been waited for is, at last, developing. Even if the humor in the next scenes does not quite come off, it is nonetheless fascinating to watch the lily-white Gerald steadily becoming more dishevelled. As he gets dirtier the character becomes more interesting. It is an oddity with Fairbanks that the dirtier he gets the better he looks. In rapid succession he battles a jawbone, a rattlesnake, and a puma. In his first real burst of defiance he states: *No lion lies down with this Lamb.* Yes, an unfortunate title, but the general message is there. Much of the interest in a Fairbanks movie is waiting for the moment when he suddenly switches off gravity and jumps over a house or something—when he is going to discard his former self like an old skin and emerge with a kick into a new daylight. We know this point has arrived with the next title, surely one of the most amazing titles in movie history. It hits us with no forewarning at all: *All of a sudden a half-caste Mexican Tribe indulged in a little rebellion. They captured a band of Mexican soldiers, and a machine gun, the latter in their eyes was mere junk.*

This title is followed, strangely enough, by a shot of Mary with Bill Cactus! The crudity of all this is a bit embarrassing. Titles used to bridge gaps in time and action are of course quite common, but the device of this title defies analysis. We feel cheated, to say the least. The only inkling we have, beside the title, is a shot of several disreputable Indians pushing soldiers around and tearing the clothes off a girl. At any rate, after the menace has been established and we have been prepared for the future involvement with the rebellious Indians, we are back with Gerald waking up in the desert: *Gerald still kept his regular Hours and Rose at Noon.* At which point he is promptly surrounded and captured by the Indians.

Mary is, in turn, captured by the Indians, and we receive all the visual panoply of nastiness— Indians are a mass of prominent teeth and long matted hair, their intentions all too obvious

31

Meanwhile, crosscutting back to Gerald, we see his character gradually hardening. His shoulders seem to set squarer now, those nervous, flighty mannerisms of the early Gerald are gone. He stands defiantly within the circle of the Indians. The shorter length of the shots quickens the story's pace, the conflict is established, and we know we are in for some exciting footage. Nor are we disappointed. Some exceptionally nasty Indians surround Mary and state their intention to "fatten her up." Gerald, too, is in a precarious situation in another part of the Indian camp. Manfully he stands before one native who advances upon him with a knife.

At this time, the Mexican troops return to recapture the renegade Indians and the resulting battle saves Gerald's life. In the ensuing conflict he manages, unseen, to loosen his bonds. As the Mexican troops are being beaten back, Gerald works his way free and—*Realizing that his father had died with his boots on he determined to follow in his footsteps.* Fairbanks is off and running. He fells several rascals, leaps out the doorway and hurtles down between the grass huts toward the camera. He turns and jumps, clambering nimbly up a house front. Just as these shots are getting up some steam, along comes another title, completely spoiling the effect: *Such a playful giddy Lamb.* The effect of this juxtaposed with the action scenes is jarring, to say the least, pointing to the constant disparity between the titles and the action. Even after we have some spectacular fistfights and such, and Fairbanks has rescued Mary, the titles persist in their patronizing tone, in an unbelievable interchange between Gerald the newly rescued Mary: *I say . . . deuced uncomfortable people these Indians . . .* And a bit later snaps at Mary who seems reluctant in his saving her: *I say, old girl, don't be huffy about that little side sideslip; we're in a deuced tight corner now, going to get you out!* Such lines would never appear in a Fairbanks film. The stilted words is far worse than the he displayed earlier. This is most because they deflate the strength of

an troops are beaten back. The back upon Gerald and Mary who in have appropriated the machine pumper." With it they beat off des of Indians, but ammunition Indians begin to creep closer ered couple after every turn crank. During these scenes ow, extensive crosscutting suspense as we see the

"government troopers" riding to the rescue. In true Griffith-fashion the two lines of action run faster toward their point of intersection.

Finally Gerald is out of "bullets." He tells Mary that he has saved the last one for her. The Indians close in for the kill. Visually, they are at their nastiest now, and we must remember that Fairbanks always had a knack for surrounding himself with the most vicious villains imaginable. The chief, in particular, is anxious for the kill: *When the chief learned it was the last of the Bullets he coveted the Brave Lamb's Living Heart.* It is at this point that director Christy Cabanne's work realizes itself. A skillful manipulation of aerial shots of the battlefield with close shots of Gerald, Mary, and the creeping Indians yields up a true montage. There is a reptilian suggestiveness to the aerial shots of the Indians' creeping bodies slithering toward and encircling the machine gun emplacement. And of course all the time the cavalry is roaring to the rescue, the camera trucking ahead of them. The aerial shot is used exclusively as the cavalry arrive and surround the natives.

After all the action it is nice to see the next shot, a close-up of Mary nestled in Gerald's arms, a relaxed smile on her face. It yields a nicely intimate breath of relief.

It is the end now and Gerald is back in his expensive home. But now he is straighter, shoulders well back, his movements quieter and full of ease and grace. He stands regarding his father's picture with a slight smile. We are offered an explanation, further, for his Arizona transformation in a title that could have been used verbatim for *The Mollycoddle* four years later: *Blood will speak–though Society may drown the Conversation.*

The problem of the titles touches the entire course of the film. As was obvious after the detailed synopsis, the tone and diction of the titles were at times completely at variance with the images. The latter part of the picture certainly suffers from the interposition of the patronizing comic tone with the aggressive images. Some of this—the capitalizations, the labelling—were indicative of the style of titling in 1915. The uneasiness we feel now about them points up the fact that the technique of silent film titling has not been studied enough. We have been at some pains to quote them because they almost steal the whole show, literally, and it gives us a chance to see what happens when the titling technique goes wrong. A good title will inform the image before and after it with a kind of counterpoint. As in music, this counterline must not always run exactly parallel with the thematic line—it should establish a kind of oscillating interdependence with it, touching it and supporting it occasionally. The titles for *The Lamb* are like canonical constructions that run on and on endlessly. There is no variation in the tone, no development to support the development of the images (mainly, Gerald's transformation). The crucial point falls completely flat when Gerald rescues Mary with the comment about the "seaside sideslip . . ." referring back to the scene on the beach when he failed to rescue the drowning man.

A first reaction to the titles was that somebody was trying to write like Anita Loos, who wrote and titled many of Fairbanks' later efforts. But a title by Loos is deceptively simple. Her art is like that of the cartoonists—easy on the eyes, but devilishly hard to duplicate. Many fine artists are notoriously bad cartoonists. Here, a forced literacy and studied humor stifle the proper spirit of the titles.

Emphasis should be upon the role of the "early" Gerald, the weakling, because it is our best chance to examine Fairbanks' acting. The dashing, reckless bravado of the later Gerald is a role that Fairbanks essayed with little trouble. In the impassive, effeminate Gerald, however, Fairbanks encounters some difficulty. The problem is, of course, how to make what could be a repellent character attractive? Perhaps no one solved this problem better than Buster Keaton. Keaton as a fop is as good as Keaton tumbling down a mountainside. The early scenes in *Steamboat Bill, Jr.* are treasures because of the suitability of such a characterization to Keaton's deceptively impassive features. With expression reduced to a minimum, every nuance and gesture of the character is more vitally significant, as when he tries hats on before a mirror, his expression betraying the slightest flicker of change with each hat. Fairbanks enjoys no such ability to concentrate such a role down to such telling detail. He improves later in his career, to be sure. His Don Diego in *The Mark of Zorro* five years later is a success. But he overdoes it here. Keaton's subtlety attracts, whereas Fairbanks' outright ham detracts in many scenes. The comic equipment is too limited here. A sense of the bizarre, so prevalent in such comedies to come as *When the Clouds Roll By* (1919) and *The Nut* (1922), remained to be discovered.

Even if we view *The Lamb* today with reservation we should not forget that it was received quite well at the time, which, at least from Fairbanks' point of view, was all that mattered. One week after the premiere on 23 September, 1915, *Variety* reported:

After viewing *The Lamb* it is no wonder the

Triangle people signed up Fairbanks for a period of three years at any salary within reason. They would even have been justified in stretching a point to secure Douglas. He "registers" on the screen as well as any regular film actor that has ever appeared in pictures and more strongly than most of them.[3]

There remains a further note about the character of Gerald. Basically, he is a rich young idler, and it is this role that was to become a typical one, although subject to many variations within the next few years. Why this kind of character seemed to appeal to movie audiences of the day can be answered in simple fashion. The character had *time*—time to pursue adventure, time to be absorbed into intricate plots. We always knew he was not *really* worthless. He loved the right girl, defeated the villain, and, in Douglas' case, displayed a pretty snappy sparring style in the process. Again, all this takes time, something most of us do not have. If our next door neighbor lived the good life without lifting a finger while we worked hard all day, we might develop a bit of animosity toward him. Not so on the screen, apparently. Today's audiences find the same kind of character in the Western drifter, the continental playboy, just as fascinating and enjoyable as in the silent days. The cinema's capacity for distorting time is one of the chief joys it affords us. Time is as basic an illusion to cinema as the images themselves. The movies—and the characters in them—have all the time in the world, even if we do not.

Fairbanks loved this kind of character. Rarely

Fairbanks and Eugene Ormond in a scene from Reaching for the Moon *(1917).*

For him the world was a theater: Doug first portrayed D'Artagnan in the dream sequences of A Modern Musketeer *(1918), a spoof on the swashbuckling style.*

do we see him actually working at anything other than playing a romantic scene or jumping a fence. The 1917 *Reaching for the Moon* ends astonishingly with him as a working man with a home and family in New Jersey. It is an appalling sight, one that jars with the character as we have come to know him. More typically, we see him throw up his hands in despair at the prospect of work *(His Picture in the Papers* (1916), *When the Clouds Roll By)*. Fairbanks, himself, was unhappy with workaday routine and before he found his niche in the movies he lost many jobs because of it. For him the world was a theater.

This tendency toward the rich idler as seen in the early films before 1920 is not really very different from tendencies seen in the characters of the later, more famous costume films, such as *Robin Hood, Don Q,* and *The Black Pirate.* In all of these he was vested with some sort of nobility prior to the events narrated. In these, too, he has servants, wealth, and social status at the outset. We are in no way led to suppose anything other than that he was rich and independent, unused to having to work to support himself.

Double Trouble appeared in another of the "Triangle Weeks" in early November of 1915. Featured with it was a Thomas Ince production, *The Golden Claw* with Bessie Barriscale. *Double Trouble* remains even today one of the oddities among all Fairbanks' films. The outdoor adventure of *The Lamb* has been changed to the more intimate locales of the modern city. In it, there is scarcely a "thrill," and compared with the later Fairbanks films it seems tame. Yet, it has a charm and intimacy less forced than in *The Lamb,* and succeeds in further consolidating the duality first seen in that first film—the ambivalence within one man of the morally irreproachable personality and the dashing, reckless personality, or, put another way, the clash between an effeminate weakness and a more aggressive drive. Booth Tarkington's comment that Fairbanks often seemed like a faun who has been to Sunday school is appropriate here.

This ambivalence is handled in *Double Trouble* by the split personality concept. Fairbanks has two alter egos, Florian Amidon—a Sunday school type with mincing, fluttery mannerisms and speech; and Eugene Brassfield, a fast-talking politician with a way for the ladies. The Florian personality is completely submerged when Fairbanks is injured by a blow to the head. Eugene takes over after this and soon his devilishly clever personality and knowing ways make him a wealthy candidate for Mayor. Five years pass and the Florian personality revives, puzzled at the new surroundings and circumstances. A medium, Madame Leclaire, is consulted. Through her devices, a series of shifts begin from one personality to the other, the question being which of the two would emerge dominant. As Eugene, Fairbanks wins the Mayoral election; as Florian, he ditches the shady associates of Eugene. Gradually a compromise between the two is effected and all is well.

The silent film abounded in dual role pictures. Pickford, Barrymore, Keaton, Chaplin—virtually all of the big stars delighted in this sort of role as a means to heighten the contrast between dramatic styles. Pickford used the device in *Stella Maris,* for instance, to enable her to play the role of an ugly, deformed young woman, in addition to the usual "golden girl" with the curls. Keaton and Fairbanks delighted in recording the process whereby the fop is galvanized into the superman, and the modes and manners are peculiar to each characterization. Fairbanks used such a device in many films, the most memorable, perhaps, the Don Diego/Zorro dichotomy in the 1920 *The Mark of Zorro.* The man of action and the man of spotless waistcoat are neatly consolidated.

One of the earliest screen treatments of the double personality was the 1913 *German of Prague,* an idea so popular that it was remade two times over in 1926 and 1936. The original 1913 version separated the protagonist, Baldwin, from his mirror reflection and made them the two contestants in a struggle not only for the favors of the heroine, but for control of the seat of power within Baldwin himself. Baldwin's liberated mirror image represents the darker aspect of his personality seeking to destroy the other half. At the end, Baldwin shoots his reflection in an attic, but the shot only kills himself.

Another German film is of more than passing interest in this context. *Der Andere* ("The Other") was a 1913 dramatization of a Jekyll and Hyde case. The Dr. Jekyll here is an enlightened Berlin lawyer, a Dr. Hallers, who smiles skeptically at the idea of the split personality. But later, the overworked lawyer suffers a fall from a horse and, as a consequence, sinks into a deep sleep, from which he emerges as "the other." This other self is a rogue and joins another burglar in attempting to break into his own flat. Later, he falls asleep and awakes as Dr. Hallers, completely unconscious of the crime. Upon subsequent questioning he collapses after being forced to identify himself as the other burglar. The story has a happy ending as Hallers regains his health and gets married—"the prototype of a citizen immune to all psychological disturbances."[4]

Double Trouble, made only two years later, reveals some interesting parallels with this plot, particularly in the ending. In each, the ending reveals a synthesis of the two characters that would seem to point toward the moral of strength through consolidation, as if the key to healthy life lay in the integration of both. This concept finds perfect expression in the Fairbanks screen persona. The Fairbanks of the precostume films would always be expounding the philosophy of clean living and sunny dispositions at the same time as he was holding up express trains and flying through the treetops. The dual characters of Florian Amidon and Eugene Brassfield exemplify both tendencies.

Florian Amidon is met at the beginning of Herbert Quick's novel not as an effeminate character at all, but "a banker, and the most attractive unmarried man of Hazelhurst." Later, he is described as "a galley slave chained to the sweep of percentages, interest tables, cash-balances, and lines of credit, to whom there came daily the vision of a native Arcadia of art, letters, and travel."

Such a characterization would become the standard Fairbanks role before another year had passed, but now it is only altered. Florian becomes a fop in the film. As a title informs, he was the *perfect gentleman of Amityville. The swish of a skirt would send his heart into a flutter of fear.* As President of the Sabbath Day Society, Fairbanks plays to the hilt the quick, fluttery gestures, the limp handshake and nervous smile. Eugene Brassfield, by contrast, is brash and aggressive, wears loud clothes, jauntily puffs cigars and is not above furtively lifting up milady's dress to scan her ankles.

Yet, Brassfield's traits are those that are needed to win the Mayoral election. One of the most arresting scenes in the film is the political rally, a chaotic situation completely beyond Florian's capabilities. With the help of a trance induced by Madame Leclair, Florian changes into Eugene who takes complete charge. His speech to the crowd on Main Street oddly reminds one of the newsreel footage of Fairbanks selling war bonds in New York some years later. At the same time, Florian's personality saves the day when he prevents the wife of a man Brassfield had had framed from committing suicide. The combination of the two, incidentally, is what is needed to consummate the romantic interest with the girl.

Double Trouble is a small-scale film, bordering on a kind of closet drama-comedy. Nothing really earthshaking happens, no opportunity to flex a muscle or take a leap, except a short tavern brawl with Brassfield. Rather, it emerges as a nicely typical example of the small-scale Triangle film and, for that matter, closer than any of his other films to the kind of play he had done on Broadway. Cabanne's direction is completely different from *The Lamb* with that picture's emphasis on outdoor romance and the large-scale architectural sweep of the last-minute rescue. Here it is toned down to the medium and close shot, the nuance of gesture, the avoidance of complex parallel editing so as to enable the quietly wacky events to unfold in their own time. *Double Trouble* is comedy of the most obvious kind. It does not have the satiric thrust or the philosophical ramifications of the later Triangle films. No foibles are ridiculed, no philosophy of optimism is preached—nor are there any gymnastic feats unveiled.

Yet, *Double Trouble* has been neglected unjustly by Fairbanks' enthusiasts. For its restraint and charm alone it has value. Certainly it represents the farthest pole from the flamboyance and action of the later costume films. The barbed wit and the flashing action would begin to surface in his third film, *His Picture in the Papers.* For now, *Double Trouble* was but a pleasant reminder of his Broadway days and a charming example of the intimate comedy that Triangle became noted for.

NOTES

1. Hancock, *The Fourth Musketeer,* p. 120.
2. *Blue Book Magazine* (April 1914), pp. 1044–1045.
3. *Variety* (1 October 1915), p. 18.
4. Siegfried Kracauer, *From Caligari to Hitler* (New Jersey: Princeton University Press, 1969), p. 34.

3
Gymnastic Evangelist
and *The Habit of Happiness*

"Well, all right, what's your fine high purpose in becoming a Man of God, Brother Gantry?"

"Well, I—Rats, it's perfectly clear. Preacher can do a lot of good—give help and—And explain religion."

* * *

"Yea! It certainly must make the common people feel awfully common to hear Brother Gantry spiel about the errors of supralapsarianism!"

"I never preach about any such doggone thing!" Elmer protested. "I just give 'em a good helpful sermon, with some jokes sprinkled in to make it interesting and some stuff about the theater or something that'll startle 'em a little and wake 'em up and help 'em to lead better and fuller daily lives."

—Sinclair Lewis, *Elmer Gantry*

The Habit of Happiness was Douglas Fairbanks' third film for Triangle. It is as unique as was *His Picture in the Papers,* but for somewhat different reasons. To find two such films back to back is indicative of the wealth of considerations we have to take into account in dealing with the early cinema of Fairbanks.

In *Habit* we have the first of the Dwan/Fairbanks collaborations. Allan Dwan, who was to direct many of the best Fairbanks films (ten in all), brought an influence different from John Emerson and Anita Loos. Today the work of Allan Dwan is being reevaluated (witness the recent retrospective at the Museum of Modern Art) and his early association with Fairbanks has proved to have produced some of his best work.

Habit is virtually the first of Fairbanks' gymnastic sermons. If in *Picture* we encountered a generally breezy attitude toward strength, health, and vigor, in *Habit* we find a much more consolidated and directed attitude toward defining the good life and the means to obtain it. *Picture* was satirical—*Habit* was a sermon. It is a bit of Teddy Roosevelt, Horatio Alger and Billy Sunday. It comes close to representing a particular American viewpoint that at the same time was uniquely Fairbanksian. Not only were goals proposed, but so were practical solutions for solving the problems encountered along the way.

Attendant upon this last is the fact that there is something we can learn personally about Fairbanks from this film. The nature of his optimism and its relation to his moody, extraordinarily aggressive inner self is not as simplistic as *Habit* might lead us to believe. Consciously or not, *Habit* is revealing about the battlements that support the edifice of cheer, optimism, and opportunism.

Upon completion of *His Picture in the Papers,* John Emerson left the Triangle studios on loan to Famous Players Company for two months in their Eastern studios. Later he came back to Los Angeles and Fairbanks. At any rate, his absence accounts for his not directing Fairbanks' next film. Directorial chores were instead given to Allan Dwan. Our examination of *Habit of Happiness* should begin with him.

Dwan had taken over as studio general in the East for Triangle in Yonkers, New York by March of 1916. Among his films for Triangle had been *Jordan Is a Hard Road,* with Frank Campeau, and *Soldiers of Fortune.* He directed several Mary Pickford features later on, among them *The Foundling,* and *Girl of Yesterday.*

Originally, Dwan had come to the Griffith studio a journeyman director and was the only "lieutenant" who was not brought up in the

Douglas Fairbanks and Dorothy West in The Habit of Happiness *(1916).*

Griffith service. He was the one exception to the Griffith rule not to go abroad for directors, and was engaged because of his excellent work in other concerns and for his close sympathy for Griffith's methods.[1] Dwan's working method stemmed in part from an influence of Griffith's—economy:

> One of the most important things was economy of gesture, which to me is a very important portion of the art of acting. To do a great deal with very little in terms of motion. The broad gestures, the scene-eating type of acting has never appealed to me. I like the little gesture. I think in anything you can give too much and if you do, you can lose all.[2]

The importance of this concept will become apparent shortly.

As early as 1909, Dwan came into his first contact with motion pictures. A professional electrician, trained at Boston Institute of Technology, he had been sent out to the Essanay studio in Chicago to install some Cooper-Hewitt lights. His interest picked up at the new industry, and while at Essanay he submitted some stories that were purchased. As a result of reorganization going on at the time, Dwan ended up with the job of scenario editor—surely a tribute to the swiftness of events in those days.

In his pictures, Dwan ruled with a kind of no-nonsense stance. Practical, calculating, he invested in his pictures a tough brand of fiber. Such qualities were well suited for the early Fairbanks films. Dwan seems to have had no trouble over artistic pretensions:

I believe only in the art which expresses and arouses human emotions and to which people react with the heart rather than the mind. I believe that the great mass of people want to live in the characters they see on the screen . . . feeling vicariously the human and the pathos of the story woven around them.

Only the critics care about taking a picture apart to see what makes the wheels go around, and they are the only ones who derive enjoyment solely from artistic workmanship.

There was a time when I had the artistic ideal but I was young then. . . . Later I got a job and went back and redeemed my overcoat with cold cash . . . when in later years I turned out some scripts for a motion picture company, I did it for so much a week in an office and when I got into the production of the business, I did it for so much a week too.

No more masterpieces! No more art for art's sake! That first experience made a realist of me and I've kept my feet on the ground ever since.[3]

Dwan almost went out of his way to disclaim anything artistic in his work:

I am a business man. I have a commercial mind. It is my personal opinion that things that are "too good" are generally not good enough. A man can make the most artistic picture ever filmed, but if it plays to empty houses it hasn't achieved a thing for Art [or] Humanity. This old stuff about not commercializing Art is the bunk.[4]

Practical and efficient—a perfect man for the fledgling Triangle to have around. Unlike many idealistic directors who had no interest or capacity for economics, Dwan knew exactly where he stood as a director:

The director is the man who has control of the money. The director is the man who can make or break a picture financially and artistically. Most directors are not business men. Therefore the films have had to arrange for

business managers, for men who, when the director had laid out the thing artistically and outlined the results he could achieve, will find out it can be done at the lowest cost. These men contract for material, set salaries, tend to all the commercial delay.[5]

What is more, Dwan turned them out fast and efficiently:

Pictures must be made fast. If you muddle around with them, you've lost your clear vision. You cannot hurry art, of course, but you can hurry commercial production. Get your art in hand before you start to produce and you'll save a lot of time and trouble.[6]

Several things emerge from these quotations that we will see echoed later by Fairbanks and Billy Sunday. One is the concept of art as a mass commodity to be treated with business acumen; another is a certain kind of pragmatism allied to the production of that art; and lastly, there is the ideal of speed. This speedy kind of opportunism was the very stuff of his films. It is no wonder that the first of Fairbanks' films to apply pragmatic philosophies to life's problems would be directed by Allan Dwan.

Habit of Happiness was begun after Dwan had completed *Betty of Grey Stone* late in 1915. In one of the most spectacular errors in journalistic annals we have ever encountered, *Triangle* reported in January of 1916 that *Habit* was to be an "Italian comedy, with a revolution and conspirators."[7] What emerged was a good deal different from that. The New York *Times* reported:

"Laugh and the world laughs with you. Don't and you're a darned old grouch" would seem to be the fable in film taught by *The Habit of Happiness*, the latest Triangle-Fine Arts feature production in which Douglas Fairbanks is being starred. This picture will undoubtedly start the happiness habit the country over, for it is one of the best comedy-dramas that has been seen on the screen in many a day. Of course the inimitable Duggy [sic] Fairbanks does a lot to make the picture go, but even at that there are certainly a host of situations created for the young comedian and he does make the best of them in a manner that would even make the veriest "grouch" in the world laugh.[8]

Before we proceed any further, a plot synopsis may be in order. Douglas portrays Sunny Wiggins, whose family is straight from Booth Tarkington. Sunny is blessed with a disposition that outshines even his surname. His father has acquired enough of a fortune through business to rise to a position where he is snubbed by all the best society. Sunny's sister, a title informs us, is one of those females who would rather have a male Salome trailing her than a flock of real, two-fisted, "regular" fellows chasing in her wake. In the Alice Adams tradition, she hopes to latch on to society, and in this pursuit, invites a pack of social scavengers to dine.

This in mind, we observe Sunny's efforts to further his own ideas, namely, aiding in the brotherhood of man. As a practical application of this, he weeds out ten of society's derelicts from the breadline and houses them temporarily in his room. When Sunny wakes one morning to find as fine a collection of down-and-outers as one might imagine anywhere outside a Bowery Mission lodging house, he promptly treats them all to a free wash and then marches them into the dining room, where the table is laid for Sis's society luncheon. Sunny and his crew, nonplussed, wade right in to the repast. When Sis and the society somebodies arrive, the chaotic confrontation leaves Sunny handing a fiver to each of the bums and sending them on their respective ways. He is then taken to task by an indignant sister and father, and makes a touching plea for the "poor guys" who never had a chance, with the result that dad tells him to go and live among them if he likes them so well. Taking dad at his word he leaves and starts a "happiness society" in his Bowery headquarters.

The scene changes to the inevitable millionaire with dyspepsia, and his pretty daughter. Like an island he is surrounded by a sea of gloom and for entertainment plays Chopin's "Funeral March" on the cello. The efforts of his physician to rouse him from this gloom fail. This same physician, while on a charity visit to the lodging house wherein Sunny is practicing his ideals of brotherhood, discovers that Sunny is teaching the unfortunates the art of laughter and makes him an offer to pull the millionaire out of his depression. Sunny tackles the job, eventually succeeding and winning the daughter along the way.

Outwardly, this kind of plot might strike one as singularly ludicrous and nonsensical. Yet, there is more than meets the eye here. It is the first film to depict Fairbanks in the role of what Alistair Cooke called the "popular philosopher." It marked the beginning of his years before 1920 as a kind of gymnastic preacher, sallying forth against all manner of social ills and medical neuroses, pretensions, stale ideas, and the other ills of an expanding America: "Fairbanks had the feel of the popular pulse—he knew to a degree the median limits of romance, prejudice, social conservatism; he knew them instinctively because they were his own."[9]

Of the many sources of virtue Fairbanks would delineate and advocate in his films, certainly optimism was of paramount importance. *Habit,* because of its conscious depiction of some of society's ills, because of its prescription of happiness to vanquish those ills, deserves to be considered as the first of the "sermon" films. Later, there would be *Mr. Fix-It, He Comes Up Smiling, When the Clouds Roll By,* and *The Nut*—all preaching similar "sermons" of optimism and enthusiasm. (The first two films, incidentally, were also directed by Allan Dwan.) One other film, *Down to Earth,* remains the ultimate extension of this philosophy.

In *Down to Earth,* the dyspeptic millionaire in *Habit* was multiplied many times over and we

A popular philosopher and practical idealist, Douglas Fairbanks, around 1916.

40

encounter nothing less than an asylum full of grouchily disabled people awaiting Fairbanks' enthusiastic cure.

It is with this vigorous and virtuous optimism that we encounter one link between Fairbanks and the times wherein he lived. Perhaps the true significance of *Habit of Happiness* lies in the way it reflects a prevailing national temperament, a kind of practical idealism known as the "Social Gospel."

During the latter half of the nineteenth century, industrialism had advanced with great strides in the United States. Its progress had been powered by a remarkable series of inventions and technological improvements. A land of mostly farmers and villagers became increasingly one of cities and roaring industrial towns. Inevitably with this came the development of a rising idea—the dignity and importance of a great American middle class. National advertising contributed to this notion. The success in the earlier twentieth century of five-cent magazines like *The Saturday Evening Post* was an important step in the rise of a classless or middle-class society. As Fredric Lewis Allen writes:

> . . .millions of Americans were getting a weekly or monthly inoculation in ways of living and of thinking that were middle-class, or classless American (as opposed to plutocratic or aristocratic or proletarian); and . . . through the same media they were being introduced to the promised delights of the automobiles, spark plugs, tires, typewriters, talking machines . . .[10]

Accompanying this was the mass production of the automobile, the swelling business of the railroad, the proliferation of the chain stores.

This is astonishing when we remember that only a few years before:

> The best journals and the best people concerned themselves very little with the fortunes of the average man, and very much with the fortunes of ladies and gentlemen, with the pomp and circumstance of Society, and with the furthering of a polite and very proper culture for the elect.[11]

As the twentieth century greeted this change, it became apparent that although a greater standard of living was sifting down through the ranks of society, there were startling differences to be found. The distance between rich and poor—in income, way of living, and status in the community—was the most significant. The gulf between wealth and poverty was immense. The most obvious way to understand this gap is to consider the parallel existence of the industrial magnates such as Morgan and Carnegie and the American workers, whose average wage was something like $400 or $500 a year.[12] This disparity became increasingly awkward as the ideal of a fair chance for all grew in strength.

The same basic feeling that the nation and its citizens must look out for the interests of all the people, not simply of a privileged few, animated a great variety of people. This revolt was not an organized movement, but it was evidenced in many ways. There were the advocates of municipal housecleaning, the experimenters with commission government of cities, the budget experts. There were the battlers for workmen's compensation laws, those trying to enact decent legislation for factory working conditions. There were the conservationists, the suffragists, the crusaders for pure food and drug laws, the investigators and chastisers of "frenzied finance" and the men who, after the Panic of 1907, labored to devise an adequate central banking system.

It was not the first time in America's history for such a phenomenon to occur. Nathaniel Hawthorne in the mid-nineteenth century had commented on this kind of all-encompassing reform in his short story, "Earth's Holocaust":

> "Well, they've put my pipe out," said an old gentleman, flinging it into the flames in a pet. "What is this world coming to? Everything rich and spicy—all the spice of life—is to be condemned as useless. Now that they have kindled the bonfire, if these nonsensical reformers would fling themselves into it, all would be well enough!"[13]

The growing middle-class could become informed now, and the "muckrakers" like Ida Tarbell and Lincoln Steffens found themselves in the position to do it. At the same time that Theodore Roosevelt moved against the Northern Securities Company in 1902, Tarbell began to publish her history of the Standard Oil Company and Steffens published his first article on municipal corruption. Unquestionably it was Roosevelt who struck the keynote for the times. The burden of his speeches about the "malefactors of great wealth" was not economic but moral. He sought the moral regeneration of the business world, the righting of wrongs perpetrated by people who unfairly got a stranglehold on business and politics. Millions of Americans in all walks of life were ready for this kind of talk. They were allergic to ideologies, academic philosophies, economic theories—highly susceptible to moral evangelism. It was Roosevelt who would instruct them that ideals were within reach and that a rich nation could effect them:

> While it was our duty, our most important duty, to maintain high standards of morality and conduct, Roosevelt robustly insisted that we should keep our ideals within range of realization. We should not, for instance, scorn material wealth, but use it for ideal ends.[14]

The method of doing this he also outlined, and a whole generation of Americans listened:

> A cultivated and intellectual paper once complained that my speeches lacked subtlety. So they do! I think that the command or entreaty to clean living and decent politics should no more be subtle than a command in battle should be subtle.[15]

The most obvious application of this credo was gymnastic evangelism, a concept, an ideal, that had an astonishing flowering in the years up to World War I. Its spokesmen would be men of the middle class, average men, shrewd, practical, enthusiastic, concerned with their respective aims in the regeneration of man. They were Billy Sunday and Douglas Fairbanks.

What was the message of the gymnastic evangelists? It was unique and was based upon a national credo peculiarly American. Articles of faith, although recently assailed by evolutionary science, had carried tenets of traditional American faith through the crisis relatively intact. These tenets were, first and foremost, the reality, certainty and eternity of moral values. Words like "truth," "justice," "patriotism," "unselfishness," and "decency" were used constantly without embarrassment. People could apply moral judgments with equal certainty to literature, art, politics, and all other areas, which means, among other things, that such judgments could be and must be applied not only to the conduct of individuals, but also to the doings of trusts and labor unions, cities and nations. In other words, the gymnastic evangelists' message concerned the *morality of the universe*. For Thomas Jefferson this morality was something innate, a matter of self-evident natural law; for Emerson, it was something that all men could find by looking either inward or outward through the eyes of the spirit; for some in the nineteenth century moralism could be demonstrated by logic. In all of these, in short, it was manifestly evident. But the shadow of evolutionary science hung over it all. It attemp-

ted to explain the existence of man and the world by chemical-physical processes that had little to do with traditional ideas of purpose or destiny. American idealism in reaction retreated to the halls of Academe and by 1912 the academic philosophers were completely out of touch with the busy, practical American mind. Philosophy had become an elegant pastime instead of a guide to life.[16] So it was that the practical, middle-class American of 1912 needed cosmic reassurance. He turned accordingly to the spokesmen of liberal religion and popular science.

One of these was Herbert Spencer, that most optimistic of the great Victorians. America naturally adopted his formulation that there were laws of evolution from the incoherent to the coherent, from the indefinite to the definite. Man was a part of this steady, unfolding moral law, a law that was bringing him closer to God, or at least to some kind of perfection. Thus, the "Social Gospel" was born. It stated that *social improvement* was necessary for man to rid himself of his brutish vestiges and society's selfishness, thereby gaining him greater proximity to God. God's method included not only biological evolution, but economic and political progress. Such philosophy had the advantage of helping many people to bear the trials of life with confidence in the unfolding purposes of God, yet was valid only as long as it was believable that mankind was improving. By 1912, it is argued by May in *The End of American Innocence* that the plain lesson of current events, not philosophy, could be used to substantiate the Social Gospel's claims that man was indeed improving. Such idealism was a "practical idealism" in that a moral universe was substantiated by real events:

> Certainly the average American of 1912 considered himself an idealist, and meant by this a man who believed in unseen goals and standards. He also considered himself a realist, which meant to him a practical man who took account of difficulties.[17]

Ideals were kept accessible. Experience, not finespun theory, was the best proof that the universe was moral. And we remember the words of that most dedicated of practical idealists, Theodore Roosevelt, that our most important duty in maintaining the high standards of morality and conduct was to keep our ideals within range of realization.

The role of the Social Gospel in reform points up a paradox. The Social Gospel assumes a belief in progress and a belief in eternal moral truth. If universal improvement was inevitable, then any kind of interference was absurd and wicked. In this light, organizations like labor unions and social legislators were sacriligious. This tough, uncompromising kind of thinking had its opponents who thought of moral evolution as one wherein men took a hand and consciously tried to reach a better world that could be imagined in the future. These people wanted to speed things up and become self-reliant and practical in the process. Of the two gymnastic evangelists in question, Billy Sunday belongs to the former group, Douglas Fairbanks to the latter.

"I am burning up to do you good and keep you out of hell," said Billy Sunday. Billy Sunday—the "Baseball Evangelist," the "Calliope of Zion" as H. L. Mencken called him. In his extraordinary life he conducted over three hundred separate revivals; he spoke to over one hundred million people in the days before radio and loudspeakers; he brought one million down the "sawdust trail," and he received, so it was said, millions of dollars in freewill offerings.[18] During the years of the Social Gospel, Sunday gained his peak popularity. The man and the period reflect and rebound off each other. He at once reflected and informed the American middle class during those years leading up to the First World War.

It is of vital importance to investigate Sunday's audience. It has been established elsewhere that the years of the cinema leading into the 1920s saw an increasing claim to legitimacy until cinema could be called the medium of the middle class. Sunday's audiences, we shall see, were also middle class, a broad, Protestant class who, as the twentieth century reached its first decade,

> led the nation and dominated its traditions . . . held the vast majority of positions at the very heart of the national power, and set the styles in arts and letters, in the universities, in sports, and in the more popular culture which governs the aspirations and values of the masses.[19]

Sunday's "decent people" constituted the overwhelming majority of Americans and were the principal objects of his concern. It was to convert this middle stratum of American society that he delivered his message. McLoughlin's biography explores his audience at some length. A composite picture of the man and woman whom Sunday used as the criterion against which he judged the sins of society was a stereotype of the middle-class suburban family. We see his type often in the early Fairbanks films:

The man was married, had two or three children, and commuted, usually in his car, from his home to his "place of business" in the city, where he had a stenographer and some clerks working for him. He spent his leisure time at his lodge meetings or "Booster Club"; he was a companion to his children, took his wife out for automobile rides, and visited his neighbors; while he might play cards or go to the movies or theater and even drink an occasional "mint julep" or glass of beer, he also went to church regularly and probably belonged to a men's Bible class.[20]

The ending to the 1917 film, *Reaching for the Moon,* immediately springs to mind. At the end, we see Fairbanks surrounded by home, picket fence, wife and kids—the local Rotary seems to smile benignly over it all, and we know that the church doors swing wide on Sundays. Ironically, it is one of the most disquieting moments in all the Fairbanks *oeuvre*, totally contrary to his bounding temperament, and points up a contradiction in the Sunday method. As we shall see, Sunday's style was extremely gymnastic and volatile—yet it was aimed toward the static ideal of the comfortable, virtuous life. Examination of the delegations that came to Sunday's tabernacle shows an overwhelming preponderance of middle-and-lower-middle-class groups, which could be called "white-collar workers" or "the salaried class." On the nights of his revival sequences, known as "Businessmen's Night," or "Out-of-Town Day" groups could be composed of bankers, manufacturers, and merchants. Delegations might represent a particular store, business firm, insurance company, or office building. The extremes of class such as the hobo, the alcoholic, on the one hand, and the amoral big businessman, the society woman, and the intellectual on the other, were always represented in his sermons as unpleasant contrasts to the "decent" citizens.

When we go about the business of tracing parallels between Fairbanks and Sunday the most important thing to bear in mind is that they virtually reached the same audience. In considering the immense popularity of both, it is impossible to ignore the fact that what they said must have been of great importance to a great many people. The two are, thus, very much a part of an American temper during the pre-World War I years and beyond.

Whether that strange creature known as the "average man" could be found in the American middle class during these years is a question posed by the social historian as well as the intellectual and cultural historian. As was pointed out earlier, in a time of reform and restless growth and academic philosophizing there was a need for the "popular philosophy" of such men as Fairbanks and Sunday. They reached a kind of mean, an average of contemporary thought. Certainly Sunday must be accepted as a man of this American type before he can be understood. People remember him, if at all, as a violently gesticulating fanatic battling the fires of hell. Today they tend to dismiss with a smile his platform antics. Certainly his religious philosophies seem simplistic and untenable now. Yet, he is infinitely more interesting as a social phenomenon than as a preacher, and it is in this light that we shall view him.

Sunday was one of the "folks." He had more points of resemblance to the common people than differences. His mind was their mind. Moreover, he had that saving sense of humor. He was born in Ames, Iowa in 1862. For four years, from 1883 to 1887, he was a professional baseball player for "Pop" Anson's Chicago Whitestockings. His "conversion" occurred in a Chicago rescue mission in 1887 and he finally gave up baseball in 1891, beginning his own preaching so that by 1905 he was already gaining a name for himself on the Chautaqua and evangelical "circuits." His peak years were from 1908–1918, which places him squarely within the philosophical bounds of the spread of the Social Gospel, practical idealism, and progressive Christianity. Quite early, his services assumed the form of "entertainments." He began imitating the oratory style of Bryan and Ingersoll and gradually assumed an almost vaudevillian tone in his proliferation of the Gospel. By 1912 Sunday had come a long way:

> . . .the shy country boy from Ames, Iowa, had become a symbol of the American way of life. In the public mind Billy Sunday was an accepted leader in the battle to maintain that way of life against the forces of evil unleashed by the twentieth century. To many people he was as important a crusader for reform as Theodore Roosevelt or William Jennings Bryan, both of whom publicly acknowledged him as their friend. Roosevelt, speaking from Sunday's tabernacle platform, once referred to him as "the most wide-awake militant preacher of Christianity I know."[21]

His message did not change, but his style bloomed.

The message in itself tried to answer for many the anxieties that were raised by some of the prevailing intellectual trends—notably the doubts issued by Darwinism. Charles Finney in the 1830s maintained that not only could man effect his own salvation (rejecting Calvinism), but that, by the use of his divinely given ability to reason, he could grow in wisdom and goodness until he achieved a state of perfection. This paved the way for nineteenth century evangelism's optimism, which, in turn, made the way easier for evangelical clergymen of all denominations to accept evolution on the grounds that it was simply God's way of bringing about that state of perfection, and which would permit his kingdom to come "on earth as it is in heaven." Sunday's creed, though it became associated with the Fundamentalist movement in Protestantism after 1916, consisted of a broad, nondenominational form of evangelicalism that represented the average American's conception of Christianity. This compromise between science and theology was too weak to withstand long the differences between Spencerian and Darwinian philosophy. Too many saw that there was no place in the Bible where God said the world was to grow better and better; conversely, it seemed to be growing worse and worse. Sunday's message was hardly profound. Once he said, "I don't know any more about theology than a jack-rabbit knows about ping-pong, but I'm on my way to glory."[22] This simplicity was one of the very factors that accounted for the success of his revivalist technique. His teachings were a kind of cross between the optimism of Herbert Spencer and the fundamentalism of Charles Finney—with the realistic observation of Dwight L. Moody thrown in for good measure. Like Finney, he was a literalistic theological conservative who saw no conflicts in the Word of the Bible and was an optimistic believer in progress. Like Moody, he recognized the ills of the world. He was at war with science and learning whenever they conflicted with a literal interpretation of the Bible: "If by evolution you mean advance, I go with you," he said; "but if you mean by evolution that I came from a monkey, good night!"[23] Eventually, in his later years, he rejected science and learning altogether. The conflict between the American way of life and American ideals he never resolved. Rather, he incessantly hammered home the necessity for man's conversion as the key for reform and the adjustment of all ills. His emphasis upon conversion superseded, to an extent, that upon social ills. The latter was dealt with only to the extent that it effected the former:

> Billy Sunday voiced the reaction of the

conservatives when he said, "Some people are trying to make a religion out of social service with Jesus Christ left out. . . . They made the Christian religion a side issue." Sunday's theory that the principal purpose of the Christian religion was to save souls and not society was still the basic creed of the majority of American church members, despite their dalliance with the Social Gospel.[24]

This, then, was where he and the Social Gospel parted company. For the straight practical applications of the Social Gospel we look to Theodore Roosevelt when he sought the "moral regeneration of the business world." Roosevelt believed in setting up a moral standard, saying:

> . . . that it was just plain wrong for some people, by tricks and wiles, to get a stranglehold on business and politics, while others were cheated out of opportunity. This was the kind of talk that millions of Americans of all walks of life—people allergic to ideologies, impatient of economic theory, but highly susceptible to moral evangelism and devoted to the idea of a fair chance for all—could understand and respond to.[25]

Sunday's zeal for reform was strongest in the realm of Prohibition; otherwise, he was content to save souls who could then take up the social business at hand.

It is Sunday's style, his delivery, his practical business sense linked to a philosophy, his sense of showmanship that are of most interest to us. He delivered a direct hook upon the jaw of a receptive American middle class—and connected resoundingly. His phenomenal success forces a detailed attention toward his technique, a consideration that places him squarely on a par with such a seemingly diverse figure as Douglas Fairbanks.

Style, style, style—the man was virtually all style. Moreover, his was a style keyed to the times. If his messages smacked too much of simplistic content, they were at least slammed across in a most unique and electrifying manner. He was a platform showman. A Billy Sunday revival resembled nothing less than a circus come to town. It usually lasted at least a week. All other religious activities ceased during that time so that the main focus would be upon his specially constructed Tabernacle. His operation was a traveling road show, his tabernacle like a Grauman's or a Roxy where the audience could come to pray. His platform was converted into a gymnasium, just as were Fairbanks' sets. The attention-catching

manipulations of Sunday's voice and the gestures and gyrations of his body led his authorized biographer to call him a "gymnast for Jesus." He learned to construct his sermons along the lines of a popular melodrama that would build slowly from climax to climax and move his auditors in rapid succession from guilt to fear, to laughter, to anger, to tears, to hate, to grim determination. He learned to use the tricks of the actor and the demagogue. Doubtless, novelist Sinclair Lewis had Sunday in mind when he penned *Elmer Gantry* in 1927. The Reverend Gantry likewise resorted to theatrical tactics:

> Every Sunday evening now people were turned from the door of Elmer's church. If they did not always have a sermon about vice, at least they enjoyed the saxophone solos, and singing "There'll be a Hot Time in the Old Town Tonight." And once they were entertained by a professional juggler who wore (it was Elmer's own idea) a placard proclaiming that he stood for "God's Word" and who showed how easy it was to pick up weights symbolically labeled "Sin" and "Sorrow" and "Ignorance" and "Papistry."[26]

We shall touch upon Sunday's sense of show business a little more later.

Sunday's physical style is undoubtedly the most famous aspect of his technique. It is here that his athletic tendencies came to the fore:

> He raced up and down the green-carpeted platform . . . waving his hands, kicking up one knee now and again, like a park walking horse, brandishing a chair, standing with one foot on the chair and another on the pulpit, bending over backwards like a springy swordblade, bobbing back and forth, and waving a handkerchief between his legs as he reeled off one of his amazing long lists of vituperative epithets and displaying as much energy, determination, and virtuous enthusiasm as Douglas Fairbanks.[27]

It was estimated that he walked a mile back and forth across the thirty foot platform in every sermon—one hundred and fifty miles in every campaign. This was not merely walking, but sliding, jumping, falling, staggering, whirling and throwing himself about the platform.

Mixing theater and baseball, he would often act out several parts in skits, scenes taken from the Bible ("The Prodigal Son," for instance), or from his life as a professional baseball player. Sometimes he would satirize foibles of modern society

Those typical American preoccupations, speed and athletic enthusiasm, found their embodiment in Billy Sunday. He cannily capitalized on both. He knew that people understand with their eyes as well as with their ears—and he preached to both:

> The intensity of his physical exertions—gestures is hardly an adequate word—certainly enhanced the effect of the preacher's earnestness. No actor on the dramatic stage worked so hard. Such passion as dominated Sunday cannot be simulated; it was the soul pouring itself out through every pore of the body.[30]

It was as if Sunday were coupling giant train cars together. He linked the vigorous life to good health and then linked that to morality. It mattered not if this coupling was naive and absurd. Far more than that, he had energy. Likewise, Fairbanks thought that all anybody needed was spirit: "Energy—the power to force himself into action! For him there is no hope unless he will take up physical training in some form that will put him in normal physical condition—after that, everything simplifies itself."[31] These people had listened well to Roosevelt's injunction—and we will quote it once again—"I think that the command or entreaty to clean living and decent politics should no more be subtle than a command in battle should be subtle."

There is a good deal of militancy in this style. Just as the intense percussiveness of such Fairbanks films as *Reggie Mixes In* is produced by it, so with Sunday a platform sermon resembled more a prizefight than a spiritual struggle. One of his methods of building himself up was to play upon the crowd's love for a fight and to assume the part of the leading protagonist. William Gerald McLoughlin quotes one observer: "No one, 'not even Mr. Roosevelt himself, has insisted so much on his personal, militant masculinity.' "[32] Conflict, we need remind no one, is the basic element of good theater.

Despite all the hoopla of his revivals, Sunday was always conscious of serving as an example of manhood that many could strive to emulate. To women he appealed as a preacher, a father, a husband, and a knight-errant who would defend womanhood against all enemies. At the end of an evening of bizarre theatrics he would bring out his big guns—his famous sermons, notably the Booze Sermon. At a stroke he would change the mood and become deadly serious. Cannily, he always stopped short this way of becoming only a clown in the audience's eyes. However cheap the hucksterism, he himself never failed to remind

(á la Anita Loos, perhaps?). Baseball, however, was *the* trademark of his athletic repertoire:

> A characteristic movement of extreme emphasis, said one observer, involves the entire body and suggests a pitcher in the act of throwing the ball. At the conclusion of his sermon to men only he always parodied the famous comic poem "Slide, Kelly, Slide" and made a running dive across the full length of the platform on his stomach. Then he would jump to his feet to imitate "the Great Umpire of the Universe" and yell, "You're out, Kelly!" This scene climaxed his account of a former teammate named Kelly who had taken to booze and thus failed to get home to heaven.[28]

All of this would have been totally absurd and unbelievable had not it possessed the ring of authority. Physically at least, Sunday was for real:

> Sunday was fast all right; his baseball years were marked by a dare-devil speed on the basepaths. He was the acknowledged champion sprinter of the National League. His slides and stolen bases were adventures beloved of the fans. He was the first man in the history of baseball to circle the bases in fourteen seconds. He could run a hundred yards from a standing start in ten seconds flat. Speed had always been his one distinction.[29]

Doug, looking his Sunday best, with Bessie Love in Reggie
Mixes In *(1916).*

everyone that the stakes were Heaven and Hell.
Elmer Gantry agreed with this method:

> I've got to figure out some way so's I keep
> dignified and yet keep folks interested. . . . I
> got to be up-stage and not smile as much as I've
> been doing. And just when the poor chumps
> think my Sunday evening is nothing but a
> vaudeville show, I'll suddenly soak 'em with a
> regular old-time hell-fire and damnation ser-
> mon, or be poetic and that stuff.[33]

Fairbanks, who also was accused of grinning a lot,
did the same thing in his films, and there is
nothing comic about the climactic battles in *Reggie
Mixes In* and *The Mollycoddle*. It was the best of two
worlds, really. Good theater means persuasive
style. Yet, it must be taken seriously if it is to be a
compelling force in our consciousness.

(Parenthetically, it is interesting to note that
Sunday's vocal equipment matched the speed
and nervousness of his body. Experienced
stenographers who tried to take down Sunday's
words verbatim stated that he often spoke at the
rate of three hundred words per minute.[34] Fairbanks, too, spoke nervously and at a great rate of
speed, occasionally lapsing into a slight lisp.)

So far, Sunday's showmanship had been
confined to the Tabernacle. Showbusiness was a
way of appealing to the rising middle class. Now it
was only a logical extension to apply his style to
Hollywood itself. Sunday and Fairbanks knew
each other, of course. In 1918 the two even

appeared in baseball uniforms at a benefit to raise funds for sports equipment for American soldiers in France. A photo exists of them at this game, standing together, arms thrust out in identical gestures of bravado and spirit. Sunday had come to Hollywood in 1915 to make a film with Columbia Film Co.—a one-reel subject bearing on his work. Lubin also released a feature called *The Evangelist*, with Arthur V. Johnson in a Sunday-type role. *Variety* took its cue and reported Sunday's noncelluloid exploits in a correspondingly theatric style:

> Sunday and his wife are both agreed that New York isn't ripe yet for saving. They are probably waiting for the dance craze to wear off so Sunday might draw a decent showing in the big town. After leaving Paterson, Sunday may play a return date in Philadelphia.[35]

Sunday even worked briefly with Allan Dwan, the director of *The Habit of Happiness*, during the filming of Dwan's *Jordan Is a Hard Road*, with Frank Campeau. Dwan describes the event:

> I got ... Billy Sunday ... as my technical adviser. We put up a huge tent over in Hollywood across from the studio and filled it full of extras—not professional ones—just people off the streets. Now, in the story, Frank Campeau is supposed to harangue them about religion and make them come to God, but I got Billy Sunday up there and he let them have one of his best hot lectures, and I had about three cameras filming only the audience. And pretty soon these people began to feel it, and the first thing you know, they were crawling up the aisles on their knees, coming up to Billy Sunday to be saved hollering "Hallelujah" and going into hysteria. A terrific scene. No bunch of million-dollar actors could have done it. You could see the frenzy in their faces. And after we cut, he actually went on with a religious revival right there. Then I was able to put Campeau up there and let him go through the gestures of talking, cutting back all the time to these people I'd already shot.[36]

The confluence in 1915 Hollywood of Dwan, Sunday and Fairbanks is remarkable. A modified kind of Social Gospel seemed to be pitching its tents in the Hollywood wilderness. Certainly the medium was consciously being used as an effective tool to reach a broad public.

Perhaps the most impressive tribute to Sunday's dramatic talent was that paid indirectly by Heywood Broun, drama critic of the New York *Tribune*. In September 1915, Broun reviewed George M. Cohan's new comedy *Hit the Trail Holliday*, wherein Cohan played Billy Holliday, a part he wrote for himself in an attempt to parody Billy Sunday. Broun wrote:

> George Cohan has forced a comparison between himself and his greatest rival in the use of dramatic slang, and strange as it may seem, it is George and not Billy who cracks under the strain ... The play was no triumph for Billy Sunday, George Cohan has neither the punch nor the pace of Billy Sunday. . . . It is true that Cohan waved the flag first, but Billy Sunday has waved it harder. . . . It is in language that the superiority of Sunday is most evident. . . . All in all, we believe that Sunday has more of the dramatic instinct than Cohan.[37]

Less than a year later, in 1916, a film version was produced with another Fairbanks director, Fred Niblo (*Mark of Zorro, The Three Musketeers*) portraying Holliday.

Sunday, like Fairbanks, came on as anything but a shrewd businessman. But, as Allan Dwan has suggested, he did not flinch from viewing "art" as a business. Practical idealism did not preclude shrewd business sense—it demanded it. Sunday, in the best tradition of the American business man (not to mention the Hollywood entrepreneur) maintained a financially sound operation. He may have been dealing with spiritual values, but they were wares as well. With the help of a permanent staff, he developed before World War I what one professor of economics ranked as one of the five most successful businesses in the country—right up there with Standard Oil Co., U.S. Steel, and National Cash Register![38]

Visually, Fairbanks and Sunday resembled each other to a surprising degree. Photographs from this time reveal that Sunday intentionally capitalized on his most flamboyant and easily identifiable characteristics in what might be best described as his "studio photos." These characteristics included a habit of raising one knee and slamming one fist into a palm, standing on chairs and pulpits, crouching with one leg drawn up and one fist flung forward, or engaging in some sort of headlong dive. His photos zero in on all of this and we are immediately struck by their similarity to a series of photos released of Fairbanks in his D'Artagnan garb, likewise standing on chairs, flexing a sword blade, etc. Newsreel footage of Sunday confirms beyond a doubt that the two even moved the same. Even allowing for slower camera-cranking in those days, Sunday jitters and twists, alive and vibrating with bodily energy.

We think of the Fairbanks in the 1917 *Down to Earth* demonstrating calisthentics to a group of "ailing" hypochondriacs: "What shall we do to be saved?" they all wail. Fairbanks shows them: He has the fat woman roll on the ground, the dyspeptic laugh and slap his arms, the man with the liver ailment gather firewood, the alcoholic (pursued by a lavender elephant) drink two quarts of water between meals, and the others climb trees and turn handsprings. Doug moves from one "patient" to another, swiftly prescribing, gesturing, grinning, slamming one fist into his palm, rocking back from the hips, thrusting forward his forearms, describing arcs in the air with his hands. . . . "You lawyers and businessmen can't exactly see leaping up steps and jumping fences and climbing trees," he said once:

> Well, Theodore Roosevelt managed to be President of the United States and to plant himself firmly in history, and to do all of these things because he knew they were worth more than this thing we call "dignity." That's the accelerator of age.[39]

Both men were under six feet and in those days parted their hair in the middle. They were slim and agile and dressed neatly. Photographs that survive from *The Habit of Happiness* reveal a Fairbanks in a conservative pinstripe suit, crouching low with one fist out, surrounded by Bowery destitutes. And *that* is the picture of Billy Sunday that comes to mind, evoked by that magical name.

Everything discussed thus far is reflected in *The Habit of Happiness*. We remember that Roosevelt insisted we should not scorn material wealth, but use it for ideal ends. Sunday's flourishing business was certainly an application of that idea. Another disciple is Sunny Wiggins who, in this film, establishes his "Happiness Society" in the Bowery. Although Sunny is wealthy we have already seen that the family has not attained a corresponding social distinction. Herein embodied is the Tarkingtonian fate of the "new rich" seen so acidly in *Alice Adams*. The point is that he does have a source of money available for ideal ends—and he uses it.

Still essentially middle class, Sunny's smile demonstrates the ready accessibility of confidence and happiness available to all—just like the nickel magazines and the automobiles. The "message" of that smile, of optimism infused with the flex of a muscle, is simplicity itself. What could be a more popular philosophy than the idea that any ailment could be cured with laughter—that making people laugh would exorcise their problems? "To be successful you must be happy," he said.

The *"popular philosopher"* in 1917: A ready grin and homilies of wisdom.

"To be happy you must be enthusiastic; to be enthusiastic you must be healthy; and to be healthy you must keep mind and body active."[40] Never mind how sublimely ludicrous these words might seem; they were simple, direct and, when linked to the bounding figure on the screen, seemed all that was needed. The Fairbanksian ideal of health and enthusiasm as a commodity not only perfectly matched the prevailing practical idealism, but was a constant factor throughout his screen work. He really nailed it down as the motto for his 1924 *Thief of Bagdad:* "Happiness must be earned." And as an agent to right social imbalance, health and vigor are seen briefly in the 1931 *Around the World in Eighty Minutes* when Fairbanks does isometrics on the deck, saying: "You pull down the Woolworth Building like this" (reaching for an imaginary object); and "you

49

lean way over and lift up social conditions like this." The ready accessibility of all this is another confirmation of Roosevelt's injunction to keep ideals within reach. Fairbanks consciously practiced this:

> . . . a goal ahead. You've got to have one to get anywhere, but don't set it too far. If you're like most human beings you can't stand it. Set your goal a little way ahead, determine not what you're going to be at sixty, but five years from now. When you catch up with your goal move it along to a new place.[41]

Lest we think any of this less than significant, we should be reminded that by 1915 the motion picture already reached a greater audience than any previous medium. As successful as Sunday's preachments were in the sawdust tabernacles erected for him across America, Fairbanks' were even more so. He reached more people for a greater cash value—Sunny Wiggins was far richer than he seemed. By 1915 some $1,500,000 was paid daily by the public to go into twenty thousand theaters; $500,000,000 was the estimated manufacturing value of the movies; and the total amount represented by the motion picture industry came to between four and five billion dollars![42]

We must never adopt the attitude that Fairbanks took any of these attitudes about health and speed and enthusiasm and a thousand other catchwords less than seriously. Later in his career, after he stopped making movies, he would look back with a kind of bitter scorn at all the "words, words, words." But in 1916, he was approaching a flood of public acceptance and popularity. He was only thirty-two and already a ranking screen star. He was naturally athletic and brimming with energy. A man preoccupied with success, he was finding it on his own terms, using his own considerable resources. At the same time, he was a shrewd businessman and knew full well a good thing when he saw it. Gymnastic evangelism was here to stay and, to paraphrase a popular maxim, it *was* a laughing matter. A person in these circumstances can readily afford to talk and grin a lot.

As early as *Habit of Happiness,* we find warning signals concerning the need for curbs on Fairbanks' optimistic zeal. Fairbanks, for some, was beginning to cloy, frankly. It is an established rhetorical principle that contends if one wants to say something compellingly, it is sometimes advisable to say it in a way opposite from the obvious. Thus, we find the horrors of war and carnage couched in the childlike vision of Ambrose Bierce's "Chickamauga." The most effective villains are always the most civil, a notable screen example being Mel Ferrer in the 1952 *Scaramouche.* As they say in the Westerns, a good poker player never overplays his hand. Fairbanks would realize this later in one of his costume films, *The Gaucho,* and temper the unalloyed exuberance with a whiff of brimstone. The swashbuckling tradition does not draw "for nothing" on the Don Juan of Tirso, Molière and Da Ponte. All the back-slapping, torso-twisting, grinning, aphorism-quoting antics of the Fairbanks of the "popular philosophy" films represents a manic energy that threatened to burst all bounds. *Photoplay* astutely pointed this out:

> Douglas Fairbanks, in common with Mary Pickford, suffers from over-exploitation of a unique personality. The Pickford gentleness and the Fairbanks smile are perhaps the two most reliable props of today's dramatic transparencies. "Habit," which starts out with the thunderingly good idea of right-side-uping a floundering grouchy old world by grinning at grief, hammers so long on the single major key that before the play's finished a bit of minor would have been high and welcome relief. . . .[43]

Perhaps anyone reading the foregoing pages would guess that there were to be black days ahead for Billy Sunday and Douglas Fairbanks. Both Sunday, and to an extent Fairbanks, were plagued in later days by restlessness and melancholy. Both had based their philosophies so heavily on physical exuberance and the declamations of youth that the passing years left them facing the visible and inevitable refutation of age. It was a hard rebuff to persons of such manic energy. Sunday turned to hardened beliefs about what constituted Americanism, propounding doctrines that left out virtually everybody. During the war he preached the madness and necessary extermination of the German race as a whole. Fairbanks' restlessness compelled many global jaunts and life became for him, as he put it, a slide down hill, an endless wandering through the thin ranks of café society. When Sunday said that he was burning up to keep people good and out of hell he was speaking not only of himself but also of Fairbanks. They both positively flared with a flame that, left untended, consumed them totally.

But if some of the sharper critics carped in 1916, the public seemed to love it all, finding no quibbles with the philosophy expressed, which is **really the whole point of this chapter**. Fairbanks' mass appeal, linked as it was to the runaway express train of his body and to the larger currents in the public temper, was firmly consolidated. Unfortunately, this public response often expressed itself in dubious ways. Consider, for example, this little ditty composed for *Photoplay* in 1916 by one Helen Joyce:

Dietician Doug

Laughing, they say,
  Takes excess flesh away;
If you're thin, it will help you gain weight.
I've found Douglas' mission—
  He's a 'Laugh Dietician'—
  A first-rate physician, I'll state!

In conclusion, we should mention Fairbanks' amusing attempt to make a practical application of the philosophy in *Habit of Happiness*. Never a retiring sort of fellow, he decided to go all the way and test out his theory that man's lot in life was improved by laughter. So he went to New Jersey . . . a dubious move perhaps, but go he did. Allan Dwan has commented at length upon the effects of Fairbanks' experiment in practical idealism:

[Doug] tried it out on a millionaire to good effect but he wanted to work it on the lower echelon so he went down to skid row and into a flophouse to see what he could do about brightening the lives of those fellows. We built a set over in our New Jersey studio and went down with some buses and brought back these bums from the real flophouses. They didn't know where they were going—half of them didn't have any mentality—they were all booze-soaked old winos. We put them in our flophouse and they all wanted to sleep. It got pretty discouraging. So I said to him, 'try a little off-color story—see if that'll work.' It was a silent picture so anything he said couldn't be heard. Well, he tried an off-color thing and one guy got a slight quirk on the side of his face—very small—it wouldn't even photograph. I said, 'Well, let's go a little further,' and we tried a real seamy one and got several grins and some teeth—or lack of teeth—appeared. Open mouths. So we came up with jokes as raw as we could find and finally we got so low-down that they really were roaring, and we had what we wanted. When we cut it, the title would say simple humorous things and then howls of laughter would come. But when we released

the picture, I began to get letters by the hundreds and finally censorship appeared in the form of a couple of executives who said, 'You've got to do something about that picture.' They were scared stiff because all the deaf-and-dumb people all over the place had read Doug's lips and were horrified at the awful things he was saying to these fellows to get them to laugh! We had to call the picture back and make different shots of Doug. And that's how I learned to be very careful about what actors said even in silent pictures.[44]

Perhaps it is entirely appropriate in the final analysis that such behind-the-scenes manipulations were necessary to produce the desired effects on the screen. The theatrical maneuverings behind Sunday's carefully staged revivals parallel this. It is a kind of politics that does not eschew doubtful processes as long as the result is "right," or at least effective. To those who do not scorn material wealth and keep ideals within sighting distance, as Roosevelt advocated, such methods are entirely appropriate. Content and form meet and each informs the other.

NOTES

1. *Photoplay* (March 1916), p. 46.
2. Peter Bogdanovich, *Allan Dwan: The Last Pioneer* (New York: Praeger, 1971), p. 25.
3. *Theater* (January 1927), p. 38.
4. *Photoplay* (August 1920), p. 57.
5. *Ibid.*, p. 109.
6. *Ibid.*
7. *Triangle* (22 January 1916), p. 6.
8. *New York Times* (13 March 1916), p. 5.
9. Alistair Cooke, *Douglas Fairbanks: The Making of a Screen Character* (New York: Museum of Modern Art, 1940), p. 18.
10. Fredric Lewis Allen, *The Big Change: America Transforms Itself, 1900–1950* (New York: Harper, 1952), p. 117.
11. *Ibid.*, p. 5.
12. *Ibid.*, p. 55.
13. In *The Complete Short Stories of Nathaniel Hawthorne* (New York: Hanover House, 1959), p. 403.
14. Henry F. May, *The End of American Innocence* (Chicago: Quadrangle Books, 1964), p. 18.
15. *Ibid.*
16. *Ibid.*, p. 11.
17. *Ibid.*, p. 14.
18. William Gerald McLoughlin, *Billy Sunday Was His Real Name* (Chicago: University of Chicago Press, 1955), p. 293.
19. E. Digby Baltzell, as quoted by G. Edward White, *The Eastern Establishment and the Western Experience* (New Haven and London: Yale University Press, 1968), p. 11.
20. McLoughlin, *Billy Sunday*, p. 221.
21. *Ibid.*, p. 224.
22. *Ibid.*, p. 123.
23. *Ibid.*, p. 121.
24. *Ibid.*, pp. 226–227.
25. Fredric Lewis Allen, *The Big Change*, p. 98.

26. Sinclair Lewis, *Elmer Gantry* (New York: Harcourt, Brace, and Co., 1927), p. 358.

27. McLoughlin, *Billy Sunday,* p. xx.

28. *Ibid.,* pp. 159–160.

29. Wm. T. Ellis, *Billy Sunday: The Man and His Message* (New York: F. W. Mead Publishing Co., 1936), p. 26.

30. *Ibid.,* p. 138.

31. Douglas Fairbanks, *Laugh and Live* (New York: Britton Publishing Co., 1917), p. 12.

32. McLoughlin, *Billy Sunday,* p. 179.

33. *Elmer Gantry,* p. 359.

34. McLoughlin, *Billy Sunday,* p. 158.

35. *Variety,* (9 April 1915), p. 5.

36. Bogdanovich, *Allan Dwan,* p. 40.

37. McLoughlin, *Billy Sunday,* p. 163.

38. *Ibid.,* p. 73.

39. Douglas Fairbanks, "How I Keep Running on High," *American Magazine* (August 1922), p. 37.

40. Ralph Hancock, *Douglas Fairbanks: The Fourth Musketeer* (New York: Henry Holt, 1953), p. 170.

41. Fairbanks, "Running on High," *American Magazine,* p. 139.

42. *Variety* (6 August 1915), p. 3.

43. *Photoplay* (August 1920), p. 57.

44. Bogdanovich, *Allan Dwan,* pp. 40–42.

4

The Social Climber

DOUGLAS FAIRBANKS AND THE AMERICAN ARISTOCRACY

"My name is Colonel Diver, sir. I am the Editor of the *New York Rowdy Journal.*

Martin received the communication with that degree of respect which an announcement so distinguished appeared to demand.

"The *New York Rowdy Journal,* sir," resumed the colonel, "is, as I expect you know, the organ of our aristocracy in this city."

"Oh! there *is* an aristocracy here, then?" said Martin. "Of what is it composed?"

"Of intelligence, sir," replied the colonel; "of intelligence and virtue. And of their necessary consequences in this republic. Dollars, sir."

—Charles Dickens, *Martin Chuzzlewit*

American Aristocracy was directed by Lloyd Ingraham in 1916 from an Anita Loos script. Watch Hill, Rhode Island is the scene for this satire upon the supposition that if America has an aristocracy at all it is founded on dollars rather than on lineage. The upper crust of the American industrial rich gather at Watch Hill in a sort of resort bounded by stuffy old ladies and high walls. The people here are not very far removed from the congregation of Dr. Jolly-em's Sanitorium in the later *Down to Earth,* in that they are bound together by a common insanity—in this case social snobbery.

One of them is a young swain named Percy Peck (played by Albert Parker), a malted-milk manufacturer. Another is Mr. Hicks, "The Hat Pin King," whose success in producing a nonsliding hat pin has earned him millions. His daughter, Geraldine (Jewel Carmen), is the object of the affections of both Percy Peck and one Cassius Lee, the scion of a first family of Virginia, an enthusiastic and penniless entomologist.

Geraldine Hicks is so bored with the female society at Narraport-by-the-Sea that she vows to kiss the first man she meets. So one day while driving, she hops out of the car and kisses Cassius. Cassius, properly stunned, seeks her out to continue the agreeable relationship. Undaunted by his lack of mobility into the Narraport society, his efforts to "crash society" consist of hurdling walls and other barriers to get in to see her, rather a neat bit of comic allegory, charming in its ingenuousness. But Cassius has a rival, Percy, who lacks the manly attributes Geraldine prefers. He asks Cassius to assist him in winning her admiration by doubling for him in some difficult stunts involving flying seaplanes and driving fast cars. The penniless Cassius needs the money and when

Douglas Fairbanks and Jewel Carmen in American Aristocracy *(1916).*

he sees who the girl is he is most willing to take on the proposal.

There are sinister doings at the resort. It develops that a mysterious porter is in league with Percy Peck concerning the "malted milk." He passes a note to Cassius dressed as Peck that states that a ship is in the harbor waiting for the malted milk to Mexico—a highly irregular missive under any circumstances. Suspicious, Cassius investigates Percy's nearby factory. The "malted milk" turns out to be gunpowder. Percy learns of the misdirected note and has Cassius disabled and imprisoned in the factory along with the Hicks, who have also been alerted to the nefarious situation. Percy cannot let well enough alone and takes Geraldine with him when he makes his escape aboard the Mexico-bound ship.

Cassius' escape from the warehouse after a terrific fight, into and up over a runaway elevator, out into the country, down a cliff, out into the seaplane and after the boat, is all fast-paced action benefitting from much location shooting. He clambors aboard the runaway ship and swings about disabling everybody single-handedly until the U.S. Navy torpedo arrives.

This film is one of the more interesting of the early films for several reasons. It is short, charming and unpretentious, yet proves to be a cogent picture not only of a great many characteristics of his screen character, but of a certain social condition and/or contradiction in American culture. It will be dealt with in these various aspects.

An aristocracy in America? It would seem to be a contradiction, but it is only one of many contradictions encountered when delving into the American temper. Discussing an aristocracy in America is merely confronting one of the major dialectic pairings in American thought: the American Adam and traditional man.

The opening question is answered to an extent in the opening title from the 1917 *American Aristocracy:*

> Has America an aristocracy? We say yes! And to prove it we take you to Narraport-by-the-Sea, where we find some of our finest families whose patents of nobility are founded on such deeds of daring as the canning of soup, the floating of soap and the borating of talcum.

In 1808 John Adams said essentially the same thing:

> We have one material which actually constitutes an aristocracy that governs the nation. That material is wealth. Talents, birth, virtues, services, sacrifices, are of little consideration with us.[1]

A reaction to court life from Reaching for the Moon *(1917), one of Doug's first films to treat the theme of royalty–satirically, in this instance.*

This indicates a difference between an intrinsically American version of aristocracy based upon money and what we automatically think of as aristocracy—that is, one based upon monarchs and the traditions of class and fealty grounded upon inherited blood lines. Both kinds of aristocracy have had their place in American history and certainly in American culture.

The word "aristocracy" comes from the Greek *aristos* (best) and *kratia* (rule) and originally meant "government by the best citizens." Of course all the trouble comes from defining the "best" citizens. Traditional aristocracy sets its standards by bloodlines.

In Crèvecoeur's famous letter, "What Is an American?" the existence of a governmental kind of aristocracy in America is denied vehemently:

> Here are no aristocratic families, no courts, no kings, no bishops, no ecclesiastical dominion, no invisible power giving to a few a very visible one . . . We have no princes, for whom we toil, starve and bleed: We are the most perfect society now existing in the world.[2]

Yet from 1776 onward, despite Adam Smith's statement that "no oppressive aristocracy has ever prevailed in the colonies,"[3] it would appear that the aristocratic *idea* refused to be downed. For instance, in 1789 a large group of admitted "aristocrats" of their day—including James Madison and Richard Henry Lee from Virginia and Thomas McKean and William Bingham of Philadelphia—met to propose a title for George Washington. Merely "President" did not seem enough. Titles proposed were "Most Serene Highness," among others. Washington himself supposedly favored "High Mightiness." At long last, of course, the simple title of "President" was decided upon; a title so bereft of respect that, it is recorded, "on at least one occasion Washington was refused lodgings at a village inn upon the assumption that he was the president of Rhode Island College."[4] This makes one wonder about the nature of the good collegian's extracurricular pursuits.

Perhaps the most typical of figures in early American history that can represent aristocratic leanings is the character of Alexander Hamilton, the Revolution's aristocrat of aristocrats. Elegant, impassioned, ingratiating, he could have fit into the Versailles of Louis XV. Yet, he was the illegitimate son of a relatively unsuccessful Scottish merchant and a daughter of the French Huguenots. From such a man, born the lowliest of the low, as they say, came the highest expression of aristocracy that America was ever to know. This kind of nobility was not the mysteriously transmitted genetic trait of generations, but arose spontaneously from the combustion of character and circumstances. While Hamilton represents an American aristocrat, he also represents the self-made man, a figure that fits quite comfortably into the nineteenth century concept of the "American Adam," a concept that viewed life and history as just beginning in America. America was the world starting up again under a fresh initiative. In R. W. B. Lewis' book *The American Adam*, American man, in this light, is described as:

> . . . an individual emancipated from history, happily bereft of ancestry, untouched and undefiled by the usual inheritances of family and race; an individual standing alone, self-reliant and self-propelling, ready to confront whatever awaited him with the aid of his unique and inherent resources.[5]

This opposite concept from the traditionally aristocratic man is the other extreme whereby we can regard a figure like Hamilton. Here we encounter a duality, one essential to an understanding of America's experience with aristocratic concepts: tradition as opposed to the American Adam.

Students of the American West know that tradition played an important part in the colonization of America. For instance, America was thought to be one more step on a traditionally outlined path leading to human salvation: the new Western lands were seen to fit into a new-Eden myth pattern. They appeared to be a stage in the realization of "terrestrial paradise." As the potential kingdom of God on earth, America was seen by the Protestant view of millenium as a step toward a desired end.[6]

At the other extreme, the "American myth" saw life as just beginning:

> America, it was said insistently from the 1820's onward, was not the end product of a long historical process (like the Augustan Rome celebrated in the *Aeneid*); it was something entirely new.[7]

This philosophy meant complete abandonment of former traditions and society. Aristocracy here is self-made, basking in the natural light of nobility as seen in the work of Whitman and in the concept of the "noble savage"; not reclining in the shade of inherited values. Such abandonment can be called "reform"; or, in Emerson's case, a call for a new nationality in culture through the abandonment of European conventions.

An observer like Nathaniel Hawthorne in 1844 foresaw that problems accompany this happy philosophy of rebirth from the ashes. The dark side of his eye noted with relish the abandonment of aristocratic tendencies in his short story "Earth's Holocaust." People of the world have gathered to consign to the flames of a huge bonfire the burden of the past in anticipation of the emancipation of the future:

> . . . some rough-looking men advanced to the verge of the bonfire, and threw in, as it appeared, all the rubbish of the herald's office—the blazonry of coat armor, the crests and devices of illustrious families . . . innumerable badges of knighthood, comprising those of all the European sovereignties . . . the patents of nobility of German counts and barons, Spanish grandees, and English peers . . . .

At the same time, while the flames soar greedily skyward, one of the spectators protests:

> "People, what have you done? This fire is consuming all that marked your advance from barbarism, or that could have prevented your relapse thither. We, the men of the privileged orders, were those who kept alive from age to age the chivalrous spirit. . . . With the nobles, too, you cast off the poet, the painter, the sculptor—all the beautiful arts; for we were their patrons, and created the atmosphere in which they flourish. In abolishing the majestic distinctions of rank, society loses not only its grace, but its steadfastness." [8]

We see the same fire in the ritual "busk" of Thoreau, in the millenium of Nathanael West's *Day of the Locust*. The reforming zeal, new beginnings, are not always comfortable with a nostalgia and a need for the traditions of the past. This is why, perhaps, America has been so rife with classical revivals in the midst of progressive growth. A good example of this duality is the motion picture, the art form of the twentieth century, a new medium of still largely unexplored potential. Vachel Lindsay's groundbreaking book, *The Art of the Motion Picture*, expresses new hopes and, at the same time, binds film to classical traditions such as painting and architecture, just as Sergei Eisenstein was to do only a decade or two later. American cinema did its best to "legitimize" itself by adopting a classical stance at the same time that Griffith was breaking conventional forms of dramatic space. One look at the cinema magazines of the 'teens shows an almost painful inclination to attach cinema to the classic arts.

If America's closest approximation to the European style lies in its leanings towards first families and its nostalgia for classical revivals, rather than a system of monarchs and inherited traditions, then no one is more indicative of such an attitude than Henry James. Although James was an American, his nostalgia for the European style of aristocracy was so intense that he lived as an expatriate in England for over thirty years. For him, as hard as America might lean toward an aristocracy, lack of tradition was the inevitable stumbling block:

> It is the hard fate of new aristocracies that the element of error, with them, has to be contemporary—not relegated to the dimness of the past, but receiving the full modern glare, a light fatal to the fond theory that the best society, everywhere, has grown, in all sorts of ways, in spite of itself. We see it in New York trying, trying its very hardest, to grow, not yet knowing (by so many indications) what to grow *on*. [9]

James was a part of that polite society that had prided itself upon its ties with European tradition, almost in defiance of the New-Worldly outlook. For him, the first step in achieving standards of individual excellence was to go abroad. As Charles Sanford says, he was representative of "reverse migration." What is the nature of his lament for the "terrible denudation" of American life?—for the absence in America of courts, sovereigns, palaces, castles, thatched cottages, ivied ruins, an aristocracy, a priesthood. It is more than an outcry of the alienated artist. It is a compelling need for tradition and order; moreover, it is the need for "encounter," for him the contact with cultures rich in experience. Perhaps it also is the need for "sanction," of traditionally ranked systems not found in America. This is a long way from the American myth that said that the European experiences a regeneration in the New World, largely owing to "access to undefiled, bountiful, sublime Nature." [10]

This "sublime Nature" for James was "thin"; in some famous remarks in his little critical biography of Nathaniel Hawthorne he condemns the author for flat remarks in his notebooks about the trivialities of the landscape such as peat smoke (sic):

> The reader says to himself that when a man turned thirty gives a place in his mind—and his inkstand—to such trifles as these, it is because nothing else of superior importance demands admission. Everything in the Notes indicates a

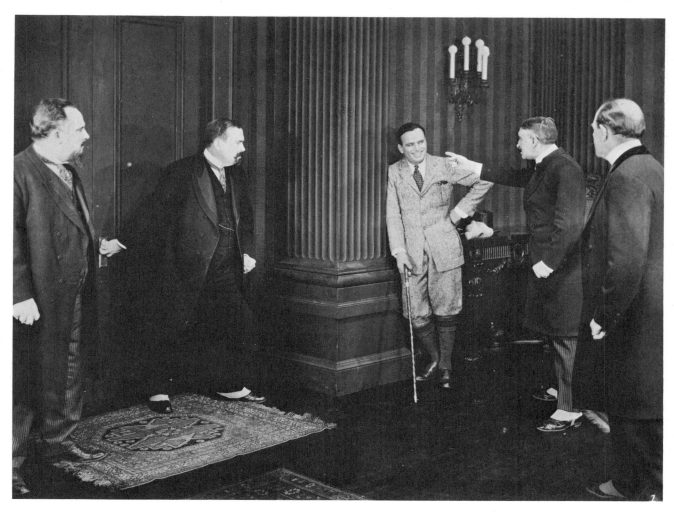

Doug as a natural aristocrat in His Majesty the American
(1919).

simple, democratic, thinly-composed society. . . .[11]

Further, Henry Seidel Canby observed about James:

... with what satisfaction he describes in his novels the delightful approach to the great English country house wide open for the week-end, each couple followed by their personal maid and valet with bags. Even nature, an American specialty from Audubon to Emerson, was no solace to this packed and ordered mind.[12]

James felt that all America had was a sense of humor, which was merely an escape from dullness. In his attitude can be seen not only the intenseness, but the complexity of the American dual attitude toward European institutions. He thought it a person's duty, for instance, to feel the "headlong rush of experience" denied an American in his own "provincial" culture. The mythology that, as we have seen, embraced nothing less than the regeneration of man in a terrestrial paradise, was bound to suffer in the harsh light of subsequent events. The unsatisfied yearning after perfection in an imperfect world might find even Hell an improvement over the obviously unfulfilled conditions in the hitherto fancied paradise of America. This kind of tragic tension caused Americans to look backward and eastward, with a heightened sense of the urgency of time and lost opportunities, toward the hellish Old World.[13] Besides, it is a fact of life that, as Mark Twain said, Hell is so much more interesting and attractive than heaven. In fiction one has only to recall Eliott Templeton in Maugham's *The Razor's Edge,* a person whose whole life, as was James's, was devoted to the pursuit of culture and society in the Old World.

Doug protects Pauline Curley in a scene from Bound in Morocco *(1918).*

America did not consign aristocracy and society to the flames. The nostalgia for its absence was there, even in the reforming spirit, as Hawthorne saw. Society founded upon certain values constituted the American aristocracy. If that society tended to discard some of the European concepts such as genetically inherited nobility and governmental sanction, it also adopted some standards of its own whereby to measure itself. In America, as was pointed out in the beginning, quite apart from the transplantation of European traditions, aristocracy showed its head in the form of money and society. America seems to have had a singular relish for both.

More than two centuries ago Lord Chesterfield defined society as "good company . . . that company which all the people of the place call, and acknowledge to be, good company, not withstanding the objections which they may form to some of the individuals who compose it." This common kind of association is counterbalanced by William Dean Howells' comment that society is intrinsically exclusive: "Inequality is as dear to the American heart as liberty itself."[14]

Nothing fed that inequality more than money. We come again to geography. The center of American society established itself as the nineteenth century passed its midpoint in the East. More correctly, the center of American society was the Eastern Industrial Establishment. This establishment embraced two kinds of "societies"—the preindustrial Eastern upper class, and the "new rich" who owed their status to industrial wealth. Henry James called the preindustrial classes "professional"; the "new rich" "commercial." They all lived "in high comfort and respectability," and, "in their small provincial

way, doubtless had pretensions to be exclusive."[15]

G. Edward White points out that this Eastern Establishment was comprised of an interrelated group of institutions—the boarding school, the Ivy League university, the college club, the metropolitan men's club, and the "Social Register"—all of which had been formed in the last quarter of the century or had altered their shape to conform to industrialism's demands. Within this context we can define the two classes of society:

> . . . the preindustrial eastern upper class—families of established wealth and long-standing social prominence who traced their ascendancy to a period before the dawn of industrialism—and the "new rich"—families of less distinguished origins to whom the industrial era had brought great wealth.[16]

In Boston, Oliver Wendell Holmes defined preindustrial society in terms of family position, education, and public service. Merchants, lawyers, and men of letters were success models. This class preserved its status by helping to maintain a system of

> . . . artificial but exclusive standards through which individuals were evaluated on a social basis, and they also consolidated power in the hands of a relatively small number of individuals and families by equating social success with occupational success.[17]

It is not difficult to believe William Black when he once said that the American young man spent five-sixths of his waking time in asking himself if he were a gentleman!

In the first decades of urban America, wealth and power came to many Americans that, in general, were not of old family, had often not attended college, and in some instances avoided public office. The apologists of these men concluded that "a rudimentary education was sufficient unto success," that college training "was positively harmful in that it made men unfit for business," and that the political arena was "unpredictable, unsound, and even immoral," which just about says it all.[18] Such are the fruits of the industrious affluent. It is not hard to see the seeds of the anti-intellectualism or at least distrust of the intellectual elite that would mark the later broad middle class that Billy Sunday reached early in the twentieth century.

The incursion of the "new rich" into the ranks of the preindustrial upper class can be seen in microcosm, in that main American standard of society, *The Social Register*. The *Register* was founded by, oddly enough, an ex-gunsmith, Louis Keller. In the post-Civil War East, the *Register* informally based its selection of candidates for admission into the ranks of society on two grounds—"descent," and "social standing." The appearance of the "New Rich" caused a third standard to appear—one cryptically called "other qualifications." The first two standards are the preindustrial concerns for community standing, but the last is particularly interesting since it recognized *economic achievement*. Clearly, money was becoming an increasingly important aspect of society. If, as James says, America was having a hard time in finding traditions for its own aristocracy, it was at least substituting its own standards. The result was a reverence for status acquired if not through blood, then at least through money.

All of the foregoing topics, the nostalgia for royalty and aristocracy, the American classes of society—the preindustrial and the "new rich"—the importance of money and industrial progress as yardsticks for such ranking, can be seen in a charming little comedy made by Douglas Fairbanks in 1917. *American Aristocracy* seems on the surface an unpretentious enough affair, but, like so many of the early Fairbanks films, it can stand up to a deeper scrutiny since it so accurately reflects the American temper around the turn of the century and beyond. Everything that has been discussed in the preceeding pages finds its reflection in *American Aristocracy*.

Earlier we mentioned Henry James as typical of the nostalgic leanings of some Americans toward the European ideals of aristocracy and society. Douglas Fairbanks likewise was typical. A consistent element in his work, this kind of thrust became more and more a part of his films, particularly in the early work seen in *The Americano* (1917), *Reaching for the Moon* (1917), *His Majesty the American* (1919), and *The Mollycoddle* (1920). He is a bit like Alexander Hamilton in that he eventually achieved a certain standard of "royalty" or "aristocracy" in his personal life (witness the dominant position his home Pickfair occupied in society and his marriage a few years before his death to an English peeress), despite rather humble origins. He is a good example of the Algeresque success story. Like Hamilton he is indicative of that basic American contradiction—the self-made man and the aristocrat—America as the embodiment of history beginning anew and as another step in a line of tradition. This duality strikes deeply into the Fairbanks temperament and can be pursued at greater length with a later film, *The Americano*. What is important here

is that this early in his career Fairbanks chooses as a character role the rough American equivalent to aristocratic man—a man of preindustrial upper class, Cassius Lee. It was in the preindustrial classes that the first families of America were found. These correspond most closely to the European ideal of blood lineage. Quite neatly, then, Fairbanks has placed himself in a dual kind of role. He is aristocratic man, yet as it turns out, he is also an American of self-made proportions.

He imparts this duality by investing the role of Cassius Lee, scion of one of Virginia's first families, with all the attributes of some kind of American Adam. Alexander Walker in his book *Stardom* seems worried about what he refers to as Fairbanks' excessive "simian" and prehensile characteristics in portraying Cassius. True enough—in this film arms and legs are used to great advantage to navigate around the landscape. His first appearance follows a title announcing him as *Cassius Lee of Virginia, amateur entomologist, who has arrived in these parts on the trail of the migratory caterpillar*. He appears from behind a rock, sits astride it, hurls himself into a front somersault down the hill and comes up with a butterfly in his grasp. He then climbs a tree, jumps from branch to branch, hangs by his knees, and in general, establishes the simian characteristics that mark some of the action to follow. We are given every characteristic of a man who is quite simply a kind of Mowgli or child of Nature. Only a little later a visual pun is perpetrated when he hangs the same way from a telephone wire after clambering onto it from the hood of a speeding automobile. In this way, the characteristics seen earlier are now transferred to an urban environment. Now all this is hardly distressing, but simply is a reinforcement of the duality of the character. That a scion of one of America's first families should find himself flying around the treetops and city streets with equal ease encompasses that duality nicely. It is interesting to remember that, also in 1917, Edgar Rice Burroughs placed a nobleman's son, Lord Greystoke, in a jungle and had him raised by apes to be called "Tarzan."

In addition to Fairbanks' preindustrial aristocrat there are other varieties of aristocracy in the film. The upper class that began to usurp the preindustrial class toward the end of the nineteenth century was, as we have seen, the "new rich," the industrialists, who in many cases, remembering Baltzell's words, believed that a rudimentary education was sufficient unto success. Wealth and power meant everything. To this was added the new element of commer-

Scene from The Americano, *directed by John Emerson in 1916.*

cialism, for it was in this direction that the propagation of business led. When the *Social Register* found its exclusive boundaries breached by the "new rich" they grudgingly accorded a diffident nod in that direction by adding the "other qualifications" standard to their list of prerequisites for admittance to Society. All was not peaceful, however, for even within the ranks of the "new rich," divisions could be seen. Snobbery is more ubiquitous than mercury.

Good examples of all this can be found in the opening scenes in Narraport-by-the-Sea wherein we are introduced to the principal characters in the play. After some shots of white-clad, parasol-carrying matrons parading in front of a beautiful white mansion, we meet the appropriately named Mrs. Greene-Rivers—"one of the leading spirits of the alcoholic set." She is contrasted with Mrs. Budhauser "whose husband has done so much to make Milwaukee famous." Mrs. Budhauser's efforts to befriend Mrs. Greene-Rivers are met with the chilling snub: "Madam, *we* are distillers." Immediately after this interchange Mrs. Greene-Rivers limply shakes fingers with another and confides, "These climbers are ruining Narraport." The pretensions and class distinctions present even within the ranks of the "new rich" are seen perfectly here, and recall to mind Mark Twain's remark that good breeding consists in concealing how much we think of ourselves and how little of the other person. In a startlingly cogent image Mrs. Budhauser flutters around the screened-in porch trying to engage these snobs in conversation. They only depart in disgust, leaving her alone to a porch full of tilting rock-ingchairs.

Not only does a distiller assume pretension over a brewer, but they both disdain the preindustrial classes, while at the same time they assume their own titles of distinction:

> *Saturday the men began to arrive at Narraport—among them the Barons of Beans, Starch, Razors, Pickles, Corn Plasters, Glue, Rubberheels, Tooth-Paste, Garters, and Chewing Gum.*

Mr. Hicks, whose daughter Geraldine provides the romantic interest, is called "The Hat Pin King," making his fortune by manufacturing the "Hat Pin with the Hump"—an ingenious little device, which, by virtue of a wrinkle halfway down the pin, prevents m'lady's hat from slipping off her head. "What is your business," demands Mr. Hicks of the would-be suitor Cassius. Cassius responds, "Why, our family never went into trade." "Young man," Hicks haughtily sniffs, "this hotel is for aristocrats. We ain't got any time for upstarts."

The theme of athleticism as virtue persists on into the main conflict of the film, that between Cassius and Percy Peck—which is to say, natural aristocracy versus industrial aristocracy. Peck, besides being the villain, is only half a man, really, in that he has Cassius substitute for him in his deeds of daring. This plot device enables Cassius to attach his athletic prowess to progressive America. Percy, for instance, persists in driving his sporty car too cautiously for Geraldine's taste—a nicely ambivalent view of the conservatism of the "new rich." Cassius, by contrast, tears around in the car as if he were Barney Oldfield (a friend of Fairbanks, incidentally). Cassius also uses Percy's seaplane to effect the rescue of Geraldine. This picture of the industrialist trapped by his own product is too obvious to delve into any further. Percy's product, the malted milk, is also a counterfeit. It is really gunpowder—an ominous kind of image for a representative of an industrial society. There are overtones here of potential conflagration that clearly imply the destructive nature of the institutions of industry. Whether this implication is intentional or not is quite beside the point—it is there, nonetheless. It is worth recalling Henry Adams' words in 1862:

> Man has mounted science and is now run away with. I firmly believe that before many centuries more, science will be the master of man. The engines he will have invented will be beyond his strength to control. Someday science may have the existence of mankind in its power, and the human race commit suicide by blowing up the world.

Alongside this sort of implication Cassius Lee stands in a favorable light indeed. If "natural aristocracy" wins out over the industrial brand, then it is only in keeping with the Fairbanksian predilection for the ideal of lineage, a theme that would emerge even more clearly in later films, notably *The Mollycoddle*.

Cassius manages to weld his first-family qualities with the Hicks's brand of society by marrying Geraldine, surely the oldest solution for containing opposites. The attainment of success was an obsession for Fairbanks in all of his films. In *American Aristocracy* he mirrors his real-life marriage to Beth Sully, daughter of the "Cotton King" of Wallstreet. The marriage offered Douglas distinct advantages both socially and economically—Daniel J. Sully had millions and a vivacious daughter (one suspects in that order). Fairbanks had to agree to quit a promising stage career and go into his father-in-law's soap business in New York to get his consent for Beth's hand. The business failed, however, and soon the enterprise was bankrupt (or is that all washed up?), forcing Fairbanks' return to the theater. Certainly the prestige of the marriage stood him in good stead in gaining a foothold in New York's club society—a fact particularly interesting since Fairbanks was partly Jewish and on those grounds alone could have been excluded from said clubs. At any rate, in *American Aristocracy* Cassius invents a new kind of hat pin and immediately thereafter marries Geraldine. The last shot is most disturbing since it shows his smiling face plastered all over an advertisement for the product. Cassius actually ends up like all the other industrialists so skillfully parodied earlier. The difference is that he embodies additionally those other aristocratic virtues in line with the American Adam. It is a truly American resolution—victory through consolidation.

NOTES

1. As quoted by Cleveland Amory, *Who Killed Society?* (New York: Harpers, 1960), p. 64.

2. As quoted by Henry Nash Smith, *Virgin Land* (New York: Vintage Books, 1950), p. 144.

3. Amory, *Society*, p. 60.

4. *Ibid.*, p. 62.

5. R.W.B. Lewis, *The American Adam* (Chicago: University of Chicago Press, 1955), p. 5.

6. Charles L. Sanford, *The Quest for Paradise* (Urbana: University of Illinois, 1961), p. 88.

*Fairbanks after completing the rescue of Jewel Carmen on
board smuggler's boat in* American Aristocracy *(1916).*

7. Lewis, *American Adam,* p. 5.

8. *The Complete Short Stories of Nathaniel Hawthorne* (New York: Hanover House, 1959) pp. 400–401.

9. Amory, *Society,* p. 24.

10. Leo Marx, *The Machine in the Garden* (New York: Oxford U.P., 1964), p. 228.

11. Henry James, *Hawthorne* (New York: St. Martin's Press, 1967), p. 56.

12. Sanford, *Quest,* p. 78.

13. *Ibid.,* p. 204.

14. Amory, *Society,* p. 9.

15. James, *Hawthorne,* p. 57.

16. G. Edward White, *The Eastern Establishment and the Western Experience* (New Haven and London: Yale University Press, 1968), p. 6.

17. *Ibid.*

18. E. Digby Baltzell, as quoted by White, *Eastern Establishment,* pp. 17–18.

5
Elastic Soil—Fairbanks and the Western Tradition

"And come to think," he concluded, "it weren't home I had went to back East, layin' round them big cities, where a man can't help but feel strange all the week. No, sir! yu' can blow in a thousand dollars like I did in New York, and it'll not give yu' any more home feelin' than what cattle has put in a stock-yard. Nor it wouldn't have in Boston neither. Now this country here" (he waved his hand towards the endless sage-brush), "seein' it onced more, I know where my home is, and I wouldn't live nowheres else. Only I ain't got no father watching for me to come up Wind River."

—Owen Wister, *Lin McLean*

When Daniel Boone kept moving westward in the face of civilization's persistent encroachments upon the wilderness, he created an enduring, yet ambivalent image of the American western experience. A part of that image delineated the stereotypical frontiersman who required unlimited "elbow room." He was said once to have complained, "I had not been two years at the licks before a d--d Yankee came, and settled down within an hundred miles of me!"[1] As a result he has become over the years the mythic symbol of man in flight from the encroachments upon his beloved wilderness. In this light he appeals to those who believed the westward movement meant the destruction of the primitive freedom of an untouched continent. But Boone can be seen in another way. He appeals to many because he blazed trails that hard-working farmers could follow. He can represent, therefore, the western movement as a victory of civilization over savagery and barbarism. In this role as empire builder he supervised the Treaty of Sycamore Shoals, which extinguished the Indian claim to much of Kentucky; he blazed the Wilderness Trail through the forest; and he stoutly defended Boonesborough in 1775 against the Indians during the Revolution.

Which was the real Boone—empire builder, or child of nature in flight from civilization? Which "West" does he truly represent—the destruction of America's natural freedom or the victory of civilization over barbarism and primitivism? We can see readily enough that the term "West" means both promise and disappointment, creation and destruction. It cannot mean one of these paired characteristics without the other.

At the core of this ambivalence lie the dual concepts of "East" and "West"—not only as geographical indicators but as philosophical referents as well. Boone as child of nature occupies the "western" regions of the American imagination, while as empire builder he advances the standards of an "eastern" establishment. This kind of understanding of the philosophical implications of geography has its direct application when we come to the western films of Douglas Fairbanks. Along the way we will examine many elements seen later in these films, such as the tough, masculine "primitivism" of the historian Francis Parkman; the naiveté of the Rooseveltian western experience; the role of the "cowboy" as an American cultural hero.

As we have seen in Boone, the terms "East" and "West" are flexible indicators. The territory that he and, later, Douglas Fairbanks, trod was, as Henry James put it, an "elastic soil," alternately Eastern and Western in its changing meanings. **Such ambivalance is a tradition in the American Western experience.**

To those fond of precise definitions the concepts of the "West" must forever remain a problem. The West embraces physical, geographical,

Doug's westerns were among the best from the silent period. His expert horsemanship could make such a scene as this one convincing.

and cultural dimensions alike. The American West in particular has been studied in many ways. For example, as G. Edward White points out, a "Western centered" study would examine the spread of democratic institutions and the role of individualism, states' rights, and the frontier in shifting western contexts. An "American centered" study would deal with the development of the West and *imaginative* constructs of that development. The West has always had a dual implication, as we saw in the case of Daniel Boone: "Since the frontier is acknowledged to be the meeting ground between *nature* and *civilization*, it proves a particularly apt metaphor to express the duality of American civilization."[2]

In intellectual history the "idea" of the West has always meant more than a geographical indicator. Edwin Russell in his famous study of the frontier effect upon American literature deals extensively with some of the confusing ramifications of "frontier," "border," "space," and other dialectic pairings. "The American West," he says, "is almost by definition indefinite and indefinable, or at least changing, pluralistic, and ambiguous in signification."[3] He goes on:

> Especially in early 19th century American thought and expression, the term "West" is not only all-inclusive but it perpetually vacillates between what might be called an absolute meaning (location) and what might be called a relative meaning (direction) . . .[4]

As far as defining "frontier," Frederick Jackson Turner carefully called attention to the way "frontier" had come to mean for America the edge of settlement rather than, as in Europe, a political boundary. The frontier was the imaginary line between American civilization and nature, or the uncreated future, and everything that came to depend upon that line was ironically reversible.

Paradoxically enough, any study of the West involves other geographical areas. Henry Nash Smith points out that:

> The process of westward expansion would create three main divisions of the society: a remote fringe of backwoods settlements, a central region of comfortable farms, and, to the East, a region of growing wealth, cities, and social stratification. Crèvecoeur believed that both the beginning and the end of the process brought about undesirable social conditions. But the middle condition offered a unique opportunity for human virtue and happiness.[5]

Doug crossing that "imaginary line between American civilization and nature" in Wild and Woolly, *directed by John Emerson in 1917.*

The West as a process is the whole point, and it remains for one to realize just what part of the process he is talking about.

As we saw with Boone the Western experience could be both creative and destructive. At once, the pioneer could be seen as a "good" and a "bad" person, while the West itself was seen as a land of promise and virtue, or as a regressive territory. In Crèvecoeur's "Letters from an American Farmer," written in 1782 the Western American is first defined as a pilgrim carrying with him the great mass of the arts; yet later, the pioneer is seen to be "the most hideous part of our society, bad people, dull, uneducated, degenerated."[6] As exciting as the West might be metaphorically, a promotional tract in the early 1800's conceded that in the actual West "the very atmosphere of society is averse to mental culture . . ."[7] The idea of Western progress could sometimes turn into cultural regression. As Fussell points out, it is not surprising that at the heart of the American language radically divergent conceptions of the national destiny were seen in conflicting notions of "back" ("Backwoodsman") and "front" ("frontiersman"). It developed, too, that as the westward movement reached the Pacific, all those areas west of the Mississippi Valley, formerly designated as the "West," underwent a new shift. Now these lands were two distinct "Wests." There was the commonplace domesticated area within the agricultural frontier with its despised social strata; and the Wild West beyond it, which was an exhilarating region of adventure and comradeship in the open air, its heroes anarchic and free.[8]

This last can be seen in Francis Parkman's antithetical attitudes toward backwoods farmers and the hunters and trappers of the wilderness. Himself a product of a complex social order and blessed with a fortune enabling him to lead a free life, he indulged in a refined hostility to progress and a penchant toward the slightly decadent cult of wildness and savagery that the nineteenth century took over from Byron. How easily are the ambivalent attitudes toward the West transferred from region to region until no one is sure just where the "West" is!

How is it that the term "West" acquired such a powerful and complex significance? As a territory of the imagination it is inhabited by the ghosts of several highly volatile traditions that haunt the mind. America received all the impetus of hundreds of years of speculation about the "West." Two of the most important sources of this stem from religious thought and from, particularly after the Enlightenment, a hostility toward materialistic progress.

Traditionally, the nonspecified territory of the "West" has come to mean nothing less than a step toward the attainment of paradise on earth. The pursuit of paradise in philosophy and literature—or, in Santayana's phrase, "the long way round to Nirvana"—stems, as the scientist would say, from nothing so basic as the tendency in living organic matter to revert to an earlier, simpler condition of being, which it has been forced to abandon by external disturbing forces, and which each additional effort to regain puts farther beyond reach. Upon this prosaic base has been constructed all the varicolored structures of the mythic West and its beckoning mansions of paradise.

Talk of an earthly paradise is firmly embedded in Western tradition. The European mind had dreamed for centuries before the Enlightenment of an absolute West, a place of refuge beyond the seas, to which the hero retreats to await rebirth. The absolute West was seen to be a "source of new life in the direction of the setting sun which seems to stand for death."[9] This is the seed that later led to the inevitable disillusionment that accompanied the achievement of Manifest Destiny, which will be discussed a bit later. If the West signified rebirth it must have meant a kind of death too.

In its simplest archetypal form, the West of religious experience affirmed that Europeans experienced a regeneration in the New World. They became new, better, happier men—they were reborn. In most versions, the regenerative power was located in the natural terrain—in the access to undefiled, bountiful, sublime Nature, accounting for the virtue and special good fortune of Americans. It was only natural that the man who lives in and is intrinsic to such an environment would likewise share in such virtuous attributes. Thus, we come to that denizen of the New World known as the "Natural Man," or "The Noble Savage."

Doug becomes a better man in the West, seen here with Frank Campeau in Headin' South *1918.*

The New World was to become the seat of new theories concerning "natural law." Were there seeds of perfectionism in nature? Yes, said Lope de Vega in his "The Discovery of the New World by Christopher Columbus," written in 1614. Therein, an Indian chieftain at one point declares "Nature and fortune have joined forces to give me happiness. Nature has given me body, intelligence, strength."[10] Only a little later America became "The Promised Land" where Columbus, with the help of the noble savage, was "to begin to achieve the redemption of the whole human race."[11] Still later, Walt Whitman located the "Natural Man" in the Pacific slopes, dedicating his *Leaves of Grass* to "the free, original life there . . . simple diet, and clean and sweet blood . . . litheness, majestic faces, clear eyes, and perfect physique there."[12] Again, we encounter a contradiction: the New World is the seat for both the natural man and the regenerated man. The former has no heritage or memory, only vision and innocence, while the latter has passed through a trial of some kind, and has history and tradition in its past. Can both dwell there?

Earlier, we asked, is the pioneer good or bad; the West progressive or regressive, creative or destructive? The real question is: Is the "natural" a source of spontaneous goodness, instinctive nobility, untutored piety, or is it the breeding ground of a demonic, destructive force hostile to our salvation? This uncertainty is not surprising since we have already seen that the West implied both creation and destruction in the figure of Boone. Leslie Fiedler points out that Nathaniel Hawthorne cannot conceive of the innocent Westerner, and that even James Fenimore

Cooper cannot be free of ignoble Indians and is forced to admit that even in the wilderness there was violence and terror, even in the natural, something dangerous to the progress of mankind. The ambivalent figure of Boone can be considered either as standard bearer of civilization with all the more ominous and destructive aspects of civilization, or as a fugitive child of nature retreating from that encroachment. In his spiritual descendents we can see some of the same contradictions. At the same time, we are brought closer to the genre of the "Western" as we shall consider it with Douglas Fairbanks.

The Western Hero in American culture progressed in a line from people like Boone and Leatherstocking—who were primarily symbols of anarchic freedom—to the wild Western hunter and scout and, of course, the cowboy. These latter figures share Boone's ambivalent attitudes toward nature and civilization. Henry Nash Smith flatly states that they reached status as heroic figures only at the cost of losing contact with nature.[13] Joe Frantz and Julian Choate refer to the cowboy's role as empire builder when they quote Joseph Nimmo:

> In the course of a few years, hundreds of thousands of cattle, almost all of them driven from the state of Texas as yearlings and two-year-olds, quietly grazing through the former haunts of the buffalo, and the cowboy, armed and equipped, a bold rider and valiant in fight, became the dominating power through the vast areas where a few years before the Indian had bidden defiance to the advancement of the arts of civilization. The question of Indian wars was thus forever settled in the region mentioned.[14]

With each surge of Western movement in America a new community came into being and gradually Western man became identified with these communities—the range rider with barbed wire territories, the trail herder with the cattle drives, the rancher and sheepman with their respective domains, the frontier scout with the advancing wagon trains. In the larger sense, the cowboy was closely allied with settlements, and by their actions, did their part in advancing those settlements.

The famous "dime-novels" idealized figures like the cowboy and range rider, bringing them closer to the Fairbanksian genre, as we shall see. We refer to the series of Erastus Beadle Westerns that began appearing in 1860, and that began to use the cowboy as hero and central protagonist in the 1880's—the same time that the figure of Buffalo Bill appeared on the national scene. In 1882 Cody presided over an "Old Glory blowout," sort of a forerunner of the Western rodeo, in North Platte, Nebraska. His brightest cowboy star was Buck Taylor, "who could ride the worst bucking horse, throw a steer by the horns or tail, and pick up a neckerchief from the ground at full speed."[15] It was Taylor, Smith writes, who was perhaps the earliest real-life model for the Beadle cowboy hero. This kind of hero brought legitimacy and distinction to a hitherto rather dreary, suspicious figure, the cowboy. Joe Frantz and Julian Choate, Jr., flatly disagree:

> In the seventies and eighties the cowboy achieved a reputation, largely unsavory, which he has never quite lived down. The yellow press, the Beadle and Adams novels . . . and Theodore Roosevelt's colorful championing all combined to present a highly distorted picture. Serious writers, therefore, have avoided the cowboy for fear they might wind up defending Zane Grey or Deadwood Dick. . . .[16]

Nevertheless, these novels did try to lift the hero up from the imbecilic. As Buck Taylor says in one of them, "We lead a wild life, get hard knocks, rough usage and our lives are in constant peril, and the settling of a difficulty is an appeal to revolver or knife; but after all we are not as black as we are painted."[17]

This kind of cowboy hero brought some new traits to the western hero. As the dime-novel series progressed, competition from other series forced outworn formulas to be elaborated by sensations and gimmicks:

> Circus tricks of horsemanship, incredible feats of shooting, more and more elaborate costumes, masks, and passwords were introduced. . . . Killing a few more Indians meant, in practice, exaggerating violence and bloodshed for their own sakes, to the point of an overt sadism. By the 1890's the western dime-novel had come to hinge almost entirely upon conflicts between detectives and bands of robbers that had little to do with the ostensibly Western locales.[18]

This kind of circus atmosphere, very much a part of the wild and fanciful fun of conscious myth-making, incurred much derision from various quarters. Even today Joe Frantz and Julian Choate can deride Buffalo Bill for the very reasons that he is significant:

> William F. Cody was as vain as a woman at Easter, as unprincipled as a race track tout, and as congenital a liar as the man who wrote those all-inclusive patent medicine ads of the

nineteenth century. Cody—or Buffalo Bill—has also come to be a symbol for the Wild West, proving again that there is considerable value and significance to any liar-promoter provided he can perform his dubious services in a grandiloquent manner. Buffalo Bill could do just that.[19]

So, for better or worse (and, admittedly, most critics readily concede it is for the worst), the Fairbanksian cowboy inherited three basic devices from the circus kind of cowboy. The first is that the cowboy hero rarely was seen in his occupation or routine workday; the second, that his pursuits lay in rather melodramatic directions not especially intrinsic to the West; third, that his costume and technique were stylizations enforced upon the subject matter.

As the cowboy began to achieve prominence as a national "type" and a mythic kind of hero, the nature of his daily occupations grew more obscured or was ignored altogether. Readers could not be bored with the tedium of the range life when they could be titillated by the thrills of desparadoes and sequined chaps. Smith concludes:

> Whatever may be the merits of the dime-novel cowboy, however, he apparently has nothing to do with cattle . . . most cowboy tales are hardly distinguishable from the Deadwood Dick and Buffalo Bill series. The professional duty of Beadle cowboys is to fight Indians, Mexicans, and outlaws. And the atmosphere created by wronged women seeking vengeance upon their false lovers, Mexican girls in men's clothing, and Army officers detailed for secret service is thoroughly typical of the decadent phase of Beadle fiction.[20]

Thus was classic melodrama substituted for dreary range life. The West was the theater of operations, all right, but apparently the daily chores were regarded in that same light that we saw much of the West was regarded earlier: in that ambivalent attitude expressed through the words "frontiersman" and "backwoodsman."

The third aspect was costume. It is really impossible to discuss Fairbanks without some word on costume. It is such an important element in his films (and he consciously made it so) that it is of interest to see how, in the Western hero at least, this kind of costume stylization that led to such monstrous twentieth century interpretations as Tom Mix's and Gene Autry's films, got started in the first place. The character of Buffalo Bill is the chief precedent. In a mammoth series of dime-novels written by Prentiss Ingraham,

Buffalo Bill was lifted entirely out of any kind of prosaic activity. His pursuits were altogether toward Indian fighting, hunting, and derring-do; his costume, accordingly, was anything but prosaic. In an effort to elaborate upon an already stylized figure the splendor of his attire grew brighter. Henry Nash Smith views him at various stages in his career, both in the novels and in real-life, and we see him, variously, in a red velvet jacket and white corduroy pants, embroidered silk shirt and gauntlet gloves, black velvet slashed with scarlet and trimmed with silver buttons and lace, etc.[21] His protégé, incidentally, the redoubtable Buck Taylor went him one better, wearing a miniature lariat about his dove-colored sombrero (in "Buck Taylor, The Saddle King").[22] All this, in real-life, and in novels, shows how showmanship came to the West. Conscious myth-making prevailed and Buffalo and others seemed literally to wear their hearts on their highly embroidered sleeves.

The foregoing are some of the ramifications brought to the Western hero during the age of the cowboy. Beyond the obvious uses of the West as myth, the ideas of removing the cowboy from his prosaic occupations, having him function as a detective or Indian fighter, and clothing him in unlikely but resplendent garb—these all reappear in the Fairbanks Westerns as we shall see. The box office appeal that appeared in such as Buffalo Bill was transferred almost intact.

So it is that this kind of hero, although seemingly anarchic and wild, really was closely tied to the East—the East of the publishers of the dime-novels, their writers, their readers. And in those stories the hero was associated with the community. Henry Nash Smith says that the spiritual meaning that we found in the West, became more and more inaccessible after the middle of the nineteenth century: "The static ideas of virtue and happiness and peace drawn from the bosom of the virgin wilderness . . . proved quite irrelevant for a society committed to the ideas of civilization and progress, and to an industrial revolution."[23] This kind of Western hero was achieving his status only at the cost of losing contact with nature.

The second powerful impetus to American Western traditions was an antimaterialistic trend occurring later in the late nineteenth century. Again, the paired terms "East" and "West" are vital. The dialectic of postbellum American civilization most clearly manifests itself in contradictory attitudes toward industry. These attitudes simultaneously embraced and rejected the industrializing process: "East" now stood for those portions of America that had assumed an industrialist, metropolitan character regardless of their geographical location; the "West" now represented those portions that remained nonindustrial—or anti-industrial and anti-metropolitan. Certain areas of America were beginning, around the 1880s, to resemble the hated Old World. This caused a bitter reaction from those who had sought to escape it. Edenic expectations were paradoxically yielding to spectacular material success—a blasphemous result. Material progress is complicated. It seemed that the more America turned away from the Old World the more material progress came its way. What began to happen was the emergence of that classical symbol of evil, the citadel of the Eastern Establishment—the city.

The provincial American has always thrilled to the promise of the city. The city's hellish nature underneath the gloss is, as can be seen in R. W. B. Lewis' study *The American Adam*, the focal point of many an American novel as well. Charles Sanford agrees:

> A favorite theme of American novelists, a theme closely related to studies of failure in our society, has been the contrast of country and city—the innocent boy or girl from the country destroyed physically and morally, and spiritually by the temptations of city life.[24]

Parenthetically, it did not take cinema very long to take up this theme, and we automatically think of such films as *Way Down East, True Heart Susie, Romance of Happy Valley*, all by Griffith, as being typical.

The anti-industrial attitude focussed upon the city and then looked quickly away—toward the West. The only problem near the end of the nineteenth century was that many of such cities now were in the regions formerly called "the West!" Nevertheless, it seemed that only in areas west of Kansas, particularly the areas of Wyoming, Montana, Arizona, could there be found respite from the city. Such regions of the west, by contrast to the cities, became in the latter nineteenth century the symbol for virtue and the cure for Eastern ailments. We saw a hint of this inclination earlier in the primitivism of Francis Parkman. He first viewed the West from a pain-wracked body within the wealthy society of the industrial East, just as Roosevelt would do only a few decades later. Parkman resolved to go West and write his history of the Canadian territory. Later, and still within Parkman's lifetime in the 1880s, we see Theodore Roosevelt leaving for a West that had already found its boundaries, but

A pampered gentleman faces the challenges of Arizona in The Mollycoddle (1919). *Note the resemblance to Teddy Roosevelt, one of Fairbank's heros. (T. R. had coined the word "mollycoddle.")*

which still had all the wildness in its spaces one could want. Roosevelt's involvement with the West stemmed from his position within the social stratification of the East—his escape from the latter led him to the former. In Roosevelt, as with Parkman and earlier with Boone, we see two opposing lifestyles bound up in opposing geographical constructs. His reconciliation of the two is a good introduction to the Western character of Douglas Fairbanks.

It will be necessary here to elaborate a bit on the links between Roosevelt and Fairbanks. Within the context of the Parkman tradition it is interesting to observe two later figures who to an extent embodied Parkman's refined but muscular revulsion to many elements in the Eastern establishment. Like the enfeebled Parkman, Roosevelt went West partially because of a weak bodily constitution.

Europe had its ocean voyage and "grand tour" as prescriptions for those mysterious, civilized illnesses of the early nineteenth century. The American counterpart was the trip west via the Pullman car and grand hotel. We have already seen that "going West" seemed to prescribe cures for Eastern ailments. Now in the example Roosevelt we are to see a practical application of this idea.

A tragedy in Roosevelt's life led him westward in search of solace and new life. Theodore Roosevelt sprang from the center of the social and occupational circle that constituted the Eastern Establishment. The Roosevelt family had had an impressive financial history. Their business ventures had stemmed from a flourishing hardware business early in the nineteenth century to the manufacturing of supplies and plate glass, and finally grew into banking. At Theodore Sr.'s death the business was valued at $750,000—a handsome valuation in those days. In the best of social traditions Theodore Jr., unlike Parkman, had a strong feeling of "class" and family. Like Fairbanks, he was preoccupied with all those things so inimical to the Western myth, including a strong tendency to look backward to antecedents, such as to the father figure and to symbols of authority.

Roosevelt, like Fairbanks and Parkman, was obsessed with physical culture. As a boy he had detested his puny body. He was ashamed of eyes so weak that one failed entirely before he was fifty. The clue to the evangelical vitality of his later years lies in those days of childhood. Roosevelt, by unending persistence, developed his body to outward, if physiologically imperfect strength. The Roosevelt Gospel of Strenuosity stemmed from this, and anybody who did less was no true patriot. It was this form of moral energy that unified such diverse figures as Parkman, Roosevelt, Billy Sunday, and Fairbanks. It found its natural outlet in the West. Whether it was affectation or not, it clung to these people all their lives, and in Roosevelt had some curious manifestations. When Roosevelt was in the White House, for instance, in the years 1903–1909, he took regular excursions with friends like Major General Leonard Wood, Luther ("Yellowstone") Kelly, James Garfield, and Major General Thomas Barry. These "outings" took the form of

swimming Rock Creek and the Potomac in the early spring, one hundred mile rides, and long hikes at other times. He formed the famous "Tennis Cabinet" for these activities and gathered together a rather wild mixture of Western friends, ambassadors, and government officials. No one was immune to a sudden expedition, and visitors came to the White House at their own risk. Parallelling this are the excursions by horseback through the California wilds by Fairbanks and whatever guests happened to be visiting Pickfair, be they visiting royalty or local gentry.

In the 1880s barely in his thirties, the city-bred Roosevelt, a graduate of Harvard and an experienced world traveler accustomed to the higher circles of society and government, lost his wife and almost went mad with grief. His bereavement, coupled with a longstanding urge to go West and "chuck" the cares of Eastern life, decided him on a trip to Dakota territory to become a cattleman. According to Leslie Fiedler, the West meant both death and life, a passage through suffering and trial resulting in renewal. Thus did Roosevelt's bereavement lead to expectations for a new life in Dakota, and true to tradition, he set out for, if not the Promised, at least the Promising lands.

Very much the dude, with a high-pitched voice, prominent teeth, spectacles, and an affected way about him, Roosevelt must have had quite an effect on the inhabitants of Dakota. One well-known story of that time describes the first time Roosevelt took part in a roundup in 1884. Some hardened cowboys about fell from their saddles when they heard his high voice admonish some of the men to "hasten forward quickly there!" The image is not so dissimilar from the Fairbanks of *The Mollycoddle.* A bespectacled fellow in morning suit moving rather stiffly among more hardened characters in Arizona, yet a man who, when called upon to prove himself, provided enough muscle and resource to save the day. Roosevelt wrote once:

> You would be amused to see me, in my broad sombrero hat, fringed and beaded buckskin shirt, horsehide chaparajos or riding trousers, and cowboy boots, with braided bridle and silver spurs.[25]

How close these words are to the costume conceptions of the dime-novel heroes like Buffalo Bill and Buck Taylor! We see them echoed visually later in a Fairbanks film, *Wild and Woolly,* when a thorough Easterner shows up in the town of

Doug as Dude in Wild and Woolly *(1917). The Artcraft production crew includes John Emerson, with megaphone, and cameraman Victor Fleming.*

Bitter Creek, Arizona, dressed to the teeth in his conception of the "proper" Wild West costume, a wild and clumsy creation of chaps and revolvers surmounted by huge neckerchief and hat.

Roosevelt's memory of his experiences out West remained vivid the rest of his life. Doubtless many an ear grew weary of his rather excessive boasting and exaggeration about the whole thing, a situation not unlike Fairbanks' boasting in his 1916 *Manhattan Madness*. An example of this kind of attitude is Roosevelt's slight boast:

It would electrify some of my friends . . . if they could see me galloping over the plains, day in and out . . . with a big sombrero over my head. For good, healthy exercise I would strongly recommend some of our gilded youth to go West and try a short course of riding bucking ponies and assisting at the branding of a lot of Texas steers.[26]

It is all here . . . the Eastern reverence for the anarchic West, the Western disdain for the Eastern "gilded" youth, the Eastern yearning for the free and muscular virtues of the cowboy's world, and Western "dime-novel" terms wherein those virtues are couched. Aside from this is a typical tone of self-consciousness so much a part of Roosevelt's (and certainly Fairbanks') personality. Such references, along with more carefully restrained comments on the hardships to be encountered in the West, abound in his books, *Hunting Trips of a Ranchman* (1885) and *Ranch Life and the Hunting Trail*.

When the city-bred Roosevelt went West he took much of the Eastern styles of speech and costume with him. When he returned to the East, he likewise tried to bring something of the West with him, which so happens to be a staple theme in most of the Fairbanks Westerns. An amusing example of this tendency is quoted by G. E. White, concerning Roosevelt's return from Montana in 1885. It points out the quite naive and certainly self-conscious way Roosevelt was liable to mix his geographies. Roosevelt had himself photographed in his beloved buckskin shirt and elaborate regalia. For a background he tried to recreate an "essential" Western setting. As White quotes Hermann Hagedorn:

> There is something hilariously funny in the visible records of that performance. The imitation grass not quite concealing the rug beneath; the painted background, the theatrical (slightly patched) rocks against which (Roosevelt) leans gazing dreamily across an imaginary prairie . . . with rifle ready and finger on the trigger, grimly facing dangerous game which is not there.[27]

This is astonishingly like the opening to Fairbanks' *Wild and Woolly.* As the picture opens, Doug sits before a campfire, eating "grub," his tent in the background. "Ah," we think, "here is the American Cowboy." But the camera draws back from its tight close-up and we see that all of this is an artificial setup within the rooms of a luxurious mansion. Similarly, in *The Mollycoddle,* the opening shot is a tight close-up of Fairbanks' dandified young sophisticate astride a prancing pony—until a medium shot reveals the pony to be of the merry-go-round variety.

In this way, we see how strange a combination of East and West at times came together in these two men, and how both were highly flexible components of their minds. Roosevelt is but one more step in the developing American attitudes toward the West. Like the railroad turning from Western shores back toward the East, Roosevelt was unique in the consolidation of East and West. He not only faced both directions, but also succeeded in interchanging them and infusing into them a kind of naive, romantic dream. The Rooseveltian character, and by parallel the Fairbanksian one, encompasses many images and concepts—the image of an outlandish Western costume against an artificial Western backdrop; the urge to leave the city to go West and return again; the self-reliance that enabled him to meet and conquer many of the hazards of the ranching life in the sometimes inhospitable range country of Montana and Wyoming; the extrapolation of

the West as a kind of "test" of endurance and virtue. They all help to explain what is happening in the Fairbanks Westerns. This last, particularly, as part of the Parkman tradition, is important.

It is a part of the tradition of the American West that the Western lands be seen in an ambivalent light. Earlier we saw the example of the noble frontiersman and the degenerated backwoodsman. The land, too, meant good and bad things at once. For Francis Parkman, the discomforts of the West were at once the test and burden of the venturing man. He concedes that there is a stretch of country which

> will answer tolerably well to . . . preconceived ideas of the prairie; for this it is from which picturesque tourists, painters, poets and novelists who have seldom penetrated further, have derived their conceptions of the whole region. But let him be as enthusiastic as he may, he will find enough to damp his ardor. His wagons will stick in the mud; his horses will break loose; harness will give way; and axletrees prove unsound.[28]

Even Theodore Roosevelt, who felt much the same way about the necessity of meeting the obstacles posed by the Old West, did not close his eyes to those aspects less glamorous than those held by the popular opinion:

> In that land we led a free and hardy life, with horse and with rifle. We worked under the scorching midsummer sun, when the wild plains shimmered and wavered in the heat; and we knew the freezing misery of riding mounted guard round the cattle in the late fall round-up . . . We knew toil and hardship and hunger and thirst; and we saw men die violent deaths as they worked among the horses and cattle, or fought in evil feuds with one another; but we felt the beat of hardy life in our veins, and ours was the glory of work and the joy of living.[29]

This predominantly masculine attitude toward the dangers of the West finds strength through conflict, and virtue in the less savory aspects of the landscape. R. W. B. Lewis notes that Parkman's West was ". . . a dedication to the unfenced, the wild, and the boundless, not out of a dream of innocence and novelty in a *vita nuova* but out of a hard, uncompromising, impatient, and severely masculine ideal of life."[30] Toughness, endurance, and other aspects of the cult of masculinity were his foremost concerns, although he remained throughout his life constitutionally feeble and at times nearly blind. His own words best illuminate his views about these aspects of the West and it is clear to see that uppermost in his mind was *the test and the burden* of the venturing man. In an autobiographical letter to Charles Ellis, Parkman, refering to himself in the third person, talks of his own life, its sufferings (which were considerable) and what he considers the triumphs of the strenuous life. Emerging out of his words is the inescapable notion that pain and triumph are inseparable:

> . . . his thoughts were always in the forests, whose features, not unmixed with softer images, possessed his waking and sleeping dreams, filling him with vague cravings impossible to satisfy. As fond of hardships as he was vain of enduring them, cherishing a sovereign scorn for every physical weakness or defect, deceived, moreover, by a rapid development of frame and sinews—which flattered him with the belief that discipline sufficiently unsparing would harden him into an athlete. . . . He tired old foresters with long marches, stopped neither for heat nor rain, and slept on the earth without a blanket.[31]

Such expectations were not to be, however. If for some the West could revive the feeble frame and otherwise prove its healthful and salutary benefits, for Parkman the effects were at best mixed. Nervous and physical maladies afflicted him and at first seemed to daunt his ambition to write the history of the American conflict between France and England—nothing less than firsthand experience in the territories involved would satisfy him. Ignoring his ill health he went West anyway, to the Rocky Mountains. Soon "complication of severe disorders here seized him" wherein at times he was "reeling in the saddle with weakness and pain."[32] By simply and doggedly keeping on with his quest for experience, with only a horse and servant for companions, he gained, at times, some lost strength, referring to "the tonic of the chase." Yet, once he returned to the settlements to recuperate, his condition grew worse and near-blindness (which was to plague him the rest of his life) all but incapacitated him. He chafed at the inactivity:

> Indeed, the change from intense activity to flat stagnation, attended with an utter demolition of air castles, may claim a place . . . in that legion of mental tortures which make the torments of the Inferno seem endurable.[33]

Clearly his energies did their part in exhausting him, yet he could still say that "on behalf of manhood and common sense," such a life was justified:

> Nor, even in the case in question, was the evil unmixed, since from the same source whence it issued came also the habits of mind and muscular vigor which saved him from a ruin absolute and irremediable.[34]

Parkman's relationship to the West, is, then, an unflinching view of the West as a conflict and test, one in which the spirit outruns the body:

> The condition was that of a rider whose horse runs headlong the bit between his teeth, or of a locomotive, built of indifferent material, under a head of steam too great for its strength, kissing at a score of crevices, yet rushing on with accelerating speed to the inevitable smash.[35]

The destructive creative dialectic clearly receives forceful definition here.

Fairbanks inherited these kinds of drives. Without exception the West in his films is a test, taxing, in most cases, Eastern weaknesses and drawing out the virtues of strength of resource. This is clear even in his first film in 1915, *The Lamb*, which for a time was to have been titled, "The Man and the Test." It is not until the slightly effete and ineffectual Easterner finds himself West that he realizes the dynamism that apparently had been there all the time. The combative and aggressive stance that informs all his films certainly finds its most extreme manifestation in some of the Westerns. Fairbanks himself commented about what we might call the Parkman tradition of toughness:

> Among the books about America for Americans, perhaps Roosevelt's *Winning of the West* is among the best. Not only has he thrown the whole vigor of his interesting personality into the writing of it, but he has given us a vivid picture of the conquest of the States by the settlers. No man could read it without being thrilled at the dangers our forefathers faced . . . at the great courage they possessed . . . at their hardihood . . . their bulldog tenacity.[36]

Now that we have seen some of the numerous and contradictory elements that have informed the American West with its peculiarly rich and suggestive quality, we can begin to link them more closely with the cinema of Douglas Fairbanks. It surprises many to see some of the early Fairbanks comedies after experiencing only the

*East meets West: Doug, essentially an urban product, poses
here while making* A Modern Musketeer.

later swashbucklers. To see the latter figure with
cloak and rapier and mustache replaced by the
peppy, urban, go-getter sans mustache comes as
something of a shock. Likewise, to many, the
rugged athletics of the Fairbanks character
would seem to point to a real life out West, to an
upbringing fraught with danger, wild horses, and
boundless horizons. In the style of Tom Mix only
a person who had lived such a life could bring it so
zestfully to the screen. Actually, Fairbanks, like
another Western star, William S. Hart, was essentially an urban product. Although his childhood
was spent in the Denver of the boom years of the
1880s, he could never pretend to a youth spent in
the Wild West. From the very beginnings, as is
plain upon examining Hancock's biography, his
sights were set on New York, and, after meeting
Fredric Warde when he appeared in Denver on
one of his perennial tours, he set his mind on

going there at the first opportunity. It is the East
that dominantly shaped his personality, not the
West. The East was a concrete reality for him:
New York was the center of his Broadway career,
his many business interludes (such as his partnership in a Wallstreet firm and the vice-presidency
in the soap company), and was the focus of his
very active social and club life. The West remained a country of the imagination, more often
than not, perhaps, shaped by the stresses of the
Eastern world. That is the way the West is
portrayed in his films—as a part of a dialectic
involving the East, and usually as a kind of dream
country best exemplified in a film like *Manhattan
Madness* or *Wild and Woolly*.

It is absolutely essential to understand Fairbanks' predilection for the East. Eileen Bowser, in
her notes for the Museum of Modern Art Film
Library booklet, states that "without doubt, a

lasting effect of his shift from Broadway to the West Coast was a keen contempt for city life." This, at best, is only half true. Fairbanks constantly returned to New York. Even after establishing himself in Triangle Pictures, he returned East many times, ostensibly to make a picture, such as *His Picture in the Papers* or later for Artcraft, *In Again, Out Again*. Like so many energetic and restless natures, he often sought out the very thing that could hem him in—city life. Yet there he found vitality and society, two things he could never be without for very long. It should be remembered, moreover, that the West for Fairbanks was Hollywood, California, for him a land of swelling economic success. Perhaps it was this connection that so firmly attached the ideals of success and prosperity—basically Eastern concepts—to his Western films.

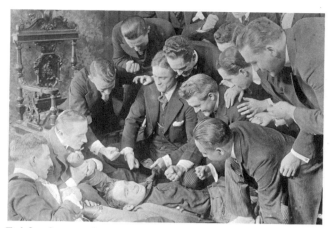

Fairbanks as Steve O'Dare among his Eastern club associates in Manhatten Madness *(1916), a lost film.*

.MANHATTAN MADNESS (Sept. 10, 1916)

Directed by Allan Dwan.
Scenario by E. V. Durling.

Fairbanks is Steve O'Dare;
Jewel Carmen is the girl;
George Beranger is the butler;
Warner P. Richmond is Jack Osborne;

At 9:30 o'clock last night Douglas Fairbanks bounded between the red draperies of the tabloid stage of the Rialto Theater, and, hands in trousers' pockets stood smiling at a large audience. He said he thought the picture was pretty good, that he nearly lost his eyesight during the taking, but that the picture on which he was now working would be better because he had already been hurt more times. . . . Mr. Fairbanks is right, *Madness* is a good picture.[37]

Insofar as its thematic content is concerned, this picture, along with *Wild and Woolly* and *Down to Earth*, has to be considered one of the major products of his early period. It plainly states and develops so many of the characteristic Fairbanks attitudes toward the "West" that it should remain with us for awhile that we may look at it more closely. In addition, its peculiar Rooseveltian quality makes it a splendid personal statement.

It is the story of Steve O'Dare, a gilded Manhattan youth who decides to go West after growing up in society. As the film opens, he is returning to New York with a carload of cattle and horses for the Russian government. Waiting for the final details of his transaction from official sources, he thoroughly annoys everyone at his club with his talk of Wyoming and its thrills. Only in the West, proselytizes Mr. O'Dare, can life be found and really lived. Soon Steve gets bored with New York. His friends are avoiding him, and everything is generally uninteresting. Every man, it seems is insipid or dishonest, there are no adventures, the life is unhealthy, there is no real sport, and absolutely no wonderful women—well, except perhaps for one girl he has his eyes on. O'Dare's situation grows worse until his friends wager that if he will stay in New York another week he will be sure to encounter a thrill.

Presently Steve is presented with a summons to come to the Russian agent's house in the outskirts of New York for a conclusion of the business transaction and payment. Once there, insipid New York disappears and he promptly detects a plot to assault and rob him. Next, he discovers that his girlfriend is a prisoner there for some mysterious reason. Before he can move to protect his life, limb, and money, as well as to rescue her, he sees two men murdered before his very eyes. A bit staggered he sets about to right all these inequities. In the process he whips a dozen men in the best Fairbanksian manner, scales walls of the house with the ease of a fly, hurdles in and out of windows, races around the eaves of the housetop as if it were a running track. At the finale, battered, bruised, bleeding but victorious, Steve winds up at a table in the sinister house's dining room, at which time, all his club acquaintances pop up quite suddenly laughing heartily at their joke, the girl louder than the rest. Admitting that there *can* be some excitement east of the Hudson, he turns the tables and sends for his friends the cowboys back at the stockyards. They arrive in a busy climax and hold off the jokers enabling O'Dare to "kidnap" the girl, race off to a departing ocean liner, and marry her at sea. Everything comes together here at the last, cowboys and city folk, concrete walls and stetson hats, high society and animal spirits.

Fairbanks had brought contemporary comedy-drama into *His Picture in the Papers*; the Western romance of the virgin soil in *The Half-Breed*. In *Manhattan Madness* he combined the two elements into a peculiar synthesis that marks the best Fairbanks Westerns as unique and worthy of further attention. It is one of the fastest paced of the pre-1920 films. Dwan's comment earlier in this study that he cut in the camera, has its verification here, in that there is no wasted motion. The scenes are quickly played, the cutting nervous and the movement extremely fast. Such a clean-limbed brand of filmmaking is rare today.

Before proceeding further, it is necessary to mention a film made later in 1917 called *Wild and Woolly,* a Western that has its own parallels with *Manhattan Madness.* Looking at them both together for a moment points up a solid motif in many of Fairbanks Westerns—East and West as a paired dialectic. In both we have a youth bored with the city and dreaming greedily of the West. According to the terms of R. W. B. Lewis, the former film would be a film of "hope," the latter a film of "memory." In *Wild and Woolly* our hero has never been West and has only a naive dream of it, picturing to himself a land of superbly romanticized action and style. His idea of a real woman, for instance, is a fiery female astride a magnificent stallion (surely a symbol for further speculation by psychologists), and for a cowtown he pictures a rip-roaring abode for outlaws, gamblers, and dance hall girls. Most of the Fairbanks Westerns spotlighted the expansive, sometimes wild animal spirits and rugged athletics of his cowboy drives, centering upon the open theater of the West. As a region of the imagination where boundless activity was the order of the day, the West was vital geography for Doug. *Wild and Woolly* is a film of the party of "hope," to extrapolate upon Mr. Lewis a bit. To those in the early nineteenth century who ascribed to this doctrine, America had fostered "a clear conscience unsullied by the past."[38] According to this creed America had no past, only a present and future, only expectation and vision. Lewis points out that the key term in this moral vocabulary is "innocence."[39] (At the time of *Wild and Woolly* the West is not really as Fairbanks dreams of it;

instead it is modern and progressive. Thus, one can argue that Fairbanks' dream is really nostalgia over a departed past, over a West as it can never be again. The point, then, and this must be emphasized, is that the West was *never* as our hero in *Wild and Woolly* dreamed of it. Rather, it is presented as an ideal lifestyle pitted against the stifling environment of the industrial East. Thus, it is not a memory of the past, merely an innocent dream of a better life.) The film in its own way is a part of an American tradition that saw America as a vision of innocence and a claim of newness. It is the imagination hungering for freedom, a basic element in the formation of the American West.

If *Wild and Woolly* is a film suggestive of hope, then *Manhattan Madness* is suggestive of memory. Steve O'Dare has been West and hungers with nostalgia. The West he remembers is much the same West that is projected in *Wild and Woolly.* That much is a constant in Fairbanks' work; nevertheless, it is a part of his memory in this case. In its capacity of a departed grace for Steve it is sharing in an American intellectual doctrine that America is *not* innocent and new, but a continuation of traditions attached to Europe.

We have earlier noted the essential contradiction in the figure of Daniel Boone as essential to an understanding of the peculiar ambiguities of the American West. Boone can be seen as either an empire builder or a child of nature. Indeed, one seems to lead into the other. When we see how these two Western films of Fairbanks participate in both the notions of hope and of memory, we can begin to see that we are really dealing in similar terms. The child of nature is the dreamer of innocence, the new being that creates around it a new experience. The empire builder is the nostalgic creature with roots in the past—he draws from it and extends it. We will see as we progress that Fairbanks shares equally in both roles.

Returning to a brief comparison of these two Westerns, we see a peculiar kind of alchemy occurring. We have two regions to deal with—three, actually. One is the effete East as contrasted with the rugged West:

If the metropolitan East is effete, Fairbanks would not be Fairbanks and would certainly not be an American, to let it go at that. He must offer an antidote, a goal the fretting city worker can aim at. Fairbanks did not have to invent it . . . It was the "West."[40]

Another region is the rugged West as contrasted

against the effete East. Hollywood has commonly defined these two regions by constantly juxtaposing them so that one is defined by characteristics (or lack of them) of the other. In addition to these two regions is that elusive region one might hesitantly call the "real" West, which makes a brief appearance in the beginning of *Wild and Woolly*. It is Arizona in 1917, a country growing steadily to meet an Eastern example, a land of modern business and industrial drives. (Ironically enough, this town was really Burbank, California.) It is seen only briefly and only as a reminder that Fairbanks' image of the rip-roaring West is only a dream.

These regions never remain static and isolated in their peculiar characteristics, rather, they change and merge at times. The West and East in a Fairbanks film seldom remain exclusive for very long, rather, they blend and are transplanted in a clever manner. In *Wild and Woolly* he goes to the Arizona town of Bitter Creek to spearhead the building of a new railroad spur for his father's railroad. He arrives accoutred in the splendor of a Western costume the like of which had doubtless not been seen that side of the Mississippi. His arrival was probably not unlike Roosevelt's in Dakota and, in a larger sense, probably echoed many similar arrivals.

> ... the range came to expect and recognize the "mail-order cowboy" who arrived already fitted in cowboy wear as he knew it from his reading and the assurances of some Middle Western store-keeper—round, soft hat, blue silk shirt, leather knee-leggings over laced boots, short straight spurs, and a glistening pistol in a "closed" scabbard.[41]

Boom times in the 70s had brought overspeculation and an influx of cattlemen and cattle. Englishmen had sought out the plateaus of Colorado (and America had learned of the new cattle-raising country through English newspapers and magazines!), and an exodus of young men, many of them collegians, from the overcrowded East came West. Towns like Bitter Creek must have seen their share of exotic transplanted easterners.[42]

The people of Bitter Creek are anxious to live up to Fairbanks' expectations (thereby securing his approval of the railroad spur) and transform their little, forward-looking town into the rip-roaring counterpart of his dreams. They paint new "authentic" signs, plan a fake railroad hold-up, arrange fights on the city streets, etc. Suddenly his innocent fancy finds its embodiment and the adventure starts. In *Manhattan Madness*

his friends try to bring the West of his memory back to New York, transforming that into a region of adventure, rescue and daring deeds.

In all this shuffling about with dream and memory it can be seen that they are essentially the same. The Fairbanksian concept of the West is not real in either case. In each film the "West" proves to be a ruse. The beautiful thing about *Wild and Woolly* is that the ruse does, in the end, generate a *real* situation with *real* Indians and villains when some enterprising villains take advantage of the city's charade. The strength and intensity of the Fairbanksian dream for a moment finds an earthly counterpart with some very real hazards and heroics. The "West" that travels to New York is a synonym for adventure and movement and is as appropriate as the "West" that was remembered from Wyoming or created in Arizona. This is exactly a definition of Fairbanks' presence in any film, particularly the Westerns and the later costume films—that it was a kind of geography unbounded based upon both hope and memory.

Again we come back to our original premise concerning Daniel Boone—that he was at once child of nature (fugitive from civilization) and standard bearer for that civilization. In *Wild and Woolly*, Jeff Hillington goes to Arizona to promote a railroad. At the same time, he wants to retreat from the Eastern establishment and seek refuge in the romance of the West. In *Manhattan Madness* he is a wealthy youth, a scion of club society, bringing horses back from Wyoming for a New York business deal, yet he hungers with nostalgia for Wyoming.

In Fairbanks' films the West is seen both as a land of promise and as a regressive territory according to the tradition we have already traced. Unfailingly, it brings out all the manly resourcefulness, physical strength, and virtuous qualities to be found in our hero. As early as *The Lamb* we see the effete, somewhat vacantly sophisticated young man transformed by the hardy Western environment. Yet, that environment is teeming with thieves, vicious Indians, and rattlesnakes. The same transformation occurs in *The Molly-coddle*, made four years later. The ultimate Fairbanksian attitude and tribute to the West is made in one scene wherein a flashback reveals one of Doug's ancestors standing on an Arizona cliff edge, arms upraised and shouting, "Hurrah for God!" As Arthur Lennig (in *The Silent Voice*) correctly states, the scene, though potentially outrageous, works with Fairbanks, and it is a tribute to him that it does. Incidentally, it had been used a year earlier in *His Majesty the Ameri-*

can, when the hero arrives and salutes the Mexican landscape in a similar manner, although he does not forget to poke fun at the whole thing and lights his cigarette by touching it to the hard-baked earth. In that same film, moreover, is given a satiric picture of a typical Mexican town, notable for its swift understatement and the following title:

Presenting Murdero, Mexico: [where he expects to find]

> *Reptiles*
> *Bullets*
> *Bandits*
> *featuring*
> *Francisco Villa*

Villa rides hell-bent through the sleepy and deserted town once a year, kicking up a lot of dust, finally disappearing until the next year. In an interchange with a native, Fairbanks asks, "Where are all the live ones in this town?" The response is: "Dead." The same kind of ambivalence of progressive and regressive territory is in *Wild and Woolly.* Although the town and subsequent events prove Fairbanks' manhood in the Parkman tradition, we also see Bitter Creek peopled with the wildest crowd of low creatures this side of Tom Mix. The Indians, particularly, suffer from an almost vicious kind of comic stereotyping—we usually see them snarling, squinting and pulling vigorously at bottles of red-eye.

The above examples from Fairbanks' Westerns will help to see just what kind of West he was trying to picture. On the one hand it brings out all the required manly qualities in our hero, while on the other, it is a territory peopled with mean, vicious (and dim-witted) scavengers. Further, it is hardly ever seen as a geography of open range, untouched by civilization. More often than not it is bounded territory in the twentieth century. In *The Mollycoddle* we see the Arizona vallies invaded by Wallace Beery's curious land cruiser, a sort of mechanized desert tank. In *Wild and Woolly, Till the Clouds Rolly By* and *Knickerbocker Buckaroo,* the hero is a wealthy youth bringing some sort of industrial know-how to the West. In *Manhattan Madness* the West is merely a part of a business venture, since the whole thrust of the film is provided by the pending business deal for the horses Fairbanks has brought back from Wyoming. Even in the "period" pieces like *The Half-Breed, The Good Bad Man,* and *Arizona,* which take place in the historical west, the hero never loses touch entirely with civilization.

This last point needs some elaboration. *The Half-Breed,* probably the purest of the Fairbanks'

Doug (as "Teddy" Drake) laughing at danger in Knickerbocker Buckaroo, *directed by Albert Parker in 1919.*

Westerns in terms of picturing man alone in the wilderness has its hero, Lo Dorman, living in a giant tree in the redwood groves of Calaveras County in California. His parentage is mixed, his Indian mother surviving his unknown father. When his mother dies, the child is forced out of the settlement and has to fend for himself in the wilds. The resolution of the film depends largely upon the identity of his father. The fear of illegitimacy as a plot device resembles the earlier *The Good Bad Man,* and reminds us that Fairbanks' films were always concerned with lineage and legitimacy—even in the Wild West. Perhaps the desertion by Doug's father of his family when Doug was only a small child helps to explain the constant use of this device in his films. At any rate, it shows how the concepts of family and community constantly pervade Fairbanks' films—concepts essentially foreign to a child of nature but essential to an empire builder.

Here Fairbanks perhaps strays from the real cowboy. Douglas Branch views the cowboy as a somewhat less than civilizing agent:

> The family, the pillar of society that rooted and stabilized the civilization that came with the passing of the range, was of little influence in shaping the society of the cow-country. Old home ties were broken almost imperceptibly, as a cowboy followed his calling for year after year. There were few of "the right kind of girls," and cowboy's wages did not permit much saving ahead against a start in domesticity. . .[43]

It is very much to the point, however, that

Fairbanks *was* conscious of the family as civilizing agent in his films. It marks all the more the ambivalence of their posture.

This contact with the community costs him his heroic status (as Henry Nash Smith pointed out concerning the dime-novel heroes). When one thinks of the concept of the community, moreover, he can see how Fairbanks' Westerns anchor themselves even more strongly to it—particularly with regard to law and order. This civilizing impulse of law and order, represented the authority of the East. Earlier we saw how Smith discovered that many of the dime-novel heroes were disguised detectives. The Fairbanks characters, notable "Passin' Through" in *The Good Bad Man,* and the title character in *Headin' South,* seem lawless, but are finally revealed to be serving a kind of system. "Passin's" deeds are motivated through compassion for unfortunates and illegitimates like himself. "Headin' South's" deeds of outlawry merely disguise a mission of a Canadian mountie to ensnare a rustler named Spanish Joe. Similarly when "Fancy" Jim Sherwood, Eastern dude and new owner of a ranch out West displays his ineptness at matters of ranch life, it is only a cover for his efforts to uncover the dastardly villain known only as "30-30." It is obvious that the Fairbanks cowboy in his function of bringing law and order to the West is merely fulfilling the function of empire builder.

In discussing the dime-novel variety of the Western hero, we noted that he rarely participated in the workaday routine of ranch life. While the cowboy gained ascendency as a hero, he gradually lost sight of his occupation. Earlier,

Doug with Katherine MacDonald in Headin' South *(1918).*

when only a secondary character in stories and novels, his background was quite apparent:

In each decade up to 1890, the ranch story could be traced, but usually the story would be the same. Ranch life is depicted with some care; the cowboy is a character but seldom a leading one. He is around, but he is in the shadows . . .[44]

One of the few books to deal with the cowboy as protagonist and at the same time maintain a highly detailed and accurate delineation of background and occupation is Andy Adams' *The Log of a Cowboy,* which details the minutiae of a trail drive of longhorns from the Rio Grande to the Blackfoot agency in Montana.

With the advent of the Wister Western novels, around the same time as the Adams work, in the early years of the century, the cowboys never seemed to work. The age of the West seemed a time ". . . when the cowboys seem throughout to spend their days in playful pranks, in love-making, in thief-hunting, in anything except work."[45] If that is only partially the case in *Lin McLean,* wherein the hero gets involved in crooked poker games, bigamous women, etc., it is surely just that way in the later *The Virginian,* which is taken up with for the most part the pursuit of lovely Molly and has nothing whatever to do with cattle-ranching.

Fairbanks' Westerns are notable for their total lack of attention to the detail of the cowboy's routine chores. The majority of cinema Westerns, however, operate according to this convention: "Nor has the cinema admitted that the cowboy was a workman, with an unmodern devotion to his world—the range, its cattle, its

All dressed in black as "Passin' Thru" in The Good Bad Man *(1916), seen here with Bessie Love.*

horses, his fellow-cowboys."[46] It is difficult to think of a single instance in the Fairbanks' Westerns when the hero herds cattle, wires fence, traps animals, blazes trails, etc. Fairbanks' cowboy might be continually associated with the community, but he manages to be absent when the time for chores comes around! Instead, like our friend Buck Taylor, Buffalo Bill's protégé, he rights wrongs to homesteaders, infiltrates bands of robbers, and, in general, performs the deeds of the dime-novel heroes with all the requisite bravado and gallantry. Never really a part of the waking West, he is essential of the dreaming one. He stands lightly on two feet, one planted in Eastern experience, the other on rugged and romantic Western space.

To this must be added a sense of flair and costume. Earlier we spoke of the Rooseveltian predilection for outrageous costume and we can recall the dude's arrival at Bitter Creek in *Wild and Woolly,* or the milksop's advent to Arizona soil in *The Mollycoddle.* The bandit all dressed in black in *The Good Bad Man* is not content to rob the Transcontinental Limited for gold but solely for the conductor's ticket punch! He uses it throughout the film for punching holes in the waistcoats of all the "bad" men he encounters—a device curiously presaging Zorro's Z trademark and Robin Hood's Three Lions symbol in later Fairbanks' films. He mounts a mustang by leaping fifteen feet to the saddle in *Man from Painted Post.* He picks up a lost toothbrush from the roadbed as he is carried along at top speed by an express train in *Knickerbocker Buckaroo.* He escapes from an embattled saloon by hanging from a rafter and kicking his way through the roof in *Wild and Woolly.* Earlier in the same film he dispatches two snakes by turning a front flip over the back of a chair while pulling two six-guns from their holsters. Details such as these along with a generally exuberant flair for roping and riding show how the Fairbanksian Western continued a sense of showmanship and deliberate myth-making found only a little earlier in the Wild West Show and the dime-novel.

Essentially a product of the Industrial East, Fairbanks found himself continuously drawn to the West. It was the masculine arena of Francis Parkman where man was tested. It was the Rooseveltian naiveté of a West of mixed geographies. It was the Wild West Show of the cowboy hero. Above all, it was the ambivalent footstep of Daniel Boone where empire builder was also child of nature. It was an arena where attitudes were hostile to industrial progress, yet where that progress inevitably dogged the heels of westward

Fairbanks with Joseph Henabery and the production crew of The Man from Painted Post *(1917).*

expansion. Somehow, the light, sometimes fanciful Western comedies of Douglas Fairbanks caught many of these ambiguities. Fairbanks can never belong to just one set of attitudes toward the West. In true American fashion he shifts around all of them too much to remain consistent to any one. This means that he shares, to an extent, in most of the Western concepts outlined. And it is this that makes his films as rich and entertaining (and as true to the American Western tradition) as they are.

NOTES

1. Henry Nash Smith, *Virgin Land* (New York: Vintage Books, 1950), p. 58.

2. Edward White, *The Eastern Establishment and the Western Experience* (New Haven and London: Yale University Press, 1968), p. 4.

3. Edwin Fussell, *Frontier: American Literature and the American West* (New Jersey: Princeton University Press, 1965), p. 4.

4. *Ibid.*

5. Smith, *Virgin Land,* p. 143.

6. As quoted by Edwin Fussell, *Frontier,* p. 7.

7. *Ibid.,* p. 11.

8. Smith, *Virgin Land,* p. 143.

9. Leslie Fiedler, *Love and Death in the American Novel* (New York: Stein and Day, 1966), p. 36.

10. Charles L. Sanford, *The Quest for Paradise* (Urbana: University of Illinois Press, 1961), p. 60.

11. *Ibid.,* p. 61.

12. Smith, *Virgin Land,* p. 48.

13. *Ibid.,* p. 77.

14. Joe Frantz and Julian Choate, Jr. *The American Cowboy, the Myth and the Reality* (Norman: University of Oklahoma Press, 1955), p. 13.

15. Smith, *Virgin Land,* p. 123.
16. Frantz and Choate, *American Cowboy,* p. 9.
17. Smith, *Virgin Land,* p. 124.
18. Frantz and Choate, *American Cowboy,* p. 9.
19. *Ibid.,* p. 121.
20. Smith, *Virgin Land,* pp. 124–125.
21. *Ibid.,* p. 120.
22. *Ibid.,* p. 124.
23. *Ibid.,* p. 135.
24. Sanford, *Quest for Paradise,* p. 205.
25. As quoted by Henry F. Pringle, *Theodore Roosevelt: A Biography* (New York: Harcourt, Brace, and Co., 1931), p. 97.
26. *Ibid.*
27. Quoted by G. E. White, *Eastern Establishment,* p. 84.
28. R.W.B. Lewis, *The American Adam,* p. 169.
29. Pringle, *Theodore Roosevelt,* pp. 93–94.
30. Lewis, *American Adam,* p. 168.
31. *Letters of Francis Parkman,* ed. Wilbur R. Jacobs (Norman: University of Oklahoma Press, 1960), I, 177.
32. *Ibid,* p. 178.
33. *Ibid.,* p. 179.
34. *Ibid.,* p. 177.
35. *Ibid.,* p. 178.
36. Fairbanks, *Laugh and Live* (New York: Britton Publishing Co., 1917), p. 96.
37. *Variety* (11 September 1916), p. 7.
38. Lewis, *American Adam,* p. 7.
39. *Ibid.*
40. Cooke, *Fairbanks,* p. 18.
41. Douglas Branch, *The Cowboy and His Interpretors* (New York: Cooper Square Publishers, Inc., 1926), p. 17.
42. *Ibid.,* p. 111.
43. *Ibid.,* pp. 156–157.
44. Frantz and Choate, *American Cowboy,* p. 143.
45. Branch, *Cowboy,* p. 198.
46. *Ibid.,* p. 232.

6
The Satire of Anita Loos and Douglas Fairbanks

ANITA LOOS

And thus we shall be quack-ridden and folly-ridden until mobocracy comes to its inescapable debacle, and the common people are relieved of their present oppressive duty of deciding what is wrong with their tummies, and what doctor is safest for them to consult, and which of his pills is most apt to cure them.

—H.L. Mencken

In the years 1916–1917 Anita Loos wrote nine films for Douglas Fairbanks. Although she had written scenarios earlier for Griffith and would later write for such stars and directors as Marion Davies, Constance Talmadge, Victor Fleming and Marshall Neilan, it is for the Fairbanks series that she is perhaps best remembered during the silent days of cinema.

These light, topical satires deserve more than a cursory glance. Not only do they tell us a good deal about the art of satire, but they also reflect a pre-World War I America with wit and cogency. Her situations grow out of everyday incidents. They concern commonplace people. Yet, these everyday incidents and commonplace people lead to witty and fanciful developments and

From The Americano *(1917): Anita Loos wrote the story of
an American engineer (Doug) who foils a revolution in a
South American country.*

characters. It is as if her pen were a divining rod
that persisted in seeking out the subterranean
significance in the most common of surfaces.

Her ability to stand with feet planted in two
worlds is of large significance in the art of satire.
Her comic sense, as Eric Bentley might point out,
"as against the farcical impulse, tries to deal with
living, with the pressures of today, with the
responsibilities of adulthood."[1] At the same time,
it can bridge out toward strange, almost surreal
situations. In this sense Henri Bergson's words
apply:

It dreams, I admit, but it conjures up in its
dreams visions that are at once accepted and
understood by the whole of a social group. Can
it then fail to throw light for us on the way that
human imagination works, and more particularly social, collective, and popular imagination?[2]

Loos' first film for Fairbanks was *His Picture in
the Papers* in 1916. It was followed by *The Half-*
Breed (script adaptation from Bret Harte's "In the
Carquinez Woods"), *American Aristocracy, Manhat-*
tan Madness*, and *The Matrimaniac* (script adaptation from Octavus Roy Cohen and J. V. Glesy). In
1917 came *The Americano, In Again, Out Again,*
Wild and Woolly, Down to Earth, and *Reaching for the*
Moon.

The combination of Loos, Fairbanks, and director John Emerson on most of the above films
was quickly appreciated by both the public at
large and the critics. As early as 1917 *Photoplay*
commented:

Thus the great triple alliance came into
being—three individuals, each of them already
successful, focusing their distinct talents upon
one task, that of showing the world how it
looks, and with the kindliest humor, stripping

---

* We have consulted three filmographies because of some confusion over the writer for this film. Gary Carey indicates that Loos
was the writer; Dewitt Bodeen, that E.V. Durling was the writer;
Alistair Cooke gave no name at all.

the tough hide of convention off the inconsistencies of life.[3]

Reference was even made to a sort of cinematic "Comédie Humaine" without the sometimes sordid elements of Balzac! True, a kind of pattern seemed to emerge from these films, as if they were parts of a systematic examination into the fabric of American society. *His Picture in the Papers,* for instance, satirized the American love of publicity; *The Americano,* the love for the romantic nonsense embodied in the Richard Harding Davis school of adventure fiction; *In Again, Out Again,* the pre-World War I conflicts between Pacifists and Activists; *Down to Earth,* hypochondria; *Reaching for the Moon,* New Thought faddism and Anglophiles.

Loos did not deal with the distorted image of burlesque, but the realistic comedy—or, as another writer defined this distinction:

> Comedy and drama tell the truth about human relations; farce and melodrama distort them for your amusement. Comedy and drama are fine, clear, French plate mirrors, in which you see yourself and your life reflected with perfect fidelity; farce and melodrama are those curved mirrors that you find in the penny arcades, casting back pictures that retain certain human features but without semblance of the original.[4]

One hastens to add that the writing of Miss Loos is informed with a notable lack of pretension. It is to be feared that this chapter may not entirely escape that failing, for while attempting to point out the unique aspects of her satire, we also wish to demonstrate its participation in certain satiric traditions and conventions.

We will first examine some of the principles of comedy defined by Henry Fielding, pointing out some astonishing resemblances between his art and Loos'. Thereafter we will deal with representative Loos/Fairbanks films in terms of their use of the subtitle, themes, and techniques outlined earlier. Hopefully in all this analysis and dissection the essential spirit of her films will not be lost. Loos was not one to seek pretentious justification for her work, yet there are profound depths there and one does not need to look too hard to touch them.

THE COMEDY OF HENRY FIELDING

In the preface to *Joseph Andrews* Henry Fielding makes an absorbing investigation into the art of comedy and satire. Many of these conclusions find their twentieth century application in the screen work of Anita Loos. Studying a few parallels will usher us into a general look at comedy and satire, preparing us for what we find practiced in much of the film satire of the silent period.

Fielding's broad classification of comedy begins with the breakdown of Epic and Dramatic narrative into two main divisions: tragedy and comedy. Comedy is then broken down into forms: the "comic romance" and the "comedy" itself. In the "comic romance" the action is expansive and comprehensive with a large circle of incident, variety of character, and elevated status of the characters. The "comedy," however, presents persons of inferior rank and manners in more intimate situations. This is done through realistic observation and detail. While the "comic romance" produces an effect of the preservation of the sublime, the latter has as its goal the preservation of the ludicrous.

It is with this "preservation of the ludicrous" that we are concerned. As we proceed, it will be apparent that this effect, as well as the way in which it is produced, links the work of such diverse writers as Fielding and Loos. They both share a profound insight into the comedy arising from common experience.

Having loosely defined the "comedy," Fielding hastens to distinguish it from its brash sister, "burlesque." Comedy arises from nature, "from the just imitation of which will flow all the pleasure we can this way convey to a sensible reader."[5] Burlesque, on the other hand, is "ever the exhibition of what is monstrous and unnatural, and where our delight, if we examine it, arises from the surprising absurdity, as in appropriating the manners of the highest to the lowest . . ."[6]

Comedy, then, is not only a matter of intimacy in scale and rank, but also of *realistic observation.* Consequently, nature is important for the comic artist:

> And perhaps there is one reason why a comic writer should of all others be the least excused for deviating from nature, since it may not be always so easy for a serious poet to meet with the great and the admirable; but life everywhere furnishes an accurate observer with the ridiculous.[7]

The poet must be aware of the importance of dealing with selective and significant detail. In comedy such detail has the effect of nailing down the situation, reining in the free-flying balloons of the ridiculous, firmly anchoring it into the everyday world. In this way comedy can grow out of everyday experience . . .

> . . . everything is copied from the book of nature, and scarce a character or action produced which I have not taken from my own observations and experience.[8]

The tradition of the Ridiculous, says Fielding, must have its roots in the real world. Comedy, the preservation of the ludicrous, can also be seen, in the satirical drawings of Daumier with their detailed topicality rather than in, say, the ballooning exaggerations of James Thurber. The Daumier drawings have a concentration of detail that nail them down to a particular situation and context. They are in effect tied down to this earth by the sandbags of concrete observation, producing the Ridiculous. In the Thurber drawings, unemcumbered by the baggage of a particular time and place, but blooming out into the *outré* realms of fancy, the caricature is the result, wherein the monstrous is preserved. Caricature's aim is "to exhibit monsters not men."[9] Realistic detail cannot produce a caricature. It can be selective, but it does not distort and twist salient characteristics into the Monstrous as the Burlesque can.

In an aside that is particularly interesting for our present purpose, Fielding even touches on the eminently *visual* nature of the Monstrous: the "Monstrous is much easier to paint than to describe, and the Ridiculous to describe than paint."[10] He cites Hogarth's ability to go beyond mere facility in the exaggeration of salient characteristics. He can portray the size of a peasant's nose so that he looks human enough to breathe. This alone would be a caricature. But, more importantly, a Hogarth can make his representation seem to *think* as well. This last is important to the comedy. As we shall see, the silent film at first took delight in its ability to capture such broad comic outlines. It was later with people like Anita Loos that film began to see its subject matter more closely and accurately.

In literature the separate traditions of the burlesque and the ridiculous can be seen, by way of an example, in much of the work of Charles Dickens and George Eliot. A character such as Mrs. Gamp is a monstrous creation. We know her solely through a handful of characteristic phrases and by her wandering umbrella. Eliot's Mr. Causabon, no less a marvelous character, is, however, carefully presented in every detail. We

not only know what he looks like at all times of the day and night, but what he says and thinks is known as well. He is intensely more cerebral and cannot be separated from his lifelong project to write a "Key to Mythology." The two different kinds of looking seen in the Ridiculous and the Monstrous are typified in these two characters.

Similarly, in films we have Chaplin to typify the burlesque tradition and such as Charlie Chase or Harold Lloyd to represent the ridiculous tradition. Chaplin is a universal. He floats free from a particular time and place. We have only a few highly visual trademarks such as the turned out feet, the mustache and cane, etc. But he is essentially incomplete, existing only for a given situation and activity—or perhaps we should say that the situation only exists for him. But with Lloyd or Chase we are swamped in all the detail of a particular time and place and how the character fits into a given milieu. Seeing Lloyd in a film like *The Kid Brother* we are struck at how much he still seems to be a typical urban man, despite the fact that this film is set on a country farm. And imagining Chase away from his world of streetcars, sidewalks and straw hats is difficult. These two are firmly anchored to the world of the Twenties.

"The only source of the true Ridiculous . . . is affectation."[11] This affectation proceeds, says Fielding, from vanity and hypocrisy. It is in hypocrisy, particularly, that we find a person turned on his head and appearing in a manner opposed to what he really is: ". . . for to discover any one to be the exact reverse of what he affects is more surprising, and consequently more ridiculous than to find him a little deficient in the quality he desires the reputation of."[12] This reversal is seen all the more clearly through the accurate depiction of elements involved. In a way, this is like one school of surrealist painting that insisted upon scrupulous fidelity to detail in order to obtain more striking effects from the juxtaposition of disparate objects. The flaming tubas of Magritte is an example. The contradictory associations tend to confuse the mind, and in comedy, impede its reactions creating a kind of suspension.

One result of this is when the Ridiculous succeeds in transforming the misfortunes and calamities of life, the imperfections of nature, into objects of ridicule. Fielding explains:

> When ugliness aims at the applause of beauty, or lameness endeavors to display agility, it is then that these unfortunate circumstances

which at first moved our compassion, tend only to raise our mirth.[13]

Thus, the attempt at normalcy within a decidedly abnormal context becomes ridiculous. We see this principle in operation constantly in literature and cinema, from Candide to Keaton. In Laurel and Hardy's *Two Tars,* there is the famous procession wherein a line of cars, all hopeless wrecks as a result of self-inflicted demolition, the last vestiges of their injured dignity fluttering from their crumpled fender, totter by with all the aplomb of new vehicles in perfect running condition. There is a superb example in a Douglas Fairbanks film *When the Clouds Roll By.* Fairbanks dives off the roof of a house set adrift by a flash flood, swims down through the flood waters to the submerged kitchen for a "snack." It seems the sensible thing to do, after all, when you are hungry, and we watch appreciatively while he consumes his meal from the underwater icebox.

Fielding has pointed out how comedy is dependent on the detail of realism, the intimacy of scope, and the preservation of the ludicrous. It remains for us to apply these ideas more fully to the work of Anita Loos in her collaborative efforts with Douglas Fairbanks.

ANITA LOOS

Before proceeding into an examination of Anita Loos' satire for Douglas Fairbanks, it is first necessary to look generally at her life and her role in the silent film of 1915.

Anita Loos was a *wunderkind* of the cinema. While barely in her teens, she sold her first scenario to the Lubin Company, an opus entitled, *The Earl and the Tomboy.* Apparently this was never filmed.[14] A month later in April of 1912 she made her first sale to Biograph of a story called *The Road to Plaindale,* which was not filmed until 1914. It was with her third sale, however, that Loos scored her first popular success. It was *The New York Hat,* which Biograph bought for $25 and had filmed with D. W. Griffith directing and Mary Pickford and Lionel Barrymore as the principal players.

After this, Loos followed Griffith from Biograph to Mutual and finally to Triangle in 1915. Despite her initial success with *The New York Hat,* her scripts were not selected by The Master, but were assigned to secondary production units. By the autumn of 1915 her career was in decline. Nevertheless, this precocious child had written by

then something like 105 scripts, of which, she claims four were never sold.

What had happened with Griffith? Her fate at his hands parallels that of her future partner, Douglas Fairbanks. Both found their forté in comedy. For her, it was the snappy, wisecracking kind of satire that could never fit in with Griffith's pastoral lyrics like *True-Heart Susie.* For Fairbanks, it was the athletic flamboyance that clashed with Griffith's experiments in restraining the gestures of his actors. Although Griffith enjoyed reading Loos' scenarios, he could not find anything cinematic in them, so he relegated her efforts to lesser directors. Of Fairbanks, he supposedly made the observation that he belonged in Keystone comedy.[15]

Now a third figure enters the picture, so to speak, one who brought Loos and Fairbanks together. John Emerson was a participant in the great influx of stage stars that came from New York to Los Angeles between 1914–1915. His career on Broadway had begun with small parts in the company of Minnie Maddern Fiske ("Mrs. Fiske"), the distinguished star of high comedy at the time. Later he joined up with Charles Frohman, then the most important of the Broadway producers. In Hollywood he was approached by Griffith about the possibility of Emerson making a film from one of his stage hits. Emerson took cinema seriously, unlike many of the newly imported stage stars, and perhaps already had an eye to becoming ultimately a film director; so he consented. Meanwhile, he had formed a friendship with Fairbanks in New York, where they were both members of the Lamb's Club. After making a few films in Los Angeles, Emerson decided to try to direct one with Fairbanks and persuaded Griffith to let him handle the film. He betook himself to the file of scripts in Frank Woods' Scenario Department. He ran across a number of stories that seemed perfect for Fairbanks. They were lightly satiric, peppy, and abounded in wisecracks.

They were written by somebody named Anita Loos.

Emerson thought them great material for Fairbanks and told Griffith so. The Great Man remained unimpressed. "All the laughs are in the lines," he said, "you can't print lines on the screen—people don't go to the movies to read." Bewildered, Emerson wanted to know why Griffith had bought so many of the stories.

"I like to read them myself," was Griffith's famous rejoinder; "They make me laugh."[16]

Emerson prevailed and a script called *His*

A publicity-hungry Doug searches for His Picture in the Papers, *the first film in which he worked with Anita Loos and John Emerson, 1916.*

Picture in the Papers was selected. In this casual way was produced the first of the great Fairbanks comedies and the first of the satires whereby we remember Anita Loos today. It represents one of the more striking confluences wherein a number of people of diverse talents happened to be in the right place at the right time.

The studio for which Loos worked at this time was one of the three production arms of Triangle Film Corporation—Triangle Fine-Arts. Also Griffith's studio, it is significant, among other things, for consistently using the professional writer on a regular basis by 1915. This was unusual for the time. Gradually all over the industry as the standards of production improved for dramatic films, better stories were sought and top writers from the field of novels and magazines were signed. A "scenario" in those days did not mean a shooting-script, but rather the sequence of scenes, the story, told in visual

cues. The continuity, with its indications for camera angles, distances, titles, was written from that.

Triangle Fine-Arts' scenario department was typical of many later departments. A special story-reading department would work a book or play into synopsis form for the director. This property was then assigned to a scenario writer. Keven Brownlow notes that this capacity was usually filled by a woman.[17] In addition to Loos, there were quite a number of first-class female writers appearing in the years before 1920, writers who would remain on the scene to become top scenarists throughout the silent era and, in some cases, beyond. A few of these were Frances Marion, Clara Beranger, Bess Meredyth, Ouida Bergere, and June Mathis.

By 1915, however, the scenario department for Fine-Arts, according to Loos, was not that advanced:

His Picture in the Papers, *their first joint success, 1915–1916.*

I worked in the scenario department. I *was* the scenario department. There was nobody else on the lot who was writing. Fine-Arts used to buy scenarios, and I think there were two or three writers who sent things in rather regularly. . . .[18]

Loos' method for writing her feature scripts was a bit unorthodox, perhaps, compared to today's high-speed assemblyline writing. By 1916 her scripts would average forty pages. She wrote them all in longhand while surrounded by rather bizarre circumstances. Her account of this effort is worth quoting in its entirety:

Seeing that typewriter desks and chairs are designed for full-grown people, I was never a typist; it was more pleasant to curl up on a chaise lounge in my room at the Hollywood Hotel and scribble my plots on a big yellow pad. The only thing that required serious thought was a basic theme; once I hit on it, the rest was child's play. After finishing an outline, I would be driven to the studio in one of the company limousines, the elegance of which I never got used to. We held our conferences in Doug's dressing room. It was equipped with a punching bag, electric horse, and boxing gloves and looked like a gymnasium. Interrupted by Doug's boisterous clowning . . . I would read my script aloud. . . .[19]

True or not, and one must take much of the incident in the Loos autobiography with the requisite helping of salt, this is certainly the way one *likes* to envision the generation of one of the Fairbanks/Loos films. Her account has all the disarming freshness and lack of pretension that mark the films themselves. *His Picture in the Papers* represented their first joint success and the beginning of a string of nine films that ranged in subject matter from outdoor drama, to salon satire, to urban man. It is these films for which Loos is best remembered today (excepting, of course, such notable titles as the 1928 Mal St. Clair version of *Gentlemen Prefer Blondes,* the 1935 *San Francisco,* and the 1939 *The Women).*

ANITA LOOS AND THE SUBTITLE

His Picture in the Papers brought a new emphasis to the screen—intimacy of gesture in a satiric film. The kind of titles it had contributed to this development. They relieved the image from the burden of carrying all the humor, which had hitherto forced much of it into broadly gestured pantomime. Moreover, the title enabled Loos to inject a kind of literal counterpoint to the image, as we shall see. For Loos the title and subtitle was by turns witty, literate, slangy, and funny. By its use she brought to the screen the "sound" of 1916 America.

Brought up on the famed Barbary Coast, Loos was particularly sensitive to the nuance and edge of American slang. In her subsequent portrayals of young Americans in a go-getting America, slang became quite important as a counterpoint to the frenetic Fairbanks image. It brought to these films an "aural" topicality and detail that make them very much a product of their time in the best tradition of the Ridiculous.

George Santayana might say that Americans "are without the vocabulary or the idiom of a cultivated people," but that would scarcely bother Loos. If America had an idiom at all it was slang. One of her early heroes on the Barbary Coast, Wilson Mizner, was famous for his cultivation of American slang. She even later characterized him as "Blackie" for Gable's role in *San Francisco.* Another of her friends, H. L. Mencken, in dealing with some of the meanings and consequences of slang in his book, *The American Language,* recounts the English horror of the American "degradation" of the King's English from colonial times to the present. It is interesting to see how in a language as well as in a Revolution, the English felt the threat of change. A good example of this disquiet with Americanisms, or slang, can be seen in the subject at hand—film.

In the silent days of American cinema, the films' importation to England occasioned a good many raised Anglo eyebrows. Titles and subtitles containing words like "hobo," "hoodlum," "dead-beat," "hold-up," "rube," "road-agent," etc., were met with some confusion. One Englishman, according to Mencken, announced in 1914 that the terminology of such films were to be denounced as "generating and encouraging mental indiscipline."[20] Such appalling literary and verbal indecencies, nevertheless continued undaunted. Apparently by 1920 something of a crisis in language communications was engendered. The London *Daily News* delivered daily invective against the exposure of children to such wickedness, and even the London bureau of the Associated Press could say, ". . . it is the subtitle of the American moving picture film which, it is feared, constitutes the most menacing threat to the vaunted English purity of speech."[21]

As if this were not enough, later there came the advent of the talking motion picture and its subsequent importation to Europe. For obvious reasons the talkie could bring in far more "Americanisms" than the silent film title, besides the fact that now the sullied accents of American speech would be audibly drawling these dreaded words. Such words and accents were "perfectly disgusting," and an "evil influence" on language and morals.[22]

Even if the English had problems assimilating these "dialects," certainly the broad American viewing public who saw Loos' films did not, which is the whole point. This was her language and she knew it was her audience's also. Yet, at first, translating this verbal humor to the screen presented some problems. The potential was not grasped even by such innovative persons as Griffith. Griffith himself was not above inserting a completely superfluous title upon the action, and he would frequently interrupt a dramatic rescue scene to inform us via title what was going to happen. But the fact remains that he was cold to her kind of cinema with its profusion of titles. His forté, as has already been pointed out, was not comedy, for one thing. For another, as Gary Carey explains, much of her humor was contained in the turn of a phrase, a witty description, even a wisecracking line or so of dialogue—all of which was lost on the silent screen.[23] Griffith felt, not without some justification, that the audience did not want to sit in a darkened room and read gags from the screen.

But he had not reckoned with the "Loosian" subtitle. In her hands, along with Emerson and Fairbanks, the incorporation of many subtitles, some verbal gags, some puns, some editorializations—all of them pungent and epigrammatic—was achieved with success and would distinguish her films from *Picture to Reaching for the Moon*. Anita Loos had made "the printed subtitle as ubiquitous as the photographic image."[24]

Loos' titles and subtitles were art forms in themselves. That dream of so many silent film aesthetes, the titleless film, was not shared by her. She would be the first to point out that even Charles Ray's experiment in titleless narrative, *The Old Swimmin' Hole*, found it necessary to incorporate information in the form of chalked-in words on a slate. If her scenarios were sometimes more interesting than the finished film, it was because the film had had to eschew the more interesting material that could only be conveyed verbally. It became necessary that more and more of this material be transferred to the screen via the subtitle.

The Loosian subtitle was a relatively novel addition to screen grammar in 1916. Of course there were titles for opening and closing credits, titles to identify a scene or character, titles for dialogue, and so on, but the Loosian subtitle, as one author at the time put it,

> ...has only been in vogue a few years. It differs from the title—the wording between scenes which describes the action of the picture that is to come—in that it need not attend to business. It is meant only for the audience, and though at times in the supposed speeches of the characters in the film, it may be a mere comment outside the picture and addressed to the audience like the aside of our fathers' theatre.[25]

The subtitle was an essential part of film form for her. In her book, *How to Write Photoplays*, she takes it quite seriously:

> The only place where the photodramatist may "spread" himself in clever verbiage and literary style is in the sub-titles, the inserts of printed matter flashed on the screen between photographed scenes. It is this matter of subtitling which is winning the continuity specialist his place as an artist.[26]

Best of all, she knew how to use these devices with restraint, and it is not until one sees a Fairbanks film where she did *not* write the titles, like *The Lamb*, that one realizes how over-indulgence with titles can lead the image astray. Loos insisted that they be written in a style that does not obtrude upon the illusion of the story. A narrative title, for instance, should be in the same mood as the scene it introduces, and, most importantly:

> The shades of meaning in the title must correspond so perfectly to the shades of the meaning of the scene in which it is inserted that the audience feels no shock at the change from a picture from the written words.[27]

Thus, a film like the 1917 *Reaching for the Moon* expresses perfectly the notion of an American adrift in European aristocracy by juxtaposing Fairbanks' slangy utterances with the stiff demeanor and diction of the rest of the cast. The satiric slant of the whole film is sufficiently seen in the one word, "bunk," that Fairbanks expresses in disgust over the endless protocol and intrigue of aristocracy.

That her work with the title was a suitable complement to Fairbanks' screen image was heartily acknowledged by the great jumper:

> Time and again I have sat through plays with Miss Loos and have heard the audience applaud her subtitles as heartily as the liveliest scenes. This has convinced me of the great value of the kind of work she does.[28]

The subtitle was a formidable weapon for Loos. It meant the power of the editorial comment, the thrust of a personal satiric vision conveyed by the pungent slang of the wisecrack. In the subtitles, her films carried on a lively kind of monologue to the audience that ran a satirical counterpoint to the action on the screen. It enabled her to prick the ballooning affectations of her characters in the best Fielding tradition.

One could expect anything to flash on the screen in a Loos/Fairbanks film. Certainly a few examples of the Loosian art are in order to see how she used the subtitle as an instrumental tool in the formulation of her comic vision.

Quotes and epithets from Shakespeare and Carlyle spice up the narrative of films like *Down to Earth* and *Reaching for the Moon*. The latter, one of Fairbanks/Loos' finest, uses these quotes to good advantage in cementing the film's thematic affinity to Shakespeare's *The Tempest*. She uses the ironic aside as a method of character introduction for a leading lady in the 1917 *In Again, Out Again:*

Pacifica Jennings—a female of the species, though not as deadly as the male.

More importantly, she levels her satiric gaze through her humor and diction. Again in *In Again, Out Again*, she pokes fun at the pacifist movement in America that came before our involvement in World War I. She juxtaposes images of the "Athenium Massage Cream" factory producing boxes of explosives and "Carter's Little Liver Pills" manufacturing mines, against that of a meeting of a group of New Jersey Pacifists ("Bless their hearts," she adds in a title). In this meeting the camera picks out a handful of signs adorning the walls and podium: "We are too comfortable to fight," says one; "Blessed are the peacemakers," says another. This last hangs below a portrait of William Jennings Bryan, a topical detail firmly placed within the America of 1917. Our own favorite sign from this little scene reads as follows:

No one can insult us but ourselves—
and we won't.

This kind of comfortable complacency might correspond to what Santayana had already in 1913 labeled as America's "genteel tradition," a term somewhat less than complimentary. It is one signifying, moreover, a spinsterish kind of "spectacled" attitude toward the world.

A single title at the beginning of *Reaching for the Moon* establishes not only the mood and tone and theme of the film but its diction as well:

Our hero—Alexis Caesar Napoleon Brown—a young man of boundless enthusiasm whose physical self is chained to a desk in a button factory, but whose spirit, led by vaulting ambition, walks with the kings of the earth—and sometimes stubs his toes.

These final words bring us up short. We know immediately that our hero's pretensions are doomed, that the general vision of the film is firmly "down to earth." The casual enumeration of the three great world conquerors would have taken a lot of tedious footage if done visually. Likewise the phrase "vaulting ambition" juxtaposed with "stubs his toes" contrasts a classical kind of diction with a more "American" kind of phraseology, a juxtaposition like those that Fielding found necessary to the preservation of the Ridiculous.

The film's no-nonsense stance, avoiding the mundane cliché is seen later in such a title as:

Every silver lining has its cloud.

In a series of dream sequences Fairbanks goes to Vulgaria to claim his crown as king of the realm. The trip there is punctuated by a series of assaults and assassination attempts. So disgusted does the would-be king become at these kingly perils that when a well-wishing subject in the crowd calls "Long live the King!", he replies sourly, "Oh, shut up!" Like a Greek chorus, this repititious declaration of "Long live the King!" counterpoints every disastrous image in the film. Finally, after a dizzying sequence of flight from traps and more assassination attempts, Fairbanks pauses and asks:

I say, couldn't we just call it a day and knock the whole thing off?

Seeing this in the form of a title gives us just the right amount of time to appreciate the point. If the film had been a talking picture we would of course have heard the comment, but the effect might not have been so striking. As it is, the switch from image to title, effects the contrast, yet appropriateness that Loos referred to earlier.

Tone and diction have been consistent with the theme of the vain-gloriousness of our typical American. Loos' emphasis upon the importance of the title's tone corresponding to the images, and, as we can see, her cogent way of working her titular commentary in a counterpoint to the image, finds justification here.

SATIRE AND ANITA LOOS

Studying the satire of Anita Loos and applying the Fielding principles of the Ridiculous means that we must first examine a very important aspect of the satiric vision—its source. As we shall see, this is extremely important in Anita Loos' case, because it tells us much about her art and how we are to judge it.

A satire may be making the same point as a sermon, yet the uncomfortable feeling we get sometimes during a sermon may result from the feeling that the minister expects us to do something about it and we may have no intention of doing so. In satire we are more comfortable because we know nobody really expects us to do anything about the subject under fire. Loos' satires, for the most part, seem to be like this. It is when Fairbanks' evangelistic zeal overrides the humor that the satire becomes strained and forced. When this happens—and it does happen—the problem is with Fairbanks and not with Loos.

To preach at all implies a norm—but whose? There has been satire on behalf of communism, fascism, and aristocracy. It appears in atheistic and religious communities alike. Whatever the context, if one says something is being done in the wrong way, he is implying that there is a right way serving as a standard. Who, then, would dare to set himself up as a spokesman for such a standard?

It was in the Loos/Fairbanks combination that we meet such a spokesman. Alistair Cooke has said that they had the feel of the national pulse and at times could express the prevailing mood of the country, while at the same time serve notice on habits and customs and attitudes that seem in need of deflation. Does this mean that they were themselves "average"? G. K. Chesterton, in his masterful study of Charles Dickens, touches upon this question, and it is worth quoting in its entirety:

> Dickens was an immoderate jester, but a moderate thinker. He was an immoderate jester because he was a moderate thinker. What we moderns call the wildness of his imagination was actually created by what we moderns call the tameness of his thought. I mean that he felt the full insanity of all extreme tendencies, because he was in the centre. We are always, in these days, asking our violent prophets to write violent satires; but violent prophets can never possibly write violent satires. In order to write satire like that of Rabelais—satire that juggles with the stars and kicks the world about like a football—it is necessary to be one's self temperate, and even mild.[29]

That Anita Loos herself valued this sense of moderation is apparent. She once disparaged its loss in American letters when subjects like sex were treated with a pretentiousness that was by turns morbid and childish:

> . . . out of this trend there developed a school of writing that reduced the American scene to the status of a bowl of worms and then reported their convolutions from the viewpoint of one of the worms.[30]

Later she says that to relate to an unbalanced school of thought, one would have to be equally off base, the implication being that the satirical vision can only result from a stance based in the norm, or center of things. Probably her most famous character, Lorelei Lee in *Gentlemen Prefer Blondes*, virtually makes an institution or normalcy, which Loos has some fun with:

Doug as Teddy Rutherford here is "in again." A scene from the Anita Loos scripted In Again, Out Again *(1917), Doug's first picture for Artcraft.*

Besides being a sound thinker, Lorelei is so normal that when, in Vienna, she undergoes analysis at the hands of Freud, the learned professor can only advise her to try to cultivate a few inhibitions.[31]

This idea of a center, after all, was stated by the man who practically invented the concept of the Common Man—Adolphe Quetelet (1796–1874) the brilliant Belgian astronomer and statistician. He wrote: "the man I consider here is analogous to the center of gravity; he is the mean about which oscillate the social elements."[32] We shall see later how Loos was able to penetrate society's disguises to the essential human form beneath— an essential element in the comic vision. But for now we can say that even in the most bizarre situation, as the central one in *Down to Earth*, she could constantly find the common humanness underneath the exotic disguise. This echoes Bergson's observation that the comic observation instinctively proceeds to what is *general*, choosing such peculiarities as admit of being reproduced, finding, in his words, ". . . a possibly common sort of uncommonness, so to say,—peculiarities that are held in common."[33]

Thus, even if the satirist is a moderate thinker fully appreciative of the wild immoderate extravagances of life, he might also be gifted with the insight into the common denominators that unite all men. If, as Bergson maintains, this is an essential direction that comedy takes, then it is one more reason why comedy is so capable of enabling us to better understand ourselves and others.

All right, so Loos, even though like Thorsten Veblen, she might be accused of wearing the mask of a "hard-boiled, scientific, savagely ironical dissenter of a moribund society,"[34] was not so at all. It is important to remember that under the savage satirical attack lies some kind of underpinning optimism toward a better condition. We mention Veblen because he was a contemporary of people like Loos and Mencken with quite a reputation for a rather savage slant on the society and civilization of America. And even he approached norms that were fundamentally optimistic. Perhaps he thought that the ugly traits of our society were survivals of the period of aristocratic barbarism. In time these might be stripped away. Beneath them were more promising material, the instincts, imbedded most deeply in the working class. Among these we might number "the parental bent, the instinct of workmanship, the instinct of idle curiosity, or in ordinary terms, disinterested love and disinterested science."[35] Henry May contends that even in such a severe observer as Veblen, who rejected moral idealism, culture when it preserved the useless, and progress, still embraced a feeling for the fundamental goodness of the human heart.

If there was anything that could link two such disparate observers as Loos and Veblen, it is this capacity to penetrate to common experience. She herself delighted in detecting these evidences of fundamental humanity in even the crustiest of people. She was not exactly a lightweight herself. She was a good friend of such people as Vachel Lindsay and H. L. Mencken and occasionally hovered around the Round Table set at the Algonquin (some of her films with Fairbanks took her and the crew to New York where they stayed at the famous hotel). She is the first to point out that someone like the terrible Mencken is at heart a believer in human instincts—"what makes New York so dreadful," she quotes him as saying, "is

the fact that its people have been forced to rid themselves of the oldest and most powerful human instinct—the love of home."[36]

The foregoing has been no attempt to reduce men of irreverence and blessed idiosyncrasy like Veblen and Mencken to a common and insipid mean; rather, it is to emphasize the necessity of an essentially sane viewpoint or average viewpoint to ferret out for scrutiny the quirks in popular behavior.

In 1919 Anita Loos wrote that some kinds of plots were out of tune with movie audiences of that day. They included the war or military story, stories of extreme poverty, cruelty to animals or children, themes justifying immorality in any form, stories of sickness or physical deformity, dope addicts. This points to the astounding rigidity and narrowness of conventions within the American motion picture at the time, and would seem to confirm Mencken's and Santayana's slashing attacks on what Mencken called the "boobus Americanus," the broad middle class that composed theater audiences and, indeed, made up the majority of that democracy both held such little regard for.

It is interesting to note that some respected films of only a few years earlier dealt with just such themes. Fairbanks' *The Mystery of the Leaping Fish* was not only about drug addiction, but was a *comedy* on the subject. Chaplin's *Easy Street* was likewise concerned amusingly with it. In 1918 came Mary Pickford's extraordinary *Stella Maris*, whose deformed main character is ugly and dies at the end a suicide. Fairbanks' 1915 *Habit of Happiness* centered on poverty and breadlines in New York slums. There, also, had been war stories like Griffith's *Hearts of the World* and Dwan's *The Traitor*, the last one filled with vicious anti-German rhetoric and graphic brutality. But these are mostly exceptions and doubtless Loos' observation was for the most part accurate.

What kind of society was she talking to, then? Certainly the vague worries of Americans in the pre-World War I period seemed to center in an old complaint—the increasing tempo of life in a mechanized and industrial society. This "fear for the national peace of mind" could lead to a long succession of "mind-cures," many of which (such as Coueism or "New Thought" which was a philosophy preferring autosuggestion as a means to attaining the slogan, "Every day in every way I am getting better and better.") were satirized by Loos. Another consequence of the pace of life was an awakened passion for facts and processes— statistics and the Model-T Assembly Line: "The heyday of the social survey was beginning; already thousands of Americans had filled out questionnaires on rural life, labor relations and urban vice."[37] Concerns of national import were disseminated as never before to everyone, as if in confirmation of our earlier remarks about the common experiences available to a large group of people. The idea of a "classless society" of common experience was operating. Anita Loos, ever the reporter of the American "process" and the aberrant statistic, chose to observe a changing society in her films. No, she did not deal with themes like drug addiction or outright immorality. Her vision operated within the framework of society itself and, in the end, with the American ideal of normalcy.

Certainly by 1919 she proved that the kind of comedy she wrote had immense popularity. On the one hand she had broken from the broad slapstick that had dominated so much of film comedy up to 1915, and, on the other, she had created a form of comedy that both appealed to and satirized the viewer—not a bad combination when one thinks of it.

What made her work unique to the period and to the movies? The world of slapstick was an essentially burlesque milieu. It was frenetic. It featured broad winks of the eye, much posturing and a very broad kind of sexual outlook. It was a tribute to Chaplin that he could elevate the stock elements of slapstick and transform them into a higher form of comic art. Slapstick's outlines were those of the cartoon. Its lineaments were those of the Monstrous. Its gestures were as broad as its scope was far-ranging. It delved with equal facility into the fantastic, the whimsical, the brutal. Above all, it participated in conventions of European farce. It clung to conventions of the boudoir. "In Europe," said George Jean Nathan, a one-time co-editor with Mencken of *The Smart Set* and prominent theater critic, "farce usually is made to concern itself for the most part with the various ramifications of amour, chiefly illicit."[38] It had little contact with the world outside the boudoir. The humorous commentary was not directed against public affairs so much as at love affairs, with a great deal of infidelity, adultery, and hiding under (or, as in Byron's *Don Juan* in) the bed!

While American farce, particularly on the screen, had been making a break with the preoccupation with this subject matter, the comedy of Anita Loos broke completely away from it. Not only was its pace much less frenetic, its gestures less broad, but it had its interest in public as opposed to mere boudoir bizarries. It exemplified what Nathan felt was "the best and most

important contribution that America has made to its own theater":

Fashionable society as American British-apes exhibit it, American advertising, American newspapers, American politics, American municipal administration, American hypocrisy, American money-madness, American business—such subjects have been the food of American farce and as a consequence the latter has frequently proved to be the most stimulating, corrective and derisorily tonic page in the native dramatic catalogue. . . . In it there has been a keener and more recognizably pointed appraisal and criticism of American life, enterprise and manners than in all the more serious plays which that theatre has shown.[39]

Loos' advent into the cinema in 1912 was a major element in this American transformation.

Now we are ready to examine some of the Loosian applications of the Fielding principles outlined earlier. We recall his emphasis upon accuracy of realistic observation, and we can now appreciate Loos' words in 1918:

Forget the symbolism and fairy stuff. Go out in the kitchen and write the history of the cook, and you will probably have a much more interesting story than any tiresome allegorical abstractions about humanity.
Write about real life even if you have to wade through the mud to do it.[40]

And Fielding's comment in the Preface to *Joseph Andrews* that everything was taken from his own "observation and experience" is echoed in Loos words:

. . . as my experience with life broadened I began to dredge real situations and real people from it. . . . *American Aristocracy,* was a satire on the big names of United States industry such as the Fords, the Heinzes, so important to the world of pickles, and the Chalmerses, who were touchingly proud of the underwear they manufactured. Eventually every experience became grist to my movie mill . . . [I] even began to make fun of the rich who had so overawed me on first acquaintance.[41]

This kind of observation did not yield dull and mundane results. It allowed the topsy-turvy world of the Ridiculous to produce fantastic images in Loos' hands—a whole sanitarium full of hypochondriacs in *Down to Earth*; a marriage ceremony performed via a three-way telephone hookup in *The Matrimaniac*; and a jail cell with the

Doug gives instruction on how to cope with nature in Down to Earth *(1917).*

comforts of home in *In Again, Out Again.* Loos could take an essentially commonplace situation and in a short time open it onto a bizarre development in the realms of the Ridiculous. G. K. Chesterton explains the process:

> The streets and shops and door-knockers of the harlequinade, which to the vulgar aesthete make it seem common-place, are in truth the very essence of the aesthetic departure. It must be an actual modern door which opens and shuts, constantly disclosing different interiors; it must be a real baker whose loaves fly up into the air without his touching them, or else the whole internal excitement of this elvish invasion of civilization, this abrupt entrance of Puck into Pimlico is lost.[42]

The energetic "gate-crashing" into the variety of social orders wherein Fairbanks indulges in many of the Loos films can be seen to be nothing less than this "elvish invasion of civilization." For example, in *Picture* he is a carnivorous creature in a world of vegetarians; in *Aristocracy,* he is a go-getter in the snobbish society of Rhode Island; in *Reaching for the Moon,* he is a typical young American suddenly thrust into the political ferment of a Balkan monarchy.

It is the detail in, say, *Picture,* that enables Loos to satirize the thinned-out existence and diet of vegetarians, such as the outrageous food substitutes and products manufactured by the Prindl family—"Prindl's Pressed Prunes" and the "Life Preserving Lentil." It whets the relish with which she confronts the hungry Fairbanks with a pallid vegetarian meal, setting up a contrast when we

later see this frustrated carnivore diving into a giant steak on the sly. He flexes his muscles, busily scatters seasoning about and, in general, enjoys himself hugely. This becomes funny within the context of the bloodless repasts usually served before his father's meatless table.

This is not to say that this kind of humor so dependent upon detailed observation, was at all the usual fare on the screens of the pre-World War I years. Knockabout comedy and grotesque costumes and characteristics were more common. The burlesque was prevalent. The screen was realizing Fielding's comment about the inherent *visualness* of burlesque. It would be years before the comic subtleties of a Harry D'Arrast or an Ernst Lubitsch would grace American screens. In the years before 1916 there was, perhaps, only one other figure in film that exercised a consistent vision into the Ridiculous—Max Linder.

Perhaps Loos' method of examination sprang from the raw twentieth century world around her. Not only was she working in that most intensely visual of mediums, but she was working in an age where scientific observation was making great strides. Robert Richardson contends in his book *Literature and Film* that the twentieth century finds creative expression in science and technology. Perhaps Loos' insistence upon the delineation of detail is a part of that broader preoccupation. If so, then Henry Bergson's words apply:

> Several authors . . . have noticed that humor delights in concrete terms, technical details, definite facts. If our analysis is correct, this is not an accidental trait of humour, it is its very essence. A humourist is a moralist disguised as a scientist, something like an anatomist who practises dissection with the sole object of filling us with disgust; so that humour, in the restricted sense in which we are here regarding the word, is really a transposition from the moral to the scientific.[43]

Doubtless, Miss Loos would be appalled at this "moralist disguised as a scientist" tag, and we offer Bergson's words merely in the spirit of conjecture. Certainly like most satirists she is mistrustful of systems. As Leonard Feinberg has observed: ". . . . most of the great satirists are anti-intellectual, distrustful of logically reached generalizations, and skeptical about the validity of all dogmas concerning men and institutions."[44]

System and dogma might be her main antipathy but it is also her chief subject. Loos approaches systems (largely of a social variety) in a film like *An American Aristocracy* and demolishes

Doug in "Vulgaria," the "average man pretending to royalty," in Reaching for the Moon *(1917), with Eugene Ormonde and Frank Campeau.*

the American drive to acquire class distinction, using society's characteristics to show it up. If she does practice her craft with the method of a scientist, it's a scientist who cheerfully admits that what we know of ourselves is woefully inadequate. Moreover, it is as a scientist who genially deflates his contemporaries with the reminder that we remain men sometimes in spite of ourselves.

According to Fielding, one characteristic of the Ridiculous is that it deals with persons of inferior rank. When Loos deals with royalty or aristocracy she never loses sight of the man inside the kingly robes. More often than not, as in *Reaching for the Moon,* she is merely dealing with the average man pretending to royalty. The emphasis is upon the man rather than the king. It is not on how the

man acts like a king but how the king acts like a man.

The common denominator here, of course, is that universal aspect of satire—the human element. How obvious it seems, yet how infrequently are we reminded that nothing is so comic as man! Indeed, Henri Bergson contends that the whole fabric of the comic is found in the human attribute and lineament:

You may laugh at an animal, but only because you have detected in it some human attitude or expression. You may laugh at a hat, but what you are making fun of, in this case, is not the piece of felt or straw, but the shape that men have given it—the human caprice whose mould it has assumed. It is strange that so important a fact, and such a simple one too, has not attracted to a greater degree the attention of philosophers.[45]

It is the shape that men give things—and vice versa—that fascinates Loos. In satirizing society's cultism and faddishness she is really reminding us of the "human caprice whose mould it has assumed."

Following this notion that nothing is so funny (or ridiculous) as the human animal, it follows that anything resembling that animal will be funny. So, too, does society take on the human shape and thereby become recognizable. When a man puts on a disguise or mask, as in the harlequinade, it is funny. Likewise when society adopts some kind of masquerade it can become laughable too. Bergson observes that anything restricting a natural flow, such as the mechanical encrusted on the living, creates a rigidity that is essentially comic. Although it would take a good deal of space to explicate his theory, it is enough here to trace its application to comedy as Loos utilizes it.

The ceremonial aspect to society, seen in its numerous clubs, lodges, parties and social registers, its celebration of conventions in rigidized patterns, corresponds to this "disguising" of an essentially human form. "The ceremonial side of social life must, therefore, always include a latent comic element, which is only waiting for an opportunity to burst into full view."[46] We can conclude that almost any form or formula serves as a ready-made frame into which the comic element operates. Scrupulous observation of that frame yields the greater comic effect when we become aware of the "disguise," or as we noted earlier, the sense of *normalcy* within the abnormal context.

It is true that her subject matter remained preoccupied with public institutions, the city, and society. It had as its fulcrum the assurance of a few basic truths concerning that society: that in a democracy "the safety of human society lies in the assumption that every individual composing it, in a given situation, will act in a manner hitherto approved as seemly."[47] Moreover, this kind of structure is held together by a very basic kind of cement—habit. Mencken states further: "This distrust of the unknown, this fear of doing something unusual, is probably at the bottom of many ideas and institutions that are commonly credited to other motives."[48]

The wrench, sometimes a destructive one, that she threw into this web of habits and prejudices, was an important factor both in the films' success with the public and with their success as effective satire. We refer, of course, to Douglas Fairbanks. His wide-open innocence and optimism, galvanic energy and stride caught the accelerating pulse of a dawning technological age. His rhythm and speed, guided by the pointed wit of Loos, delivered more than one shaft at a nation's posturings.

Loos always takes care to inform us that although Fairbanks pretends to high society and aristocracy, he is still a man of self-made values. In short, beneath his disguise of convention he is still essentially a man. The same holds true for her depictions of society. In *American Aristocracy* we encounter a rigid system of high society that is founded upon wealth and position—essentially artificial masks upon essentially commonplace people. Although they all register the correct deportment and correct clothes, they are not at all above the petty and mean actions that characterize us all. In one scene, the wife of a prominent businessman snubs the wife of a brewer with the chilling words, "Madam, *we* are distillers." The hapless brewer's wife likewise finds herself snubbed by all the rest of the industrialists' wives and is finally left alone in a screened-in porch full of empty (but still tilting) rocking chairs. This unusual visual metaphor for the empty and mechanical movements of society is typical of Loos' ability to give us glimpses into the "human condition" underneath a person's scarlet, flowing robe and mask. This society in the film of which we speak is a "bean-can nobility" that is founded upon the all-American dollar, but which has all the caste and exclusiveness of "The 400." Indeed, the same kind of levelling conformity operates—any deviancy means expulsion. It is practically impossible when confronted by such a vast horde to change any aspect of it, and even if one could, the people would not be likely to move out of their accustomed grooves, unable to shake loose from the unintelligible prejudices and mental vices that condition ninety percent of his thinking.[49]

We turn now to the society she depicts in *Down to Earth*. It is a kind of microcosm wherein a number of severely ill people reside in "Dr. JollyEm's Sanitarium." Their ills are entirely imaginary, yet they cling to them with all the earnestness of youth clinging to illusions. Thus does Loos show the habit and prejudices of social life to be both illusory and firmly confined. Similarly, in *Wild and Woolly*, the townsfolk of Bitter Creek, Arizona, transform their progressive little town into an imaginative construct of the "Romantic West" that a wealthy railroad official has envisioned it to be. In this way they hope that the industrialist will be pleased with the town and build a railroad spur there. This rush to shape *a whole town* into a living stereotype or convention is again demonstrative of her treatment of the pretense and artificiality and conformity of society.

In each of the above examples there is affectation—the "true source of the Ridiculous" in Fielding's view. From the vanity of "bean-can Nobility" to the hypocrisy of the Bitter Creek townsfolk, Loos succeeds in turning each topsy-turvy by showing the truth under the mask, or the humanness under the convention. The example of *Down to Earth* is a mild excursion into Fielding's comment that the Ridiculous can transform the misfortunes of life and nature into objects of ridicule. Loos reverses the process, and we see abnormalcy operating within a decidedly healthy (and normal) situation.

Loos' concerns with some of the shapes engendered in people by a technological age, as well by society, her predilection with the currents of American life that George Santayana called the "vast modern mechanical momentum" and the "rushing tide of instrumentalities"—is lightly apparent in the 1916 film *The Matrimaniac*, a little gem linking everyday life with the machine muscle of America. Fairbanks portrays an altar-bound swain who is separated from his fiance by the agencies of fate and her irate father. He tries to rejoin her by utilizing all the various methods of transportation at 1916 man's disposal. These include, variously, a motor railcar, a switch engine, the brake rods of a freight train, the transcontinental limited, three brands of autos, and a wheelbarrow! The film is a paean to speed, and, most importantly, to man's adaptation to and of the agencies of technology to further his ends. This last is seen fully developed in the final sequence. Loos beautifully engineers events so that the film ends with Doug trying to elude his pursuers by clambering about an urban forest of rooftops and fire escapes and crawling across a series of telephone wires to a pole under repair by a workman. There, perched amid the crossarms and wires, he has the lineman put through a multiple hook-up to his fiance in her hotel room where she is being kept a virtual prisoner by her father and to a minister who is being likewise detained in a jail cell. The wedding is thus conducted by long distance while a lineman, a maid, and deputy sheriff are witnesses. Loos has been at some pains to contrive such a situation and when we see here a man's passion being transmitted through an electric power cable, we

can be sure she is saying something worth paying attention to. Effecting the marriage union is in this case more like connecting a circuit. The possible mechanization of man's impulses is at least one possible consequence of the machine age. Whether this example from *The Matrimaniac* shows normality operating within and through the abnormality of the machine, or the just the reverse, is not quite clear. The film either echoes Pope's declaration:

> Ye gods!
> Annihilate but space and time
> And make two lovers happy.

or the chain gang supervisor's words at the end of *Cool Hand Luke*:

"What we have here is a failure to communicate."

In any case, the events of the film would seem to bear out Santayana's withering criticism of the "genteel American" in 1913: "He is a materialist in morals: he esteems things and he esteems himself, for mechanical uses and energies."[50]

Earlier we discussed the importance of the norm in satire in general, and with Loos in particular. There remains but to take this consideration to its final stage. To do this one may briefly consider two of the Loos films, *In Again, Out Again* and *Reaching for the Moon*.

In the first film the striking thing that happens is not necessarily that Loos is satirizing the pacifist movement before World War I, rather, it is the secondary plot about a man who wants to break *into* jail instead of out. This motif, vaguely reminiscent of O. Henry's earlier short story, "The Cop and the Anthem," is in itself a pointed barb at the American's love of confining convention as a way of life and of the efforts to secure it at any cost. Fairbanks' attempts to get back into jail (wherein resides, incidentally, the sheriff's beautiful daughter) are quite hilarious. After discovering that his stay in the cooler has its advantages, he greets the judge's sentence of thirty days with a broad smile and a vigorous handshake. At the same time a title states:

At the end of a perfect trial.

Once inside, he transforms his cold and bleak cell into a cozy nook with curtains, oval pictures on the walls, flowers, and a couch upon which he reclines with a pipe and ukulele, his beloved beside him. What more telling image of the middle-class dream than this—paradise recaptured in domestic bliss.

The same kind of end befalls our hero more than once in Loos. It constitutes seemingly a paradox in her work, but is actually one of the truly interesting aspects of her satire. In *Reaching for the Moon*, Fairbanks, after being disillusioned by his pretensions toward the aristocracy of Vulgaria, is happy to accept his little home in New Jersey—picket fence, bouncing babies, and all. Loos greets this somewhat less than glowing image with the words from a travel booklet:

Why exist in New York? Come to Jersey and live.

"This is the essence of the comic," H. L. Mencken said: "The unmasking of fraud, its destruction by worse fraud."[51] As we have seen with our series of Loos examples, man is a pretentious animal, subject to both the vagaries of whims and fads and the iron-bound conventions of societies and customs. If, as in *In Again, Out Again, American Aristocracy,* and *Reaching for the Moon,* we see Fairbanks shadowboxing with the illusions of class and structure, we, of course, will laugh at the ridiculousness of such ambitions. But at the same time the "norm" that is implied, the center about which these pretensions revolve—in other words, that which is advocated or at least accepted by the characters as the "right" American way of life—is likewise a fraud. Doubtless, Mencken would have applauded the endings to these films. In *Aristocracy* Fairbanks successfully crashes society's barriers and even founds his own wealth upon a modest little invention of his own—the double-hump hat pin. In *Reaching for the Moon,* he learns to accept the American epitome of middle-class life—the little house in New Jersey. In *In Again, Out Again,* he succeeds in getting back into jail and getting the girl. We appreciate the Fairbanks vitality during all this—and so does Loos. And for a time we are fooled. Yet, in the final analysis Loos has pulled a fast one on us. Fairbanks has gone toward rather than away from the stuffed shirts. The journey toward individual expression has been seen from the wrong end of the telescope. The American Dream, in short, has turned out to be the fraud at the end of the rainbow instead of the fabled pot of gold.

She has shown, it would seem, the ridiculousness of all things. Santayana's blast at materialism and idealism in America might be a salute to her in a way, for he, too, holds dearly the gift of laughter in the face of all things:

. . . the constant sense of the incongruous, even if artificially stimulated and found only in trivial things is an admission that existence is absurd; it is therefore a liberation of the spirit over and against this absurd world; it is a laughing liberation because the spirit is glad to be free.[52]

NOTES

1. Eric Bentley, *The Life of the Drama* (New York: Atheneum, 1967), p. 296.
2. Henri Bergson, "Laughter" in *Comedy* (New York: Doubleday Anchor Books, 1956), p. 62.
3. *Photoplay*, December, 1917, p. 48.
4. Paul Grant, "John, Anita, and the Giftie," *Photoplay*, December, 1917, p. 50.
5. Henry Fielding, *The History of the Adventures of Joseph Andrews* (New York: Modern Library, 1950), p. xxxiii.
6. *Ibid.*, p. xxxiii.
7. *Ibid.*, p. xxxiii.
8. *Ibid.*, p. xxxix.
9. *Ibid.*, p. xxxiv.
10. *Ibid.*, p. xxxv.
11. *Ibid.*, p. xxxvi.
12. *Ibid.*, p. xxxvii.
13. *Ibid.*, p. xxxviii.
14. Gary Carey, "Written on the Screen," *Film Comment*, Winter, 1970–1971, p. 51.
15. Ralph Hancock, *The Fourth Musketeer* (New York: Henry Holt and Co., 1953), p. 121.
16. Anita Loos, *A Girl Like I* (New York: Viking Press, 1966), pp. 98–99.
17. Kevin Brownlow, *The Parade's Gone By . . .* (New York; Bantam Books, 1969), p. 22.
18. *Ibid.*, p. 313.
19. Anita Loos, *A Girl*, p. 154.
20. H. L. Mencken, "The American Language," reprinted in Huntington Cairns (ed.) *The American Scene* (New York: Alfred A. Knopf, 1965), p. 314.
21. *Ibid.*, p. 315.
22. *Ibid.*, pp. 308–309.
23. Gary Carey, "Written," p. 51.
24. *Ibid.*, p. 51.
25. Karl Schmidt in *Everybody's*, May, 1917, p. 622.
26. John Emerson and Anita Loos, *How to Write Photoplays* (Philadelphia: George W. Jacobs and Co., 1923), p. 39.
27. *Photoplay*, July, 1918, pp. 88–89.
28. *Everybody's*, May, 1917, p. 622.
29. G. K. Chesterton, *The Last of the Great Men*.
30. Anita Loos, *A Girl*, p. 221.
31. *Ibid.*, p. 273.
32. Clifton Fadiman, *Any Number Can Play* (Cleveland: World Publishing Co., 1957), p. 115.
33. Henri Bergson, *Laughter*, p. 170.
34. Henry F. May, *The End of American Innocence* (Chicago: Quadrangle Books, 1964), p. 181.
35. *Ibid.*, p. 180.
36. Anita Loos, *A Girl*, p. 215.
37. Henry May, *The End*, p. 157.
38. George Jean Nathan, *Testament of a Critic* (New York and London: Alfred A. Knopf, 1931), p. 253.
39. *Ibid.*, pp. 253–254.
40. Anita Loos in *Picture-Play Magazine*, October, 1918, p. 251.
41. Anita Loos, *A Girl*, p. 73.
42. G. K. Chesterton, *The Defendant* (London: J. M. Dent and Sons, 1901), pp. 125–126.

43. Henri Bergson, *Laughter,* pp. 142–143.

44. Leonard Feinberg, *Introduction to Satire* (Ames: Iowa State University Press, 1967), p. 5.

45. Henri Bergson, *Laughter,* p. 62.

46. *Ibid.,* p. 89.

47. H. L. Mencken, *Prejudices,* First Series (New York: Knopf, 1920), pp. 162-163.

48. *Ibid.,* pp. 162–163.

49. *Ibid.,* pp. 163–164.

50. George Santayana, in Douglas L. Wilson (ed.), *The Genteel Tradition* (Massachusetts: Harvard University Press, 1967), p. 126.

51. H. L. Mencken, *The American Scene,* p. 202.

52. George Santayana in *The Genteel Tradition,* p. 151.

7

The Founding of United Artists

In 1918, Los Angeles was a city of about half a million population. Ten years later this number would double. The movie industry had adopted it as its own. Triangle had built a large studio at Culver City; Carl Laemmle had moved Universal to a site in the San Fernando Valley; the Lasky Company bought acreage near Universal; the Metro plant in Hollywood was expanding; Vitagraph was in East Hollywood; Fox had purchased a studio on Sunset Boulevard; Mary Pickford and Charles Chaplin were producing in Hollywood.

To understand the genesis of United Artists, we first need to ask, what is "open" booking or what is "closed" booking? Since around 1915, distributors had booked films to exhibiters on a block basis, a type of closed booking. This meant that the exhibitor had to buy up a number of films from a company that were relatively bad in order to get those few that were relatively good. The rise of the star system contributed to this bind, because stars sold the picture more than anything else, apparently. A movie-goer had only to know that a Chaplin was coming to town and the exhibitor was assured of gold at the box office. This was true to a lesser extent of directors, such as Griffith, Tourneur, Dwan. Through closed booking the exhibitor was forced to book the lesser films to obtain the few good ones.

There were a number of exceptions to this rule, of course. United Artists is one of them. But to a lesser extent there were at least three efforts previous to United Artists that attempted a system of "open booking," i.e., booking films individually on their own merit rather than in a series. Lewis Selznick did this with the pictures of Clara Kimball Young when he rented them singly and made a sizeable profit. The "Clara Kimball Young Pictures Company" did quite well in those years 1915–1916.[1] And there was William Hodkinson who in 1919 was attempting the "first open-market policy adopted by a distributing organization," according to *Variety* at that time. This is ironic since it was Hodkinson who originated the "series" contract with Mary Pickford in 1915. (Briefly, when Hodkinson was head of Paramount he had to meet Pickford's demands for more salary raises and was forced to sell the Pickford pictures as a "series," charging more for them than for the regular Paramount features.) It made possible higher salaries for actors, increases in admittance prices to the great new theaters, and increases in price for the exhibitor to show such a series of films. The open-market booking was complex by the fact that contractual arrangements were made for individual titles, and paperwork and headaches were multiplied on both the distributing and exhibiting end.

United they stand: Douglas Fairbanks, Mary Pickford, D. W. Griffith, and Charlie Chaplin, the "United Artists."

The idea of open booking seems to have hinged originally on both the quality of the picture and the prestige of the star. As we shall see, it was because of the overwhelming popularity of the star system that United Artists was founded at all. The stars' demands for higher salaries were becoming so numerous that efforts to get them under contract were nothing less than pitched battles between star and employer. It all came to a head in 1918–1919 when the struggles to ensnare the likes of Mary Pickford, Charlie Chaplin, and Douglas Fairbanks were at their bitterest. It was from these struggles that general agreement seems to have been reached among these stars that the only way to receive more money and at the same time to avoid the restrictions and time limits of studio contracts was to form a company of their own and release their pictures singly, rather than as a series in a closed-booking plan. Let us try to deal briefly with the individuals and events leading up to the actual formation of United Artists on 5 February 1919. It will be seen that it was the star system and increasing demands of the stars that were the leading factors in its formation.

In tracing the career of Mary Pickford one understands immediately that a remarkable tenacity and drive contributed to her rise as the most popular screen star in the world, a position solidly consolidated by 1919. Probably the screen has seen no other star as fiercely businesswise as she was. Still in her midteens under David Belasco she announced that her goal was "to earn five hundred dollars a week by the time I am twenty."[2] Later, she would recall, under Zukor's Famous Players:

In the next few years my salary staged several spectacular leaps, going from one thousand to two thousand; then from two thousand to four thousand, and, finally, to what was then, and, I believe, remained for some time, the ceiling of motion-picture salaries, ten thousand dollars a week. These were not only salaries, but were weekly guarantees against 50 per cent of the profits.[3]

By 1916 she had amply proved that the audience came to see the star regardless of the picture, and that she could command higher and higher wages and be worth it. She then insisted that her pictures through the Artcraft Company (a producing wing of Famous Players) be sold separately. This was an innovation and the theater owners began to wonder if this revolutionary departure from the program system meant an increase in rentals. Her films were trebled in price right at the start and the exhibitors went wild. But gradually the exhibitors learned that people would pay increased admission prices, that in fact the films were increasing in quality, that at higher prices their profits (not to mention the profits of Artcraft) were higher than before. Thus already we see her interest in this kind of system. It would come to fruition with United Artists. Because of more contractual disputes she joined with First National in 1918, being offered complete independence in the distribution of her films and a raise in her salary. It is easy to see that her popularity as a star and her drive for independence were vital factors in her success.

And then there was Chaplin. Like Pickford he rose to the peak of his success by 1918. Like Pickford, an incredible drive for independence and money swept him past the most obstinate and cautious of producers. He went from Keystone to Essanay to Mutual to First National, his salary soaring all the while. Like Pickford, whoever owned him controlled top box office receipts. But Chaplin's contracts called for short films, two-reelers, and it was not until *Shoulder Arms* in 1918 that he was to make even a three-reel picture (excepting the 1915 *Tillie's Punctured Romance*), and the freedom and time necessary for features was not to be found even under First National, though he did do *The Kid* in 1921. It was under United Artists that this drive for independence and the freedom from contractual restrictions would enable him to take his time turning out features.

Of the Big Four under discussion here, D. W. Griffith is the least important in terms of contribution to United Artists. Since 1916 he had been saddled with debts incurred since *Intolerance's* failure at the box office. Still indisputably the Master Director, he nevertheless had been making disappointing pictures after the 1918 *Hearts of the World,* nor was there any box office success to speak of until he released through United Artists his *Broken Blossoms* in 1919. His name lent considerable prestige to the undertaking of UA and he was able to isolate himself and his production crew out at Mamaroneck, New York for several years. In 1926 he would break with UA, go to Paramount, then to Universal, then back to UA, then away again. If there is any particular benefit derived from his association with United Artists it is his own studio at Mamaroneck.

Now a figure suddenly leaps into view and almost immediately is gone. He is Douglas Fairbanks, of course, a junior member of the film industry compared to his good friends, Chaplin and Pickford. But in only two years, between 1916 and 1918, he had become a star of the first-rank. Shrewd, resourceful, agile and dynamic, he turned the industry on its ear, had his own production company, Douglas Fairbanks Pictures under the aegis of Paramount Pictures. The theater's proscenium arch could never have contained him for long and the motion picture was the necessary medium to capture his personality. By 1918 many production companies eagerly sought him from Zukor, the most outstanding of these—First National. Fairbanks was ready for more money and more independence.

During the latter part of 1918 the dickering had been bitter to sign up Chaplin and Pickford to new contracts. Out of the smoke of battle emerged the "upstart" company, First National, with them in tow. But a comparatively new star was approaching a zenith and the acquisition of him was also vital if a company was to control the box office. So First National turned greedy eyes to that star, Douglas Fairbanks. It would appear, as subsequent events proved, that it was because of him and his timely rise to prominence that the idea of United Artists was born.

It happened this way: Throughout January of 1919 Los Angeles was the center of a spectacular film parade. The heads of nearly all the film companies were there, and most of the reason was First National. They were buying up every star in sight and naturally other producers wanted to be on hand to protect their own stars. We already know that Chaplin and Pickford were sewn up by First National, but Fairbanks was as yet unsigned. Two producers that were on the scene were Hiram Abrams and B. P. Schulberg,

recently resigned from Zukor's Famous Players-Lasky. They, too, had their eyes on Fairbanks. According to Benjamin Hampton, they came up with a plan based upon what they knew of the power of a star at the box office. So "they went to Los Angeles and submitted it to Charlotte and Mary Pickford and Douglas Fairbanks, all of whom were pleased with the idea."[4] "Pleased" is hardly the word. . . . This first outright move toward the formation of United Artists consisted of a plan calling for the removal of their films from association with any company distributing-program or series of films, forcing the exhibitor to pay almost any price set upon them. From Pickford and Fairbanks the plan spread to include Chaplin and Griffith—that they form their own company to make and sell their own pictures. *Variety* reported on 24 January 1919, that:

> . . . while the producers were wrangling, the big stars, headed by Griffith, Chaplin, Fairbanks, Hart, Pickford and Arbuckle, effected a temporary organization to combat the producers. Each star pledged to forfeit a big sum of money if they tried breaking away. They plan to make their own pictures and sell to the releasing organization bidding the highest for same.

And Arthur Mayer recalls:

> Now the stars . . . decided that the movie firmament revolved about them. If First National could afford to pay millions for their services why should they not make and distribute their own product and retain all of the profits that were being appropriated by greedy entrepreneurs such as the producers and the exhibitors.[5]

We should note here that Fairbanks was important at this time for several reasons: (1) He was the only one of the aforementioned stars not under a long-term contract—his present contract would expire in May of 1919 to Paramount. Chaplin still had five pictures to do for First National and he was working slowly; Pickford still had four pictures for First National; Griffith had three for the same company. The burden of producing for any new company would inevitably fall to Fairbanks therefore, since the others would be tied up for some time. (2) It was Fairbanks who suggested that a man of national prominence head the company, someone whose name would bring respect and prestige to the still fledgling industry. That Doug was a shrewd businessman is evident here as this was years before Hays was brought in on the heels of scandal-wracked Hollywood to lend dignity through his name to the film colony. Thus, Douglas suggested William Gibbs McAdoo as an ideal head (he was son-in-law of President Wilson, had been a former Secretary of the Treasury and was at that time Director General of the railroads). Douglas knew McAdoo, had staged a rodeo for him once, and, with Mary Pickford, had sold a lot of Liberty Bonds under his eye.

At any rate, Fairbanks refused to sign with any of the producing companies until he learned what would come of their own proposed alliance. Meanwhile the expected rumors began to fly around Hollywood, such as that Fairbanks had signed with First National, that Zukor had engineered the whole alliance out of the air to weaken the appeals made by said First National, that even if the big stars banded together, the films made under their present contracts would be withheld and run in competition with films made by them for their new company.[6] Another rumor referred to "several big money interests mentioned as backers of the scheme. Among those whose names are freely mentioned as financially interested in it are Henry Ford. . . . Du Pont and Morgan are also mentioned."[7] This rumor was based on fact, and, according to Terry Ramsaye, this was part of a theater project intended to assure the stars of a sure avenue to viewers. This scheme included the millions of the Du Pont interests, James and Nicholas Brady, E. E. Smathers, a wealthy oil operator, Joseph Godsol, and a consolidation with the then still-active Goldwyn concern. This fell through.[8]

One thing that remains certain during this confusing period is that the stars were interested in "open booking" their films—"the Fairbanks plan of direct making and selling from bids is reported to have been favorably looked upon the other stars when hearing of it. . . ."[9] But they had to consider exhibitors and with the proposed merger of Paramount and First National underway they knew that at least sixty percent of the exhibitors would be sewn up by the combination. The independent, under which heading the stars might come if they banded together, would have only a forty percent field—decidedly unprofitable. Thus, the failure of the aforementioned theater plan was most unfortunate.

On 19 January a meeting was held at Fairbanks' home in Beverly Hills. McAdoo was officially approached to head an organization that would market their film wares. He declined, but said that if they could get Oscar Price for president he would take an advisory capacity as counsel.[10]

Price had been McAdoo's press agent during his treasury administration and was now his assistant in administration of the government's railroad affairs. Apparently everyone wished to keep things in the family.

Finally on Monday night, 5 February 1919 a conference was held again at Fairbanks' home. Present were Fairbanks (needless to say), Griffith, Chaplin, Pickford, and William S. Hart. Chaplin was represented by Arthur Wright, Griffith by Albert H. T. Banzhaf, Fairbanks and Pickford by Dennis F. O'Brien. There it was announced that William Gibbs McAdoo had been retained as general counsel for the "Big Five." Their company would be called United Artists. After the conference in Fairbanks' home he released the following statement as to the aims:

> . . . I have agreed to become general counsel for the United Artists Association, the independent company which they are organizing for the protection of their interests. They have determined not to permit any trust to destroy competition or to blight or interfere with the high quality of their work. They feel it is of the utmost importance to secure the artistic development of the moving picture industry and they believe that this will be impossible if any trust should get possession of the field and wholly commercialize the business.[11]

So the United Artists Association was formed at last, in spite of the potential problems over distribution mentioned earlier. There were two concerns actually. The first was the *United Artists Association,* not a corporation, but an association of four producers banded together with clauses providing for federal injunction in the event any of them tried to withdraw. Then there was the *United Artists Corporation,* which had the producers as the principal stockholders, and which held a contract to distribute the pictures with the agreement that each of the four stars (Arbuckle had withdrawn and Hart had decided to retire) produce two pictures per year. As was soon evident, this last stipulation was not a binding one.

The setup was as follows:

McAdoo was general counsel
Oscar Price was President
George Clifton was Secretary and Treasurer
Dennis O'Brien was Vice-President
Hiram Abrams was General Manager

For the distributing corporation the preferred

Doug and William S. Hart. They both worked for Triangle and later would be briefly associated at United Artists.

stock was divided evenly among the four who agreed to put up $125,000 apiece, paying for it over a period of years. McAdoo got his common stock at the beginning, but the others were supposed to get theirs in one-ninth lots, as they completed each of the nine pictures they originally contracted for. The essence of the plan of distributing was based on a percentage arrangement with the theaters, computed on a sliding scale. The exhibitor would be asked to contract a film on a percentage of the gross, the percentage to the picture increasing as the receipts jumped. We should point out the striking departure between this system and the previous systems used by producers: (1) UA was in earnest about selling each picture individually—no star series, no contract for the four stars, but each picture separately. With the exceptions already cited, this was vastly different from the prevailing style of series booking. (2) Exhibitors were given an opportunity to see the features in advance, with permission to cancel if they failed to come up to expectations, the rentor being the sole arbiter in this respect.[12] Now, in a company like Paramount, the vast output of pictures alone would have made these two factors unfeasible. Paramount would release "super" pictures like the Pickfords along with lesser features and downright mediocre ones at the same time. United Artists would concentrate on a relative few, each one handcrafted, so to speak. Only such an organization could have had such a distributing system. The only problem still was to find those exhibitors.

Heretofore producers and distributors had been the employers (with the exception of First National) paying salaries and sometimes a share of the profits to the star. But, as Terry Ramsaye states: "Now that the inventors, cameramen, exchangemen, and exhibitors had taken their fling at motion picture control, it was the actor's turn."[13] Now the stars were their own employers.

They had to do their own financing, but they received the producer profits that had heretofore gone to their employers, and each received his share of the proceeds of the distributing organization. This had been their goal all along. They represented the peak of the star system and were demonstrating just how powerful it was.

Fairbanks and Pickford established their studio on Santa Monica Boulevard in West Hollywood. As soon as their contracts were up with First National and Paramount, they started to make their own pictures and distribute them through UA. Chaplin established his studio at Sunset and LaBrea in West Hollywood, which he used throughout his years in the U.S. Griffith moved his entire company to Mamaroneck, N.Y., where he quickly filmed his required three films for First National. He bought an estate there at Orienta Point, a peninsula of land jutting into Long Island Sound, and converted everything into a studio.

The first two years no doubt were critical. Can anything be seen in the first films by the Big Four that are indicative of the success and independence that each hungered so much for? Let's take a brief look—

United Artists now had a handsome new front with McAdoo and Price. But it was Hiram Abrams who was the real power behind the initial success. Abrams, it will be remembered, had been the first to approach Fairbanks and Pickford with the idea of forming their own company. His long association with Paramount and Zukor enterprises provided him with an atmosphere of success and healthy payrolls that no doubt filled the hearts of the Big Four with gladness. When he left Paramount to work for United Artists he brought with him all the perspicacity and business acumen that had made him invaluable for Zukor. For our purposes he is most noteworthy in that as General Manager he was able to persuade most exhibitors to book the early United Artists films. In smaller cities the company had to show in second-rate theaters, and it was shut out of some areas completely. In some of these areas Abrams rented theaters and played his pictures on extended runs in a vigorous effort to prove that UA pictures were a profitable product. That Abrams was effective is shown when he "dazzled many exhibitors into putting up deposits against future rentals, with the result that they kicked in with enough money in advance to finance the first United Artists Fairbanks picture, *His Majesty the American*." [14] In a matter of months McAdoo and Price had left UA because of various disputes and Abrams assumed the helm of UA, a position he

held until his death in 1926.

In the beginning, the burden of production fell on Fairbanks. By the next year Pickford was able to assume some of the weight. Chaplin was tied up until 1922 with First National and did not produce anything for UA until the now legendary *Woman of Paris* in 1923. Griffith was producing on the East Coast. Fairbanks kicked the whole thing off with two pictures in 1919, *His Majesty the American* and *When the Clouds Roll By*. He was at this time approaching the peak of his career and his popularity evidently was sufficient to assure a good representation at the box office. He had made his mark with exactly this kind of film—breezy, contemporary comedy that at times took on the vigor and enthusiasm of a race horse. He specialized in a kind of gymnastic sermon, making topical comments and satiric thrusts while performing incredible athletic stunts. The latter film, particularly, is one of his happiest creations. There is an unflagging joy and enthusiasm coupled with a truly inventive fantasy that is all quite captivating. But so far he had not strayed far from his well-established format. He was playing it safe. But in 1920 he made the first of several moves in an effort to take advantage of his autonomy as producer and freedom as an actor. Surveying his first twenty-nine pictures, Fairbanks observed:

There comes a sure day when you are struck by doubts whether what you are doing is after all worth the effort, whether the world is in the slightest degree better for what you have done. And doubts and fears are the two things that enthusiasm cannot survive. [15]

His thirtieth film—*The Mark of Zorro*. Here was a clean departure from contemporary satire and jazz-age message, here was historical romance and escapism. It can be argued that Fairbanks needed the independence of UA to do costume films. Griffith's failure at the box office with *Intolerance* had put the taboo on such films since 1916. But Fairbanks had had leanings in this direction before. In the 1918 *A Modern Musketeer* was a five-minute dream sequence lampooning D'Artagnan. But it was not until the advent of United Artists that he dare take the risk of a full-length costume film. *Zorro* (since then hackneyed by any number of second-rate remakes) was fine, adventurous stuff and but the first of a series of experiments in production. In 1922 he would construct the biggest set in Hollywood (for *Robin Hood*) smack during the "depression" that had gripped the industry with unemployment and malaise since the Reid and Arbuckle scandals a year earlier. In 1924 he would make an "art" picture that, in technical effects at least, bettered any European product—*The Thief of Bagdad.* In 1926 he would make the first feature in the then highly unpredictable and untried process of Technicolor, *The Black Pirate*—a terrific risk that cost him millions. Needless to say, it is easy to see how UA was good for a man with the vigor and determination of Fairbanks. *Zorro* was the turning point. 1921 saw two more films, *The Nut* (the last of the contemporary comedies) and *The Three Musketeers.*

Mary Pickford, who in 1920 had become Mrs. Fairbanks, surely the screen's most famous business and romantic consolidation in history, made two films in 1920—*Pollyanna* and *Suds.* 1921 saw three films—*Love Light, Through the Back Door,* and *Little Lord Fauntleroy.* These were all typical of her product in that they embodied the "sweet young thing that every man desires some day to have for himself."[16] In her thirties by this time, Pickford was still playing little girls of fifteen or so, who, by virtue of bright optimism and a fiery sense of injustice could be counted on to right all sorts of pervading evils. That she was aware of her stereotyping is obvious from the success with which she manipulated it and the bitterness under which she privately chafed at it. In other words, as yet there were no apparent differences between her UA films and those for Paramount or First National. But, for her, UA provided two advantages over her career under other producers. First, as her own producer, she could make fewer films and make them to higher standards. Secondly, she could "experiment" too. But while Fairbanks broke the mold after only one year with UA, Pickford waited for four years before making *Rosita,* importing Ernst Lubitsch for it. A year later she made *Dorothy Vernon of Haddon Hall.* In both films she was a mature young woman with appetites quite different from those of Pollyanna. Unfortunately, her attempts to change her screen image did not meet with the success that her husband's similar efforts did—they bombed at the box office. Even Pickford looks back at *Rosita* and groans.

Kevin Brownlow says of Mr. and Mrs. Fairbanks during the Twenties:

> Pickford and Fairbanks were able to recognize talent, and they had business acumen enough to be able to employ it. Their choice was dictated as much by commercial considerations as by artistic merit, yet their films attained the highest possible standards in every de-

partment. Mary Pickford employed the finest cameramen, Charles Rosher. Douglas Fairbanks used brilliant men like Arthur Edeson. . . . They both signed top directors . . . and they drew from lesser-known directors the best pictures of their careers.[17]

The impetus to make quality films for United Artists lasted throughout the Twenties. They are truly products of their creators. In no other studio could a similar feat have been performed because the other major studios were rapidly assuming the characteristics of a machine, quickly turning out a slick product, each film greatly resembling the other.

Griffith was experimenting too, in a number of ways. 1919 saw one of his greatest efforts, both financially and artistically, *Broken Blossoms.* This was one of Abrams' greatest challenges when the distribution end of UA was still nebulous. The subject matter (from Thomas Burke's *Limehouse Nights*) was a little questionable. "It was the forerunner of the sordid, dilapidated slum theme that has been present in the cinema ever since Griffith suggested it."[18] In addition, Griffith, with his cameraman, Hendrik Sartov, utilized "soft-focus" photography, a process of filtering light before it reached the camera lens so the image seemed clouded and fuzzy. This was the first time such a process was consciously used and exploited. 1921's *Dream Street* brought another experiment—sound. Although many think sound came in 1927 with the *Jazz Singer,* it had been around for some time with Lee DeForest's Phonofilms. *Dream Street,* however, is one of the granddaddies of the process and as a film was a fantasy to boot! It was Griffith's only experiment with sound until *Abraham Lincoln* in 1930. *Way Down East* in 1922 was a different kind of experiment. Griffith looked backward to a hoary old stage melodrama and paid hundreds of thousands for the rights to it. Those that called him crazy stopped laughing when the box office gold started pouring in. His years with United Artists were hardly his best ones, but at least he did achieve his own studio and did continue in the tradition of expansion and experimentation in the cinema that distinguished him from the first days at Biograph.

Although the scope of this chapter does not extend beyond 1922 and Chaplin did not begin producing for United Artists until 1923, we should note his initial picture for UA since it does indicate the independence he had achieved. *Woman of Paris* does not even star Chaplin, nor is it a comedy. Made in 1923, it is one of Chaplin's strongest assertions to be considered as artist *first* and funnyman second. Now this happens in all his films from then on—the dramatic element exercises a stronger hold upon the comedy, the pathos is more pronounced. *Woman* gave Chaplin full opportunity to fully control the directing and writing. Not until the recent *Countess from Hong Kong* would he stray from the front of the lens. For any other production company such a straight dramatic film without even an appearance by Chaplin would have been questionable, to say the least. His previous contracts wanted Chaplin pictures, comedies, *with* Chaplin. As his own boss he saw fit to get away from that and *Woman* is the brilliant result. As the usually ascerbic Paul Rotha says:

> He attacked both man and womanhood in this unforgettable film. He showed an understanding of the machinery of human mentality that hitherto had been merely suspected from his own comedies. He was reminiscent, if the comparison may be allowed, of the wit and skill of Wilde.[19]

Mary Pickford and Douglas Fairbanks and Charles Chaplin and D. W. Griffith—all superstars, bizarre creatures who formed their own company as the ultimate step in their demonstration of the power of the personality at the box office. They were themselves no product of the "star system," but they made their own way until, paradoxically enough, they came to be regarded as the epitome of the star system.

At its inception Hollywood tended to sneer at the enterprise known as United Artists. Richard Rowlands of Metro dryly commented, "The Lunatics have taken over the asylum." "But the idea worked. The producers made money, and United Artists began to make money. Before long, United Artists became known as 'The Tiffany of Hollywood!' "[20] Apart from its capacity to "make money" we have tried to show that such a system also granted the Big Four a necessary independence and, in the case of Fairbanks and Chaplin, a valuable boost to greater efforts. It is well to call this kind of result "success" also.

NOTES

1. Benjamin B. Hampton, *A History of the Movies* (New York: Covici, Friede Publishers, 1931), p. 135.

2. Mary Pickford, *Sunshine and Shadow* (Garden City: Doubleday and Co., 1955), p. 161.

3. *Ibid.,* p. 168.

4. Benjamin B. Hampton, *A History,* p. 229.

5. Arthur Mayer, *Merely Colossal* (New York: Simon and Schuster, 1953), p. 156.

6. *Variety,* 31 January 1919, p. 58.

7. *Ibid.,* p. 58.

8. Terry Ramsaye, *A Million and One Nights* (New York: Simon and Schuster, 1926), p. 796.

9. *Variety,* January 31, 1919, p. 58.

10. Terry Ramsaye, *A Million,* pp. 794–795.

11. *Variety,* 7 February 1919, p. 65.

12. *Variety,* 16 May 1919, p. 57.

13. Terry Ramsaye, *A Million,* p. 794.

14. "United Artists—Final Shooting Script," *Fortune,* (December 1940), p. 170.

15. Ralph Hancock, *The Fourth Musketeer* (New York: Henry Holt and Co., 1953), p. 172.

16. Paul Rotha, *The Film Till Now* (London: Spring Books, 1949), p. 176.

17. Kevin Brownlow, *The Parade's Gone By . . .* (New York: Ballantine Books, 1969), p. 140.

18. Paul Rotha, *The Film,* p. 153.

19. *Ibid.,* p. 169.

20. "United Artists . . ." *Fortune,* p. 170.

8
On an Odd Note—
The Nut and *When the Clouds Roll By*

Man is possessed by a darkness, by monsters of dark zones. He cannot enter those zones, but at times night sends out rather terrifying ambassadors, through the mediation of poets. These ambassadors fascinate you. They attract you and repulse you. You try to understand their language, and not understanding it, you ask the poets to translate it for you. Alas! the poets do not understand it any better and they are satisfied with being the humble servants of these ambassadors, the mediums of these individualistic phantoms who haunt you and upset you and whom you would like to unionize.

—Jean Cocteau

A *man walks* down the street carrying the rigid figure of a policeman under his arm; or he clambers over a ten-story building to avoid a black cat; or he walks upside down on the ceiling of a house. A house behaves like a giant machine, articles of food assume lifelike proportions, and two people get married on a rooftop while a flood sweeps the world away. These are events in two of the last comedies Douglas Fairbanks made before the costume cycle. These films hold a uniquely bizarre place in his work and deserve special mention on their own.

The concept of normalcy in Fairbanks' work is at once central and indispensable. The satirical touch in the films depended a great deal upon the presumed normalcy of the man. If the man behaved oddly it was by a curious alchemy that the oddness seemed acceptable and even necessary. Despite his superhuman physical capabilities, his occasional susceptibility to fads and foibles of the time, his audience never mistook him for a freak, fool, or superman. In the face of athletic feats and incredible agility, he always remained a "normal" man, one with whom the audience could identify and confide for reinforcement of the sanctity of the American ideal of the "average" and the "normal." This then is the most remarkable aspect of his screen popularity, that he remained so definitive of "norms" despite his growing preoccupation with fantasy and exotic incident and superhuman physical feats. "If Fairbanks had any neuroses, they, then, were the chronic ones of the average man who will never become pathological," wrote Alistair Cooke.

The word "normal" can truly be used of Fairbanks in this sense as well as in the literal sense of being, like a man with "normal" vision, the one man in a million who registers the exact norm from which most of us vary more or less.[1]

The Nut and *When the Clouds Roll By* both display, however, a considerable strain upon this idea of normalcy. Both films present a Fairbanksian character who not always acts sanely and who moves within a world that for some reason has been turned inside out. These strains upon the tethers of normalcy are perhaps clear evidence that a major shift in Fairbanks' style of filmmaking was underway. The breaking up of the normal universe was first necessary before there could be established another, more exotic and colorful world, a world like that of *The Thief of Bagdad* that seemed more a gorgeous dream, a suitable landscape for the epic and the fantastic.

The opening scenes of *The Nut* and *When the Clouds Roll By* both display some of the ways wherein the protagonist has lost his position within a normal world. In *The Nut* the figure who awakens and rises in the morning is not so much a man as he is a machine. Ropes lift off his bedcovers, the bed tilts him down into a pool where a revolving brush spins him clean, and later a revolving towel brushes him dry. He walks onto a treadmill that takes him to a closet where hooks thrust out to him his shirt, pants, coat and neckerchief. No, not the first handkerchief (he rejects that), but the *second* one that appears. This kind of sequence would be used by Buster Keaton in films like *The Electric House* and the opening reel of *The Navigator*. Later Pierre Etaix would pay it tribute in the opening of *Yo Yo* (1965). During this assemblyline sequence Fairbanks himself remains perfectly impassive.

In *When the Clouds Roll By* an even more ominous atmosphere is established. An opening title says, "Guinea pigs and rabbits are often sacrificed for scientific purposes. But here is a new one . . ." The following shot discloses the back of a lecturer addressing some kind of convention. This man if identified as one "Dr. Metz" who is propounding a theory "of evil design." "I mean to take a human life in the cause of science," he says. "The power of suggestion can destroy both mind and body. But first I weaken the power of resistance in my subject by implanting psychic germs of fear, worry, superstition and kindred annoyances." His object is Daniel Boone Brown (Fairbanks) who is described by a title as an "average young man." What happens to Brown throughout the course of the film is

engineered by the evil Dr. Metz with the aid of assistants. These assistants, unbeknownst to Brown, insinuate themselves into his daily life. Thus, Brown becomes the helpless object of a perverse world of science, the counterpart of the man on the treadmill in *The Nut*.

From these initial scenes both films undergo different developments. The similarity remains, however, that in both, our hero finds himself in a world that seems to behave in extraordinary ways and with which he must cope. In *The Nut* the conflict is hilarious and fanciful. In *Clouds* the confrontation is frightening and even a little profound.

Fairbanks' girl friend in *The Nut* has an idea about social reform. Estrell's theory is that if only slum children are given a chance to grow and develop in a "refined" home and under normal circumstances, they would turn out to be productive and useful citizens. Again, the emphasis is that normal circumstances are all that is needed for a person to grow up successfully. In espousing her cause, Charlie Jackson (Fairbanks) places himself at the service of this normalcy. Yet, as has already been seen, Charlie is anything but normal himself. There is an interesting device working here—the achievement of normalcy through abnormal means, a device that has figured often in the Fairbanks comedies.

Charlie gives a party for prospective patrons of Estrell's plan. He will try to sell them on the idea of opening their homes to unfortunate children. So far so good, but what results is the first of two great set-piece scenes that dominate the whole of the film. Before the assembled people, Charlie puts on a series of impersonations. He comes and goes behind a screen, successively appearing as Napoleon, General Grant, Lincoln, Tom Thumb, and finally as Charlie Chaplin. The gag is that Fairbanks is obviously not any of them—the changes are so fast, the impersonations so obviously *un*like Charlie that no one is surprised when Charlie accidentally knocks down the screen to reveal all five characters crouching there. The Chaplin character, moreover, is obviously *really* Chaplin and Fairbanks cheerfully kicks him off the little stage. This double kind of masquerade (even the act of disguising is itself a sham) sets the tone for the numerous conceits of identity and illusion in the rest of the film.

The party is disrupted when the bumbling Charlie unlooses fireworks in the house and the guests run for cover, diving out windows while their pants go up in smoke. Charlie's own suit is now a pile of ashes and he flees down the night streets of the city clad only in his underwear.

Greatly embarrassed he attempts another "disguise": he tears a number "23" off a poster and pastes it on the back of his tee-shirt. Looking for all the world like a track runner he jogs about. Seconds later he has to adopt another disguise. This time he cuts out the pasteboard figure of a man from a bill board, cuts off the head, inserts his own into the opening, and, with the torso held in front of him, saunters about always careful to keep his front toward any passersby. In this way he returns to his house.

As fast as these illusions have come there are many more ahead. Trying to reach the distraught Estrell in order to placate her, he has to resort to other ruses. Someone who has fainted at the disastrous party has been carried out on a stretcher supine under a sheet. Charlie rigs up a similar effect by holding his hands and shoes out in front of him while the draped sheet conceals his real legs. By rocking back his head and keeping the shoes thrust out before him, he is able to fool a squad of policemen who, alerted by the townspeople that a naked maniac is running through the streets, have come to carry him away. After dodging about a great deal and unable to see Estrell, he finally takes refuge in a truck parked outside. Of course the truck turns out to be a police wagon and Charlie's despairing face peers through the rear window as the truck drives away.

This whole sequence of events happens so fast that it is easy to let them go by without noticing the really clever ways in which the gags are developed. What is of central concern here, however, are the numerous variants on the disguise theme set up by Charlie's earlier impersonations at the party. The artifice of magic—the illusion—stands at the core of *The Nut*.

The same is true of the other set-piece sequence, this one occurring later in the film. But first some of the plot must be related. While in jail, Charlie strikes up an acquaintance with a dapper, affluent-looking fellow who sympathizes with Charlie's cause. He agrees to enlist his society friends in the effort to find good homes for Estrell's scheme. Charlie in turn will donate $2500 for any charity of the gentleman's choice. Of course this is another masquerade as the gentleman in question is really one "Gentleman George," a conman who senses an easy mark in Charlie.

Gentleman George joins forces with one Mr. Feeney, himself a rascal with designs of his own on Estrell. Feeney and George plan another masquerade to fool Charlie. Charlie visits the "society" people Gentleman George has prom-

ised to supply. Of course these social lions are really only George and Feeney's accomplices pretending to be the eminent personages. Charlie discovers the ruse and leaves in anger.

Still desperately trying to placate Estrell, Charlie hits upon another idea. He visits Warren's Wax Works. And here transpires the second major sequence. At the Wax Works Charlie is himself fooled by the lifelike wax figures. Near closing time Charlie freezes into a position so that the caretaker mistakes him for one of the display figures and locks up the gallery. To see Charlie frozen among the waxworks and then suddenly move about is eerie. The viewer by this time is quite prepared for *all* the figures to walk about, a device used later, incidentally, in the marvellous short story by John Collier, "Evening Primrose."

Bustling about, Charlie swipes two of the figures and for good measure appropriates a fake policeman that he uses later to direct traffic while he carries the other two figures across the street. The sight of Charlie with these figures under his arm attracts a lot of attention of course and a call is sent out to the police station that another maniac is loose.

Back home Charlie positions his dummies in the parlor. He will pass them off to Estrell as two prominent social personages who have come to listen to her idea. By this ruse he hopes to win back Estrell's love. He carefully sets up the illusion, seating the dummies and placing a cigarette in the hand of one. Estrell arrives and Charlie pretends to talk with the dummies about her idea. The effect is successful and she is fooled until the burning cigarette sets one of the dummies on fire. Furious with Charlie, Estrell leaves in a huff.

Events finally straighten themselves out when Estrell sees through yet another ruse. Mr. Feeney tries to set himself up as a society person interested in Estrell's idea. His lecherous intentions become all too clear at last and she is rescued by Charlie in one last masquerade. This time he has donned the dummy policeman's clothes and brashly invades Feeney's den and defeats him and his cronies after a furious struggle.

This striking succession of masquerade motifs lends *The Nut* a zany, magical quality that not only spotlights Fairbanks' considerable talents as a comedian, but gives *The Nut* a unique position among all his films. In no other film, save *When the Clouds Roll By*, are such devices employed so well, so consistently, and so often. The whole film displays a brittle, mirrorlike surface that constantly keeps the viewer off balance. Estrell's theory about the normal, secure world is all but buried under the dazzling, quirky avalanche of bizarre incident and illusion that Charlie seems to represent.

If the bizarre world of illusion in *The Nut* is immensely enjoyable for all its fancy and charm, the world seen in *When the Clouds Roll By,* while just as strange and illusory, is a darker and more troubling one. It achieves in a few scenes an almost harrowing feel of an individual trapped in a world gone mad. The "average young man," Daniel Boone Brown, is the object of the sinister researches of Dr. Metz. As was seen earlier, Dr. Metz seeks to weaken Brown's resistance to the power of suggestion and then implant suggestions that will eventually drive the subject into madness and suicide. He carries out his project by capitalizing on Brown's peculiar susceptibility to superstitions, contriving to make Brown jealous of the attentions of another man toward his girl friend, and finally in implicating Brown in a plot to cheat the girl's father of some valuable real estate.

Dr. Metz' efforts make daily life a hell for Brown. All the normal activities of eating, getting up in the morning, going to work, making love to his girl friend, are suddenly disrupted by the machinations of the infernal doctor. This is best conveyed in the two central sequences that highlight the film. In the first, one of Metz' accomplices goes to work as Brown's servant. The servant persuades the hapless Brown to imbibe quantities of food, such as onions, lobster, Welsh Rarebit, and mince pie just before retiring one evening. Not surprisingly Brown goes into convulsions, finally settling into a troubled sleep. At this point, fantasy takes over and Brown begins to dream. What follows emerges as one of the single most exhilarating sequences in any of Fairbanks' films.

Helpless before the onslaught of all the food in his stomach (a number of shots show the various foodstuffs tumbling around in there), he suffers a violent nightmare. He sits up in bed. A distorted, tall, figure has materialized beside the bed and glares at him. Brown pushes at it and it falls to the floor stiffly like cardboard, but it springs up again. Elongated white hands appear all over the room reaching for him. Then Brown leaps out of bed and dives *through* the wall. Now he is in the midst of some kind of ladies' meeting. Tugging at his falling pajamas, he moves through the crowd in two leaps. He dives toward a painting (a seascape) and again passes through the wall, falling with a splash into a pool of water. He climbs out of the pool. Suddenly the various articles of food appear, enlarged to man-size and,

moving in accelerated motion, they pursue Brown. He flees and suddenly is running in slow motion as he jumps some timber fences, clears another fence with a front somersault and tuck, leaps onto a waiting horse, then leaps off through another wall.

Now he finds himself in a room in a strange house. The viewer watches as if watching a cutaway of a doll's house with the two walls, ceiling and floor kept in medium long shot. Brown crosses the floor to frame right, walks *up* the wall, across the ceiling, down the left wall, runs across the floor, and back up the right wall. The door opens and the pursuing foods tumble in. Brown "stands" on his hands from the ceiling. Back "on his feet" he reaches down and grips the bannister of a staircase. After circling around the ceiling again he runs out of the room.

The next shot shows Brown running toward the camera, again in slow motion. He hurdles a number of barriers as he runs toward a chimney. He leaps into the air, descends through the chimney opening, falls through the long shaft and lands in a large metal cylinder or drum at the bottom. People are standing outside the cylinder banging upon its surface. At this point Brown wakes up. The banging is coming from another of Dr. Metz' aides who is standing outside Brown's room.

This entire sequence is one of the more successful efforts of pure fantasy the silent film has given us. The abrupt changes in locale, the changes in camera speed, and certainly the bizarre sequence in the house all contribute to the dreamlike quality of the whole thing. There would be nothing this fantastic in the costume films, not even in *The Thief of Bagdad* (although *Thief* would employ some slow motion in the "Old Man of the Sea" episode). The house sequence utilized an early attempt to work with revolving sets (recent examples being the Fred Astaire *The Royal Wedding* (1951) and Stanley Kubrick's *2001*). A magazine at the time related the techniques employed in this sequence:

> They built at his studio a set showing a room open at one side and revolving on an axis like a squirrel cage. As Doug walked over to the side wall and placed his foot on it for the first step, the camera, also set with special equipment so that it would revolve, likewise turned, and so on as he walked up one side, over the ceiling, and down the other side.
>
> To the turned camera he appeared always to be walking along the floor, head up, but in the picture registered on the film, always vertical, the star had his head out horizontally or

downward, as the case happened to be. The pursuers rushing into the room were introduced by double exposure.[2]

The art of this technique is of course to get the mechanism of the room and the camera adjusted to such a mathematical nicety that the artifice would not be given away at some point in the revolution. The effect remains today quite startling.

From here on, even Brown's waking world seems to have gone mad. Dr. Metz manages to play upon Brown's belief in superstitions. A shaving mirror breaks, the servant opens an umbrella in the apartment. Metz' agent turns off the apartment water. Brown leaves the tap on and when the water is turned on again the bathroom is flooded. These disasters follow Brown all the way to work at his uncle's office.

The superstition motif is handled quite charmingly when Brown meets his girl friend-to-be, Lucette, in the park. Their meeting is accompanied by little rituals. They circle each other warily, waving their hands in all the little movements traditionally used to ward off evil spirits. This penchant for superstitions is satirized later when they both crouch over a ouija board. The homilies that issue forth from the board are odd indeed. At one point she drops a letter and the board says,

What falls to the floor
Comes to the door.

Sure enough a postman arrives with a letter. She is so startled that she drops a paper knife. The board responds,

A falling knife is a dead sure hunch
That some young man will come to lunch.

Of course Brown is only too glad to oblige *that* one.

Meanwhile Dr. Metz furthers his scheme by bringing Brown, his new girl friend (Lucette), her father, and Brown's uncle together at a party. Metz stands back and seems to pull invisible strings while disaster breaks out. It seems Lucette's father owns some property that, unbeknownst to him, contains oil. Lucette's *former* boy friend is a swindler bent on getting Brown's firm to buy the property for a pittance. The secret comes out and the swindler in trying to protect himself, implicates the innocent Brown in the fraud. In the midst of all this both Lucette and Brown's uncle walk out in a rage. Brown, unfairly blamed, tries to explain, but things are made worse when the police show up to arrest him! The police of course are also accomplices of the good doctor, provided as the crowning touch to the whole charade. Frantic, Brown runs from room to room, the policeman popping up behind windows and doors blocking his every move. The film cuts to Dr. Metz gazing upon a model of a brain. Back to Brown who is clearly going crazy. He stumbles into a closet, his forehead coming close to the camera. Dissolve to figures racing about in his head. Pictured are a woman designated as "Reason" atop a throne, a figure as "Sense of Humor" cringing at her feet. Two more figures, "Worry" and "Discord" appear and abduct the lady "Reason" from her throne.

Brown now stumbles out of the closet. The lights are out (Metz has conveniently turned them off). He staggers aimlessly and in the gloom the shadows of bars are thrown across his face. Out in the corridor he meets Dr. Metz who furtively slips a revolver into Brown's pocket. The plot is almost consummated.

This sequence, while amusing, is nonetheless quite frightening in a way. Everyone has at some time or another felt that his actions were all too fruitless, that some thwarting kind of fate seemed to block his every action. Every movement seems to lead deeper into a maze. This kind of situation has been magnificently depicted in the Fellini episode from the Poe trilogy film, *Spirits of the Dead.* In the Fairbanks film the momentary paranoia is quite effective. There is no boundary line that separates this waking dream from the dream earlier in the film. Although the visual metaphor of toppling "Reason" detracts from the thrust of the sequence, it does, nonetheless, indicate clearly the intentions of the filmmakers to retain a note of whimsy during the proceedings and at the same time make sure no one is missing the point. If the viewer is prepared to accept a giant Welsh Rarebit running around, then he is not likely to be troubled by this.

Minutes later, as Brown is contemplating suicide, he sees the evil Doctor Metz carried away by attendants from the local insane asylum. One more charlatan is unmasked. At this point Brown's brain clears (inside his brain the figure "Sense of Humor" appears to restore "Reason" to the throne and immediately tells her a joke— "Have you heard the one about the old maid in the sleeping car?") and he dashes away to rejoin Lucette.

One is prepared for anything by this time. And he is not disappointed. Waiting in the wings is a hurricane and flood that now sweeps over the countryside. In a whirlwind finish Brown rescues Lucette in the flood. The finale is, if anything, just as bizarre as the preceeding two sequences. Lucette is trapped by the flood on the roof of a house floating down the current. Fairbanks floats by, hanging from the branches of a tree. He sees Lucette, dives into the water, swims toward the house, clambers onto the roof and joins her. He may by this time be freed from all susceptibility to superstitions, he may have cleared his good name, he may have recovered his "Reason and Sense of Humor"—but he still is hungry. What could be more normal than to raid the refrigerator? The fact that the whole house is floating away in a flood seems not to matter at all. So he cheerfully dives off the roof, swims down into a window, down the watery stairway, and into the kitchen for a snack. (Perhaps this was the origination of the "submarine" sandwich.) The finishing stroke occurs when a preacher comes floating by atop the church steeple and marries them.

Even such a casual description of the film (and many details and scenes have been omitted here, such as when Brown clambers over a ten-story building to avoid a black cat) cannot fail to convey something of the almost surreal nature of its events and characters. Like *The Nut* its characters are either charlatans or victims of a ruse. The magician's art of illusion powers the action in both. If normalcy is restored at the end of each film, it exists at best under questionable circumstances. Norms in both are certainly relative, whereas the main intent and purpose in each film seems to lie not in the depiction of normalcy, but in the delineation of the absurd and the dreamlike. *The Nut* and *When the Clouds Roll By* are two of Fairbanks' most interesting, amusing, and even troubling films. One delights in them both as he would before the snapping of the prestidigitator's fingers. The images, so strange and at times troubling, foreshadow the end of a world—and the beginning of the fantasyland soon to be created in the costume films to come. Monsters walk in these regions, men defy gravity, darkness falls, but people continue to laugh.

NOTES

1. Alistaire Cooke, *Douglas Fairbanks: The Making of a Screen Character* (New York: Museum of Modern Art, 1940), p. 18.

2. "Technical Effects for *When The Clouds Roll By*," *Literary Digest*, (3 July 1920), p. 75.

the Costume Films

Part II: *The Costume Films and Beyond*

9

Zorro and *Don Q:* The Mark of Greatness

The founding of United Artists in 1919 marks an important stage in Douglas Fairbanks' career. The next year, however, is even more important in the effect it had on the type of films he was to continue to make. For in 1920 Fairbanks discovered the perfect vehicle to carry his flamboyance and exuberance. Although we do not exactly find a radical shift in style, it is apparent that Fairbanks, by stepping into costume, emerged as a character that was uniquely his own. All through the 1920's the character reappears—in a fanciful Bagdad, in Sherwood Forest, on a painted ocean—but, clearly, it was born in the New World, though deriving from and nurtured by the Old.

The Mark of Zorro was released in 1920 and inaugurated the series of costume films for which Fairbanks is most famous today. Fairbanks at first was uncertain about the change to the costumed character and went ahead to make another light comedy of the type already well known to his fans. *The Nut* appeared after *The Mark of Zorro,* but even though it was one of his best comedies, it failed to evoke anything near the response that *Zorro* did. It was, therefore, the success and dash of *The Mark of Zorro* that was to set the style for Fairbanks' next seven films.

Fairbanks in costume as Zorro courts danger, baiting the Governor's soldiers early in The Mark of Zorro *(1920).*

The popular success of Señor Zorro cannot be denied. He has almost become a part of American folklore. The mythic, masked figure who galloped and slashed his way through Old California has, like Robin Hood, become a symbol of the elusive outlaw who confounds the villains in

Fairbanks as Zorro making an acrobatic escape from soldiers he has dared to capture him in The Mark of Zorro.

Zorro makes a fool of Sergeant Gonzales (played by Noah Beery, Wallace Beery's brother).

charge, in order to right injustices done to the common people. Douglas Fairbanks established for all time the definitive interpretation of Zorro in his 1920 filmization. Subsequent versions by Tyrone Power, Reed Hadley, and Guy Williams seem stolid in comparison. Fairbanks' flashing smile, agile body, and quick sword give the character a power and dark humor that has never been equalled.

The character of Zorro made his first appearance in the magazine *All-Story Weekly* on 9 August 1919. Johnston McCulley's five-part story was called "The Curse of Capistrano." It dealt with the corruption in politics in Old California, the landed power of the blooded caballeros, the fading empire of the missions around Reina de Los Angeles. Dashing in to right injustices wrought by the corrupt political system is a mysterious Señor Zorro. Disguised by a black mask and a purple cloak, he comes and goes like a graveyard ghost, avenging wrongs all along El Camino Real. Eventually, he enlists the caballeros in his cause and the corrupt Governor and his military power are overthrown. Zorro is in reality one Don Diego Vega, son of one of the most powerful houses in Old California. Diego finds it necessary to disguise his activities by pretending to be a foppish, indifferent young man more interested in music and the poets than in righting wrongs and dueling with the sword.

This story brought Johnston McCulley, already a prolific writer of romances, much fame; however, it also brought a "curse" of its own. McCul-

ley became identified with the Zorro stories and ever thereafter was called upon to provide sequel after sequel for the pulp magazines. Fairbanks bought the rights to the character in 1920 and eventually became likewise identified with Señor Zorro. He changed the story's title when he released *The Mark of Zorro* in 1920. In 1925 he himself made a sequel called *Don Q.*, featuring both Zorro and his son. Later in the Twenties Fairbanks even purchased three thousand acres of San Diego County real estate that he planned to turn into a hacienda called Rancho Zorro. The project got as far as a few buildings, several hundred acres of orange groves, and the completion of a dam to provide a vast overhead irrigation system for the groves.

Danger lurks 'round the corner, as a cautious soldier approaches Señor Zorro (Douglas Fairbanks).

The other face of Zorro: Fairbanks as the mild-mannered and foppish Don Diego disapproves of Sergeant Gonzales' show of force.

McCulley's original story, "The Curse of Capistrano," stands squarely in the action-romance tradition of the pulp magazines before 1920. This style of adventure story got its real impetus from the Edgar Rice Burroughs stories that began to appear in 1912. Burroughs' first "Mars" story, *Under the Two Moons of Mars* (later published as *The Princess of Mars*) appeared in *All-Story* magazine during the months of February through July of 1912 under his pseudonym of "Normal Bean." This saga of the earthling John Carter adrift among the wild landscapes and people of Barsoom established the classic pattern for such adventures. Like "Curse of Capistrano," its hero is uncommonly agile and proficient with the sword. He knows not the meaning of cowardice, treachery, or deceit. His swordarm wins him a place in the aristocracy of his world. The heroine, moreover, is forever being abducted by the villains and the hero is constantly off in hot pursuit. The pattern becomes a representation of abduction-pursuit-recapture-and abduction again. If it were not for the lady fair, it seems, villains and heroes alike would have nothing to do but eat and get fat, their swords rusting in the attic.

The glories of roistering, bloody combat and camaraderie disguise only thinly a stern morality in these tales. John Carter of Mars and Zorro of Reina de Los Angeles alike act with their blades to right injustice, aid the oppressed, and, of course, rescue the ever-threatened heroine. Whether

hero or villain, there is always a code to be followed. Only when a character acts contrary to this code (is cowardly or lustful or deceitful) does he become truly despicable. Pirates and heroes alike are worthy protagonists as long as they adhere each to his own code. The pirate Barbados in a McCulley sequel called *The Further Adventures of Zorro* says at one point in the action, "If a thief, be a thief! If a pirate, be a pirate! But do not play at being an honest man and try to be thief and pirate at the same time."[1]

Johnston McCulley was fascinated by the setting of Old California during the days of the mission empire. His career as a writer saw him work on the Kansas City *Star* in 1913, travel extensively throughout the country in later years,

The pattern of the abduction-pursuit-recapture: Fairbanks as Zorro, defends Lolita (Marguerite de la Motte) from Captain Ramon (Robert McKim).

*The dual courtship of Lolita Pulido (Marguerite de la Motte),
here courted by Fairbanks as Zorro.*

and finally settle into an apartment in New York, from which flowed his narratives of swordplay and romance. His novel *Captain Fly-by-Night* had already anticipated the events and setting of "The Curse of Capistrano." The purchase of the film rights to the latter by Fairbanks, the publication of the Grosset and Dunlap Photoplay Edition in hard covers (by now, the title had irrevocably become *The Mark of Zorro*), and the demand for sequels saw his most famous character become a worldwide favorite.

McCulley's sequel appeared in 1922 and was called "The Further Adventures of Zorro." *All-Story Weekly* had by then become *Argosy All-Story Weekly,* and the story appeared there in six parts. It needs to be mentioned here because it is proof-positive of the effects of Douglas Fairbanks' filmization upon the original. Here is a

case of the interpreter of a character influencing the development of that character. For example, in the original "Curse of Capistrano" there is no mention of Zorro's famous "mark"—the "Z" carved into the forehead of his victims. That "mark" was apparently invented for the film. Fairbanks utilizes this innovation as a kind of visual trademark, the kind of thing he had already done in earlier films like *The Good Bad Man.* The effectiveness of this idea is demonstrated in one scene wherein Zorro carves a "Z" into Captain Ramon's cheek and then shows Ramon his blade, the impression of the "Z" delineated in blood along the blade. Further, there is no mention in the original of a bit of business featured prominently in the film. Don Diego's foppishness is emphasized by foolish little parlor tricks with a handkerchief, accompanied

123

"Have you seen this one?" Fairbanks as Don Diego courts Lolita (Marguerite de la Motte), obviously unimpressed with his foppish tricks.

by the words, "Have you seen this one?" McCulley's own sequel, appearing after the film, incorporates both of these elements into the narrative. Suddenly, McCulley's own hero is carving "Z's" all over the place, and, suddenly, Don Diego is whipping out his handkerchief at every opportunity and saying, "Have you seen this one?" Clearly, McCulley has been influenced by the Fairbanks interpretation.

This sequel of McCulley's would in turn influence later work by Fairbanks. Featured prominently on the cover of the *Argosy All-Story Weekly* issue carrying the sequel are the words, "In which Douglas Fairbanks Will Again Play the Hero." Fairbanks, in fact, never made a Zorro film with plot elements from this story. Instead, the story appears somewhat altered in Doug's 1926 film *The Black Pirate*. Similarities between McCulley's sequel and the Fairbanks pirate film include scenes wherein the heroine is captured by pirates, the hero scampering about the rigging of a pirate ship, a rescue effected by allies of the hero in a pursuing ship. Even the character of Barbados is echoed somewhat in Donald Crisp's portrayal of a tough old pirate with a heart of gold. McCulley has acknowledged that his "Further Adventures of Zorro" was utilized for *The Black Pirate*.[2]

So firmly was Fairbanks identified with Zorro that one can see a gradual change in artwork that accompanied the Zorro stories from 1919 on through the Thirties. The J. P. Monahan conception adorning the cover of the 1919 *All-Story*

Weekly has no similarity to the Fairbanks image. After the film, however, subsequent drawings, particularly the Sam Cahan artwork, clearly show the Zorro character as interpreted by Fairbanks. The costumes and facial characteristics all closely resemble him.

Despite the changes or additions Fairbanks brought to his film, it is nevertheless a very close adaptation of the story. The sequence of events is the same, the characters are the same, details such as the boasting of Sergeant Gonzales, the whipping of the Padre, the indifference of the caballeros to the Governor's injustice, the rescue of Lolita from the prison, even much of the dialogue, are all almost identical.

The visualization of the story is at once clever and entirely in the spirit of the original. Already mentioned are the devices of the "Z" mark and Don Diego's handkerchief. In addition, Don Diego enjoys casting hand shadows on walls and manipulating his hat to emphasize his foppishness. Fairbanks' acrobatics leaven the action with a dazzling sense of airborne agility. The confrontation between Zorro and Ramon after Ramon has tried to "compromise" Lolita Pulido has Zorro literally falling into the frame from the top. The chase sequence at the end of the story is considerably elaborated with emphasis upon Zorro's bravado. With the Governor's men in hot pursuit, Zorro still has time to attach a note with his sword to the bole of a tree. It advises his pursuers that this is his last weapon, that he has gone into town to have breakfast, and that he dares them to capture him! The subsequent chase reminds one of Fairbanks' most successful trajec-

The image of Zorro confronts authority, here in the person of Captain Ramon (Robert McKim).

Don Diego, with handkerchief, shrinks from Gonzales.
Fairbanks' definition of the character influenced the author.

tories, taking his agile form and his bumbling pursuers over stile, walls, rooftops, through windows, etc. In the middle of all this frenzied action, Fairbanks takes a characteristic pause for refreshment. Reclining on a window sill, he advises a peasant woman, "Never do anything on an empty stomach," before whirling away again back into the chase. Although none of this is in the original, it seems entirely right and satisfactory in the film.

The conflict is resolved in the story by the caballeros banding together and informing the Governor that his oppression must stop and Zorro be exonerated for his outlawry. The resolution is much more satisfactory in the film. Don Diego confronts Captain Ramon and finally reveals his identity. They cross swords. After Ramon is bested, Zorro hurls his sword upward to the ceiling, declaring, "'Till I need you again!" That need is later to be demonstrated in the sequel *Don Q., the Son of Zorro.*

According to the film's credits, the story of *Don Q.* derives from the novel *Don Q's Love Story*, by K. and Hesketh Prichard. The original *Zorro* was directed by Fred Niblo, while *Don Q.* was directed by Donald Crisp. Nonetheless, there is a remarkable consistency between the two films, even though the adventure formula in the later film has been sophisticated and the cast enlarged. No one remembering *The Mark of Zorro* would be disappointed by this sequel.

The events of the sequel may be summarized as follows: Don Cesar de Vega has come to Madrid to complete his education. His courage and heroic action attract the attention of the Queen of Spain and her visiting cousin, The Archduke of

Fairbanks as Don César in Don Q., The Son of Zorro
(1925): the sequel was no disappointment.

Austria, who befriends him. Don Cesar falls in love with Doloros de Muro, daughter to the Queen's closest advisor and, it is finally disclosed, a friend of Don Cesar's father. Don Cesar also makes a dangerous enemy, Don Sebastian of the Queen's Guard.

At a ball given in honor of the Archduke Paul, the surly Don Sebastian is inadvertently insulted by the Archduke, and, losing his temper, he murders him. Circumstantial evidence points to Don Cesar as the murderer, even though there is a witness, the corrupt Don Fabrique, who holds the key to the mystery—a note the Archduke scribbles just before his death, naming his assassin.

Stating his preference for death before dishonor, Don Cesar heroically feigns suicide, jump-ing from the casement of the castle to the sea far below. Against these impossible odds he survives, of course, to redeem the family name. Don Fabrique, meanwhile, uses the Archduke's note to blackmail Don Sebastian and to insinuate himself into a government position whereby he can exploit others. Don Q. summons his father from California and together, at the end, they undo the villains and clear the name of de Vega.

How often has the sequel to a popular film lived up to the original it imitates? Frequently the second film will be little more than a shadow of the first, attempting to duplicate the tried-and-true formula, to exploit the success and reputa-tion of the original. This is not quite the case, however, with *Don Q., The Son of Zorro*; for a number of reasons this movie may be considered

126

*Fairbanks confronts Don Sebastian (Donald Crisp) as Do-
lores (Mary Astor) looks on at the ball in honor of Archduke
Paul in* Don Q.

both a more entertaining and a better film than
the original *Mark of Zorro* made five years earlier.

In 1920 Fairbanks was just moving into his
costume period. The original *Zorro* is highly
significant in the development of the actor's
screen career as Doug seemingly searched for a
character that would embody his romantic aspira-
tions, both as a man and as a representative of his
country, the New World. The swashbuckling
persona that romps through all of his films of the
Twenties was in a period of gestation when *The
Mark of Zorro* was made, but it had not been
brought to perfection. By the time *Don Q.* was
made, however, it had emerged, fully developed,
more flamboyant and comic than ever and
infinitely more amusing. Almost all of the little

tricks and touches that define the character,
regardless of the specific costume it may wear or
the particular historical period into which it has
been placed, we now find developed and per-
fected in 1925. These are used to particularly
good effect in *Don Q.*, as they are later in *The
Gaucho*. In these films, as in most of the other
costume pieces, we find a performer who is
supremely confident of his abilities.

There are significant differences in both the
conception of character and setting between the
two *Zorro* films. The first film is set in California,
the second in Spain. The aristocratic lineage
explained in the first film curves back paraboli-
cally upon itself in the second. The senior Zorro
represents the New Man in the New World. His

actions, bearing, and dignity harken back to an older, aristocratic tradition. His son, however, embodies the perfect synthesis of the two cultures. Zorro had brought the best traditions of aristocratic Spain—honor, courage, courtly manners, heroic style—to the New World. Don Cesar, his son, takes the best qualities of the New World—honesty, directness, vigor—back to Spain and puts them to work in Madrid, where the Court itself is in danger of falling into corruption (or at least is threatened by the likes of such lowly characters as Don Fabrique). Don Cesar is heroic and manly and does not affect the effeminate mannerisms that his father had used to cloak his true identity. But it takes father and son together, finally, to reform the Court, remedy the situation, and exonerate the name of de Vega. There is, in short, a thematic as well as an obvious monetary reason for having Zorro appear in both films. The film's conclusion is both comic and melodramatic, as honor and justice are restored by two legendary figures who represent the moral order that must prevail—the "best" America has to offer for the ultimate salvation of the Old Country.

Don César with whip in Don Q. *the "best" America has to offer.*

The influence of the father is stressed from the very beginning of the film. When Don Cesar is asked where he learned the whip, he responds: "In California—my father taught me. My father is the greatest man in America." And a bit later, as Don Cesar duels with Don Sebastian, the American casually remarks to the student audience: "You know, my father is the greatest swordsman in America." Most important, however, is the moral instruction that has passed from father to son. This is demonstrated early in the film when Don Cesar's whip quite by accident removes the tassle from Don Sebastian's cap. The American apologizes with the following words: "My father always said: 'When you are in the right, fight; when you are in the wrong, acknowledge it.' " This advice both prefigures and determines Don Cesar's behavior in the film.

Don Q. is organized around a number of trials and demonstrations of courage that give the Fairbanks figure ample opportunity to outwit and to outfight villains that appear to be more physically imposing, on the one hand, and more sophisticated and dissembling on the other. As usual, these dangers are calculated to put Doug's cavalier recklessness on exhibit. He fights Don Sebastian, who is no worthy opponent—in swordplay or in love, it turns out—so a maddened, rampaging bull is allowed to escape to threaten him further. He takes the bull by the horns with ease, of course, but his combined means of cape, whip, and lasso, provide a highly unlikely (and therefore comic) solution. And for good measure, he also saves the injured Don Sebastian's life. This impressive show of courage results in his personal invitation to meet the Archduke Paul of Austria. It also establishes early in the film that this young whippersnapper is fashioned in his father's image, and perhaps even more daring and outgoing in his devil-may-care attitude. He is able to take situations and mold them to his own ends. After restraining the bull he wins the acclaim and adulation of the crowd, but he sprints and vaults away from them, partly for his own amusement (and eternally for ours) to show that he can escape the pursuing masses—a star good-naturedly fleeing his public.

This sequence, in turn, foreshadows the later escapes that are required in more serious situations. It establishes our confidence in the character, just as the character asserts and reasserts his confidence in himself. Later, for example, we see Doug expose himself to danger again when he escorts Paul to a lowly tavern in the sequence entitled "An Archduke's Night Out." His highness is debonair (as always) and slightly tipsy. In

Don César duels with Don Sebastian (Donald Crisp) early in
Don Q.

the tavern they notice commoners singing and a young woman dancing. As Fairbanks imitates her dance, with his Gaucho outfit and his ever-present cigarette, he does a rather obvious—and successful—parody of Valentino. It is a very funny routine. When the dancer begins to flirt with the Archduke, however, her jealous lover draws his weapon, but Fairbanks is there in time to block his move with a tabletop. While four thugs, armed with knives, force Doug into a corner, Don Sebastion ushers the Archduke out, leaving Fairbanks to face the consequences. "You think you will leave this place, eh?" one of the thugs says. "When I am ready," Fairbanks responds, typically laughing at the danger. The audience, meanwhile, knows that he will escape without difficulty, just as they know he will later escape the murderous situation that develops at the ball, for the character is indomitable.

Obviously Fairbanks is now ready to leave the tavern. He tricks the thugs by putting his sword in a sling (these cutthroats, after all, are not worthy opponents), and he sprints off to court Dolores in his typically flamboyant fashion ("With Love's light wings did I ore' perch these walls"). Meanwhile, inside the de Muro house Don Sebastian is making arrangements with General de Muro for his daughter's hand. Archduke Paul, who is still with Sebastian and can see Don Cesar courting Dolores through the window, knows what Sebastian is up against—Sebastian, however, does not. Warner Oland's Archduke Paul is one of the most appealing characters in this movie, and it is a pity that the plot requires his assassination so early.

The escape from the Tavern: Fairbanks "supremely confident of his abilities" in Don Q.

Warner Oland's Archduke Paul, one of the most appealing characters in Don Q., *with Fairbanks and Mary Astor.*

The film ends with that magnificent reunion between father and son. Interestingly, Fairbanks here steps into the role of the elder Zorro, but it is with a greater zest than when he becomes the elder D'Artagnan in *The Iron Mask*. Though presumably old, he is still spry and happy as he retrieves the sword that was placed in that rafter in 1920 at the conclusion of *The Mark of Zorro*. The father arrives in time to help the son, but the son, whose picture this is, has the situation pretty well under control. The reunion is mainly a sentimental and happy one.

In conclusion, the evolution of the Zorro character demonstrates a peculiar collaboration between Douglas Fairbanks and Johnston McCulley and represents a marriage between popular fiction and popular film. It is a good example of book and movie working together, of that rare kind of rapport that was able to create and then sustain one of the most popular figures in the romance fiction of this century.

NOTES

1. *Argosy All-Story Weekly,* 6 May 1922, p. 484.
2. Acknowledgment from a letter dated 2 April 1946, from McCulley to Vernell Coriell of Kansas City, Missouri.

10

Robin Hood: A Dance of Free Men in a Forest

ené Clair was charmed by Douglas Fairbanks' *Robin Hood* when he saw it in 1923. It was, he stated, a film that "disarms criticism." The French director expressed doubts that the spirit of the Middle Ages could accurately be revived, but he nonetheless favored "the interpretation of the Middle Ages given by Fairbanks' film as much as a history book."[1] This film, quoting Charles Kingsley,[2] begins with a romantic evocation of the past: "So fleet the works of men/ Back to their earth again/ Ancient and holy things/ Fade like a dream"—while shots of a ruined castle dissolve into shots of a restored castle and Allan Dwan's pictorial magic transports us back to the Age of Chivalry, or, as the titles insist, to the "Age of Faith."

This "impression" of the Middle Ages begins with the knights of King Richard assembled for a grand tournament that is to mark their departure the following day on a Holy Crusade. Thus, we are at once overwhelmed with pageantry and spectacle and action as Robert, the Earl of Huntingdon (Fairbanks) jousts with the devious Sir Guy of Gisbourne (Paul Dickey). By swift strokes of action the main characters of this movie are immediately sketched—Huntingdon, brave and

Doug as Robin Hood: the half-eaten apple will soon be flung in the face of the Nottingham sheriff.

Robin Hood

An "impression" of the Middle Ages: Fairbanks as the Earl of Huntingdon with Wallace Beery as Richard the Lion-Hearted in Robin Hood *(1922).*

strong, but naive and shy; Gisbourne, spurned by Lady Marian Fitzwalter (whom he lusts after), a villain who refuses to play fair (he straps himself to his saddle), and a sore loser. Most important here, however, is Wallace Beery's King Richard, "impulsive, generous, and brave," but also down-to-earth, direct, honest, a king who exudes humanity and common understanding, juxtaposed visually to his sneering, wicked brother, "sinister, dour, his heart inflamed with an unholy desire to succeed to Richard's throne." And therein hangs the tale.

Of course Huntingdon readily defeats Gisbourne and is appointed Richard's second-in-command. As he goes to be crowned victor, Huntingdon admits to being "afraid of women." (This must have amused Doug's following at the time.) Prince John promises Gisbourne his choice of maidens, but Huntingdon interferes and becomes Lady Marian's protector. And melodramatic motives are established. John gives Gisbourne

Fairbanks as Huntingdon with Lady Marion Fitzwalter, played by Enid Bennett in Robin Hood.

orders that neither Richard nor Huntingdon is to return from the crusade. Just as John is motivated by his unholy lust for power, so Gisbourne is motivated by his unholy lust for Lady Marian.

These are no ordinary villains. John sets his cruel, oppressive tyranny in motion almost at once as Richard disappears over the horizon. The images Dwan uses to demonstrate his tyranny are not matched in effectiveness until a decade later in the montage suggesting the cruelty of Imperial Russia in von Sternberg's *Scarlet Empress.* The "High Sheriff of Nottingham" is John's agent in these evil designs, but in this version of the legend the Sheriff is only a minor villain, his villainy being far eclipsed, for dramatic reasons, by that of Prince John and Sir Guy.

Meanwhile, Lady Marian goes before Prince John to plead for "mercy for the people of England." Ignored, she sends word for Huntingdon to return. John, sensing danger, tortures her servant woman and finds that word has been sent. He then sends soldiers to capture Marian. Forewarned by her loyal servant, however, she escapes, and the soldiers are led to believe her horse threw her over a cliff. She takes refuge, meanwhile, in a convent.

Huntingdon's servant brings him the news from Lady Marian, and Huntingdon is torn between love and honor. He must return to England, that is clear, but he cannot tell Richard the reason, for the King must not be diverted from his "holy mission." Huntingdon sends word

"By some pretext I shall persuade the King to allow me to return." Fairbanks as Huntingdon caught between Love and Honor as King Richard (Wallace Beery) reminds him of his Christian duty as a crusader.

135

to Marian that he will work a guise for abandoning the crusade ("By some pretext I shall persuade the King to allow me to return"), but his carrier pigeon is intercepted by Gisbourne's falcon, as bird imagery enforces stereotyping. Richard writes Huntingdon off as a coward after Gisbourne shows him the intercepted note, and imprisons him in a tower. Gisbourne leaves instructions that Huntingdon be starved in the tower. Soon, however, Huntingdon's loyal servant rescues his wounded master. Huntingdon returns to England, only to be told that Lady Marian has met with a fatal accident. Thus, he gives up his noble past to be reincarnated as Robin Hood, the champion of the common man, the role Fairbanks was created for.

This is a very carefully plotted movie. All of this business consumes nearly an hour's screen time. Even so, the early part of the film is not without action, and character motivation has been meticulously prepared. At the same time, the atmosphere of medieval England has been carefully drawn. To do this effectively, the pace of the film is slowed to the extent that it is momentarily halted, providing a visual caesura to emphasize the key turning point of both plot and character

Huntingdon reincarnated as Robin Hood, "the role Douglas Fairbanks was created for."

development. We last see Huntingdon at the location of Marian's presumed death. This scene becomes a visual tableau as the knight stands in the mists of the past, holding his sword and shield, desolate at the news of his true-love's death. This is the last time we shall see Huntingdon before the end of the film.

Screen time must now pass in order to give Huntingdon a chance to recover from his grief so that Robin Hood can be born. A band of "Merry Men" cannot have a brokenhearted leader. Thus we follow King Richard on his successful crusade. Then we see Gisbourne enter the King's chamber and stab the figure sleeping in the King's bed. Gisbourne immediately sets off for England, thinking his mission accomplished. We learn, however, that the King's jester was sleeping in his master's bed and that Richard now knows the treachery plotted against him. He also learns of conditions in England and of the exploits of Robin Hood. He realizes at once that Robin Hood must be his old friend Huntingdon. He sets off for England, thinking to join the band of Merry Men. What becomes of his army in the Holy Land is left oddly unresolved.

All this, and Robin Hood has yet to appear. There is dramatic foreshadowing here that resembles the legendary treatment of Zorro. People are aware of his presence and speak excitedly about him. The spent shaft and the emblem of King Richard become Robin Hood's "signature" in this film, in much the same way the slashed "Z" became the signature of Zorro.

Then, finally, we see Robin Hood impishly invading John's castle. In this sequence, our first chance to see him in action, the narrative is done entirely through visuals and emblems. For something like ten minutes of screen time, Fairbanks' movements are not interrupted by subtitles. Only after he escapes the castle are the subtitles resumed, then to introduce his men in the forest—Will Scarlett, Friar Tuck, Little John— soon to be joined by their leaping leader. From this point forward, the film becomes a ballet of motion, a "fairy-pantomime" in an enchanted Sherwood Forest, or, as René Clair so aptly described it, "free men dancing in a forest."[3] Their good-natured lawlessness is happily captured in the following title: "We rob the rich, relieve distressed/On damnèd John to score./ We'll take a life, if sorely pressed/ Till Richard reign once more."

Prince John's men steal church vestments from the Priory of St. Catherine's. Later, they are intercepted in the forest by Robin and his men, who return the goods to the convent. Their good

Robin Hood and his Merry Men: "Free Men dancing in a Forest."

Production shot showing the set for Robin Hood *(1922), the largest that had yet been constructed during the Twenties in Hollywood.*

deed is repaid. One of the nuns recognizes Robin as Robert, the Earl of Huntingdon, and leads him to Lady Marian, who has lived with the sisters in secrecy. The reunion of the knight and his lady freezes into a second tableau, for this visual device is used to etherialize the ideal of courtly love, here, as before, when the grieved Huntingdon took his oath.

The plot then moves rather rapidly toward its conclusion. Gisbourne returns to England. John discovers Lady Marian and has her taken into his custody (establishing the need for her later rescue); and "A mysterious stranger invades Sherwood Forest," a helmeted knight who seeks Robin Hood, "Mayhap to join him—mayhap to slay him." We know this to be King Richard. He crosses longstaffs with Friar Tuck, and defeats that formidable opponent. The narrative is true here to the spirit of medieval legend, as the enigmatic challenger tests the mettle of Robin's

men. One is reminded of the coming of the Green Knight to Arthur's court, as we find in this film a visual blending of legend and chivalric myth.

Of course there is no question that Richard shall reign anon—but that is not exactly the point, even though the film does build to an exciting, fast-moving rescue and climax. The point is that rarely has the magic of the cinema been utilized to better effect than in this astonishing treatment of medieval legend. In all, this is one of the most satisfying of Fairbanks' costume dramas.

NOTES

1. René Clair, *Cinema, Yesterday and Today*. Trans. Stanley Appelbaum. Ed. R.C. Dale (New York: Dover Publications, Inc., 1972), p. 60.

2. Peter Bogdanovich, *Allan Dwan: The Last Pioneer* (New York: Praeger, 1971), p. 63.

3. Clair, *Cinema*, p. 61.

11
Architecture in Motion: *The Thief of Bagdad*

This astonishing motion picture is best described by its subtitle—"An Arabian Nights Fantasy"—and it becomes the perfect instrument for cinematic magic and spectacle. The rags-to-riches motif is here fantasized in a most peculiar and exotic way, but the film is nonetheless linked to the basic Fairbanksian philosophy of success as the opening motto of the film declares: "Happiness must be earned." And before we are taken to the imaginary streets of Bagdad, "dream city of the ancient East," we are subjected to still another message from the titlist, this one, presumably, from the *Arabian Nights*: "Verily, the works of those gone before us have become instances and examples to men of our modern day, that folk may view what admonishing chances befel other folk and may therefore take warning." Now this all sounds potentially pious, uplifting, and instructive, but, finally, one wonders what, in fact, one may learn from the bizarre and unusual "examples" this fantasy has to offer. It is rather silly, in short, to attempt to find a didactic purpose behind what is most certainly an entertainment vehicle.

The main characters of this film represent polar extremes of fairytale society. On the one

Fairbanks in character for The Thief of Bagdad *(1924): "What I want–I take."*

hand, we have oriental potentates who are generally flawed by their indulgence and luxury, such as the stout Prince of Persia (one is reminded of the indulgent rich in the early comedies, by the way), or by their conniving political ambition, as is true of the villain of the piece, Cham Shang, The Great Prince of the Mongols, King of Ho Sho, and Governor of Wah Hoo and the Island of Wak. At the other social extreme, we have Doug's Thief, a clever, pragmatic fellow who lives by his wits and is clearly successful at his "profession." He appears as an appealing and energetic entrepreneur in baggy pants, out for himself, a rather greedy realist who states his philosophy as follows: "What I want—I take. My reward is *here*. Paradise is a fool's dream and Allah is a myth." In the next sequence, at the Palace at Ho Sho, this philosophy is echoed by the Mongol Prince, demonstrating that cynical ambition is not limited to the lower classes. The Prince proclaims that the Palace at Bagdad "shall be mine. What I want, I take," and prepares to travel to Bagdad as suitor to the princess there. Hence, the Thief thinks like a Prince, or the Prince thinks like a Thief. Both, at any rate, shall contend later for the hand and favor of the princess.

Therefore, one wonders initially what will set these two figures apart as deserving suitors. But, in typical courtly fashion, the Thief is soon to be ennobled by his passion for the Princess, and later claims to be "transformed" by his love for her. Having bluffed his way into the Palace, he confesses, contritely to the Princess that the comely "Ahmed, Prince of the Isles of the Seas, and of the Seven Palaces" is no more than "a wretched outcast—a thief." But he is no less manly, for all that: "I can bear a thousand tortures," he tells her, "endure a thousand deaths—but not thy tears." Moved, the Princess helps him to escape (after he has been discovered, flogged, and is about to be thrown to the palace ape). She also presents him with her ring, and professes her love. Thus, the Fairbanks figure leaps over social barriers as well as physical ones.

The "test" is then devised for the choosing of her proper suitor: "Send them to distant lands to seek some rare treasure. At the Seventh Moon let them return. Who brings the rarest treasure I will wed." The "transformed" Thief goes to the Mosque for solace and advice. He is told there: "Allah hath made thy soul to yearn for happiness, but thou must earn it," and the film's little motto is therefore enforced.

In none of the other costume films is the episodic structure so obvious as in this one during the extended sequence of the "Seven Moons." The scenes change rapidly from one magical setting for spectacular action to another—from "The Valley of Fire," for example, to "The Valley of the Monsters," to "The Cavern of the Enchanted Trees," the "Old Man of the Midnight

Doug as "Ahmed, Prince of the Isles of the Seas and of the Seven Palaces," courting the Princess, Julanne Johnstone, in The Thief of Bagdad. *Still, courtesy of the Killiam Collection.*

Sea," the "Abode of the Winged Horse" (which resembles nothing so much as a drawn set out of a later Disney animated feature). Equally strange and exotic and wonderful are the prizes won in this "Search for Rare Treasure" that occupies the central portion of the film. All of the prizes—the Prince of the Indies' magical crystal (plucked from the eye of a "forgotten idol near Kandahar at the expense of an agile servant's life"), the Persian Prince's magic carpet, the Mongol Prince's magic apple from the "Island of Wak"—all of these enter into the film's dynamic conclusion involving the rescue of the poisoned Princess. The villainous Mongol Prince who has taken Bagdad with twenty thousand men is then thwarted by the carefree and devious Thief, who, having the seeds to power, sows them, conjuring up one hundred thousand soldiers in no time at all.

At points such as this one the film excels in its special effects photography as this army materializes from puffs of smoke. The magic of its technological achievement was not missed by

Fairbanks as the impudent thief before his transformation.

contemporary audiences. The *New York Times* reviewer, after seeing this film open to an appreciative audience at the Liberty Theater, wrote (on 19 March 1924): "There are some wonderfully well-worked-out double exposure photographic effects, and even to an experienced eye the illusion is in nearly every instance kept up to a state of perfection."[1] The writer goes on to comment on the uniqueness of the cinematic illusion that is created here, remarking that it is "something that one could never see upon a stage." Such illusions as Fairbanks' dive to the depths of the sea and his battle with the sea monster, and other seemingly "magical" effects set this film apart as a triumph of artifice. Of course, the trickery was not always entirely photographic. The *Times* reviewer noted, for example, that the effect of the Thief's dive to the bottom of the sea was "obtained through the aid of the slow motion camera and glass." But obviously the production crews' ingenuity was taxed at several points in the making of this picture. How, for example, does one make a magic carpet fly convincingly? Is this the sort of trick that can be created through the camera? Raoul Walsh, the director of the film, finally found the solution to this problem while observing a group of steelworkers at a construction site in Hollywood, one of whom was riding a load of girders. Back at the studio, he found the right kind of crane, and was left only with the difficulty of lifting the carpet from the floor. The director

solved that problem by installing an overhead pulley and a hand winch (both off camera) and using a burly extra to wind the crank. The result [Walsh reports] was better than I had expected. The carpet had a steel frame and

Energy confronts lethargy: the Thief in defiance of a sleeping eunuch.

boom (and a double for Miss Johnston). The crane cables were painted white, which rendered them invisible. Beyond this, the "reality" of the effect is informed by the director's cinematic sense:

> To strengthen the illusion of flying, I made low-angle shots, added cut-ins of the people staring up from the streets—obtained by perching cameramen and myself on a platform at the top boom and shouting down—then resumed the slow pan showing the travelers on their way.[3]

As was often the case in these costume spectacles, cost was not spared if exactly the "right" effect had to be created. One recalls the tremendous expense that went into the building of the set for *Robin Hood,* and the costly experimentation with Technicolor that was deemed necessary to create the appropriate atmosphere for *The Black Pirate.* According to Raoul Walsh, *The Thief of Bagdad* was the first picture to cost a million dollars. Much of the expense, no doubt, went into the creation of the exotic costumes (designed by Mitchell Leisen) and the set designs of William Cameron Menzies. For this is largely a film of architecture and atmosphere, to the extent that the Fairbanks figure is frequently subordinated to the sets as well as to the spectacle. Ornamentation becomes an end in itself, the film a spectacular and popularized masque for the millions. The Fairbanksian charm is there, to be sure, but of primary importance is the manner in which the design values excite and delight the visual sense. In conception, the Art Nouveau influence (as evidenced by the curving lines, the consciously developed surface patterns) is central. It is as if a set of mobile black-and-white, pen-and-ink drawings has come to life, creating an animated *mise-en-scéne.* Some fifty years later it seems that one of the essential formulas for popular success that the Disney Studio was later to exploit is here given its most effective early rendering.

In his study *The Art of the Moving Picture,* Vachel Lindsay contemplates the idea of "Architecture-in-Motion" and goes so far as to emphasize "that the architects, above all, are the men to advance the work in the ultra-creative photoplay."[4] Lindsay earlier points out that

> it is a quality, not a defect, of the photoplays that while the actors tend to become types and hieroglyphics and dolls, on the other hand, dolls and hieroglyphics and mechanisms tend to become human. By an extension of this

steel cross-strapping underneath. When the drum winch began to turn, the whole thing, with Fairbanks and Miss Johnston sitting cross-legged on it, rose before the eyes of the suitably astonished spectators and thin wires pulled it toward the window.[2]

Putting the carpet and its occupants through the window could then be done by suggestion, by cutting from the shot where the carpet reaches the window to the next shot of the carpet outside the palace on its journey over the city of Bagdad. For this outside shot, Walsh used an eighty foot

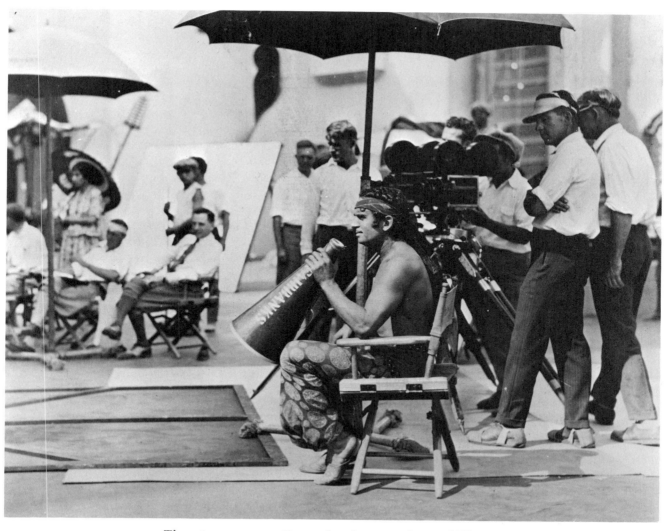

The actor as auteur. *Doug takes charge on the set of* The Thief of Bagdad: *"Cost was not spared."*

Doug on the set of Thief *with Frank Case and Mary Pickford.*

Actor and architecture: Thief of Bagdad *was the perfect vehicle for his athletic versatility.*

The set for Thief of Bagdad *under construction. According to Vachel Lindsay, the architects had "to advance the work in the ultra-creative photoplay."*

principle, non-human tones, textures, lines, and spaces take on a vitality almost like that of flesh and blood.[5]

This is very like the effect created in *The Thief of Bagdad,* and this distinction would sustain the film even if Fairbanks were not in it. However, one cannot imagine such a film being made at this particular period *without* Fairbanks in the lead, for it is his kind of picture. In many respects it is the perfect vehicle for his athletic versatility. The sets become an oriental and exotic playground that almost matches the potential of the *Robin Hood* situation and is sometimes even more astonishing.

Robert E. Sherwood considered *The Thief of Bagdad* "the farthest and most sudden advance that the movie has ever made," and this is substantial praise.[6] The trick is, as Sherwood goes on to explain, to be able to perform such wizardry and somehow make it all seem probable. The criticism offered in the *New York Times* has withstood the years and is still nearly valid, for *Thief of Bagdad* remains "a feat of motion picture art which has never been equaled and one which itself will enthrall persons time and again."[7] One might reasonably argue that the technology has perhaps been "equalled," but the film itself continues to cast its unique spell of enchantment for audiences far removed from the times that produced it.

NOTES

1. As quoted by George C. Pratt, *Spellbound in Darkness: A History of the Silent Film* (Greenwich: New York Graphic Society, Ltd., 1973), p. 298.

2. Raoul Walsh, *Each Man in His Time: The Life Story of a Director* (New York: Farrar, Straus, Giroux, 1974), p. 168.

3. *Ibid.,* p. 168.

4. Vachel Lindsay, *The Art of the Moving Picture* (New York: Liveright Publishing Corp., 1970), p. 162.

5. *Ibid.,* p. 161.

6. Writing in *Life,* 3 April 1924, p. 32, as quoted in *Spellbound in Darkness,* p. 298.

7. As quoted in *Spellbound in Darkness,* p. 298.

12

A Painted Ship on a Painted Ocean:
The Black Pirate

Color is vice, although it can be one of the finest virtues. When controlled by a firm hand, well guided by her master, Drawing, Color is then like a splendid woman with a mate worthy of her—her lover but also her master—the most magnificent mistress possible. . . . But when united with uncertainty, with a weak drawing, timid, deficient, easily satisfied, Color becomes a bold whore, makes fun of her little fellow, isn't this so?—And gallivants as she pleases, taking the thing lightly as long as everything is pleasing to her, treating her poor companion like a simpleton who is bothering her—which, moreover, is true, too. The result is visible: a chaos of drunkenness, cheats, regrets, things left unfinished! All right now, enough!

—James McNeill Whistler

*T*he Black Pirate, like all of Fairbanks' costume films, offers a wide range of interests. Much has already been written about the famous acrobatics—such as the slide down the sail on the knife, the final undersea rescue. But *The Black Pirate,* for other reasons, is a unique product of Fairbanks' art. He had been working more and more in the direction of the studio-made film, exerting more and more control upon the set designing and the art direction. The summit of these efforts was reached with *The Black Pirate.* It was a color film in the process of Two-Color Technicolor. The process itself forced the filmmakers to resort to extreme methods in shooting, making *The Black Pirate* the most carefully controlled and executed of all Fairbanks' films.

The limitations and advantages of this two-strip process directly influenced the look, pace and impact of the film. These will be considered here. The story of the filming of *The Black Pirate* remains a fascinating, yet relatively unknown chapter in the development of the color film. It had considerable impact in the eventual success of Technicolor.

It is almost impossible to view the film today in its original state. Up to this time only black and white prints could be located. Recently, however, a negative with the dyes intact has been found and processed by Technicolor in England. The transfer was made from a bi-pack film strip to a single strip. At this writing, the film is being exhibited in selected theaters both here and

Doug in costume for The Black Pirate *(1926).*

abroad, including the American Film Institute Theater in Washington, D.C.

TECHNICOLOR

The history of the Technicolor process is really the history of the so-called "natural color" film. A distinction must be made between the general term "color film" and the "natural color" film. The "color film" may refer to two standard practices during the silent film period—tinting and toning. Tinting merely was the application of a liquid dye either to the entire surface of the film or to part of it. This was a common practice with silent films. Most films contained a number of color "keys"—amber color for daylight scenes, red for fire scenes, gold for early morning scenes. Sometimes the emotion within a scene determined the use of specific tints—blues or reds for passionate scenes for instance. It has been estimated that as many as nine colors would be employed throughout a tinted film.[1] Toning is a process that corrects one limitation of the tinting process. It converted the black gradations to a color, but left the whites untouched. If yet another tint were added to the toned stock, a two-color effect was obtained.

These two processes have been with the motion picture from the very beginnings. What is not so well known, however, is that "natural color" processes have been around for almost as long. These processes refer to films wherein the colors are imparted to the film stock or to the screen by mechanical or optical means. There may be no color at all on the film, as was the case with some early processes. The color appearing on the screen would be created by a combination of special printing processes and the use of color filters in front of the projector. Such processes are as old as tinting and toning. There are two main classifications of natural color films: additive and subtractive. The history of Technicolor embraces both techniques.

The additive processes literally added colors to light. The film strip carried no color. The color values were created by projection, by placing appropriately colored filters between the film and the screen. As early as 1855, Clerk Maxwell, an English physicist, discovered that if a scene were filmed separately on three different black-and-white negatives through filters that transmitted the blue, green and red sections of the spectrum, the scene could be rebuilt in its original colors by superimposing the three positive images onto a screen through the same filters as those used in making the respective negatives.[2] Again, there was no color on these three·positive images. The color resulted from the filters through which each of the three images was projected onto the screen.

The subtractive process records the three images in the same way—by breaking down the scene into the three primary colors. The synthesis used in reproduction is quite different. The primary colors are subtracted from the color spectrum. Again, three negatives are made by photographing an object through red, green, and blue filters. But in this process the positives are printed in the *complementary* hues of the respective negatives. Thus, a negative that recorded light with a blue filter would be printed into a positive image that contained the opposite of blue-yellow. Moreover, that positive image would be printed and dyed in that color. Color is now on the film itself.[3] The subtractive process needs no filters or special apparatus for projection. It is the process that predominates today.

The history of Technicolor reveals the limitations and advantages of each process. When

Fairbanks shot *The Black Pirate,* Technicolor had been using the subtractive process for some years, but before that an additive process had been tried. This last takes us back to 1913.

Three graduates of the Massachusetts Institute of Technology named Herbert Kalmus, Daniel F. Comstock, and W. Burton Westcott, had organized a firm of technical consultants in 1913. In the course of a consultation with a client named William H. Coolidge the idea for a new kind of motion picture camera was presented. Comstock had already designed a camera that could photograph a scene in two colors—red and green. Two negatives, one sensitive to red, the other to green, received simultaneously the light that came through the single-lens camera. The light was "divided" by a prismatic device onto these respective negatives.[4] The two images were then superimposed onto a screen by "projecting through two apertures, each with a color filter, bringing the two components into register on the screen by means of a thin adjusting glass element.[5] This was an additive process. The client Coolidge was impressed with this idea and, with a partner put up the $10,000 that enabled the Technicolor Motion Picture Corporation to come into existence in 1915.

After a year of research the fledgling company decided to make its first feature film in Jacksonville, Florida in order to take advantage of the semitropical sunlight. The first Technicolor lab was mounted on a remodelled railroad passenger car. It contained a laboratory with darkroom, a fireproof safe, a power plant, and an office. New colleagues were added to the staff including Professor E. J. Wall, a veteran experimenter in color photography, and Joseph A. Ball, who later became a key director of Technicolor research. That first film was called *The Gulf Between* and was completed in the summer of 1917. Its first exhibition was a private one at Aeolian Hall in New York City on 21 September. Subsequent exhibition was limited and some flaws marred its debut.

The problems Technicolor encountered with *The Gulf Between* are typical of the additive processes. The main problem was "fringing." This refers to the separation of the two colors on the image so they no longer registered. Suddenly a man would have two shirts, one of red and the other of green. An image, whether it be of a single object or a large landscape, will contain all of the primary colors. If the colors get out of register on the screen, fringing is the result. Another problem lay in the special equipment for projection. The twin-aperture kind of projector was expensive. This meant that regularly equipped movie theaters would have to install the new equipment at great expense.

1918 saw efforts underway to solve these problems. The result was that Technicolor began working with a subtractive color process. This meant that a method had to be worked out to stamp color dyes on the film, eliminating the encumbrance of projector filters. Professor Wall had suggested as early as 1916 that the subtractive process was the answer to the color problem. Now it remained to devise an effective method of printing the color dyes onto the film.

In 1920 Coolidge was replaced as principal backer by one William Travers Jerome who remained for many years chairman of Technicolor's board. It was under Jerome that Technicolor's subtractive two-strip process was further developed. The positive film strip was really two strips cemented together, each strip contained the color dyes for the colors of red and green respectively. The dyes were stamped onto the film strips by a process called *imbibition,* wherein a dye absorbed in gelatin is transferred by contact and pressure to blank film. The first film made in this process was *Toll of the Sea* in 1922. The film industry closely watched the progress. Rex Ingram expressed interest in re-shooting his *Prisoner of Zenda* in Technicolor, D. W. Griffith considered shooting *Faust* in it. Both projects never came to pass. Douglas Fairbanks likewise expressed interest. Plans of making a pirate picture were already forming. A few more years would pass, however, before he would do so.

With plans for extending its foothold into the film industry, Technicolor established a laboratory and photographic unit in Hollywood in 1923. The subtractive, imbibition process was expensive. The cameras used were costly and only a few were in existence. Personnel had to be specially trained to use them. Up to this point Technicolor had to finance its own ventures since it was difficult to persuade a Hollywood producer to foot the added expenses. But soon some producers, impressed by the quality of *Toll of the Sea,* began to underwrite Technicolor's services for sequences in films. The exodus of the Israelites from Egypt in DeMille's 1923 *The Ten Commandments,* for instance, was shot in the two-color process. In 1924 Technicolor had a chance to shoot some interior sequences for George Fitzmaurice's *Cytherea.* Shooting color under artificial light as opposed to natural sunlight posed more problems for the process. It was found that at least twice as much light was needed on the set than for the regular black-and-white film stock.

The next break for Technicolor came in 1924 when Zane Grey's *Wanderers of the Wasteland* was adapted for the screen for Famous Players. Zane Grey's contract stipulated that the novel be shot entirely in color.[6] The Technicolor crew worked day and night for six weeks. The negative was processed in a plant in Boston and took almost a year to produce enough prints for theatrical distribution. Technicolor actually lost money on the deal due to increased expenses. It was decided not to shoot any more features for a while. Work would be limited to sequences in a number of films spanning 1924–25. *Wanderers of the Wasteland,* however, left no doubt in the minds of many that the two-color imbibition process was here to stay. More and more producers sought out the company and soon sequences appeared in such diverse films as *The Phantom of the Opera* and *The Merry Widow*. More importantly, the time was right for Douglas Fairbanks to realize a lifelong dream. He would make a pirate picture. It would be in color.

TECHNICOLOR AND *THE BLACK PIRATE*

The association between Fairbanks and Technicolor reveals the typical interdependence between art and business that has shaped Hollywood's growth. Fairbanks had wanted to do a pirate picture as early as 1923. He had previously voiced doubts about the film in natural colors:

> The film in natural colors seems to me another fetish. Every now and then someone discovers a new process for making colored photographs, but the photograph which goes on being taken and purchased the world over is not the photograph in supposedly natural colors. We have our own medium in the films, and I see no particular reason for wanting to alter it.[7]

This comment may have been influenced by the available color processes at the time. By the time *Toll of the Sea* had been produced a year later he knew that such processes were steadily improving. At any rate in 1923 when he first considered doing a pirate picture, color was very much on his mind:

> Pirates demand color. Stories of modern life, war stories, even romances like *Robin Hood* and *Thief of Bagdad* might be told in black and white, but what pirates needed was something more vivid. It was impossible to imagine them without color.[8]

Technicolor at that time was a struggling concern, burdened by the expenses of color, looking for producers to foot the bills. If Fairbanks was waiting for a color process to mature, Technicolor was likewise waiting for a producer of imagination, daring, and—yes—wealth to take the risks of producing an expensive commercial feature in the still relatively untried process. Success on either hand would enhance the success of the other. The combination of business sense, personal artistry, and foresight is a rare one. *The Black Pirate* is an example.

With *Robin Hood* finished, Fairbanks in 1923 considered turning to a pirate subject. He hired as director Raoul Walsh and as leading lady Evelyn Brent. He let his hair grow down to his shoulders in anticipation of the role of the bold buccaneer. Plans stalled, however. One reason, previously cited, was the lack of a dependable color process. But there were other factors that worried Fairbanks' always shrewd business sense. Chief among these was the fact that pirate pictures were very popular at the time. Everybody, it seemed, was making them. Fred Niblo was working on a picture to be called *Captain Applejack* (later titled *Strangers of the Night*), Fox was producing *Treasure Island,* and Charles Ray was sinking (!) everything he had on his super-picture, *The Courtship of Miles Standish,* which would feature some pirate sequences. Fairbanks' hesitation about flooding the market with yet another pirate picture were perhaps borne out by the failure of Ray's film. It failed so badly at the box-office that the popular star never quite regained his financial balance. Fairbanks postponed his own picture and waited while Edward Knoblock, the author of *Kismet* prepared for him the storyline for the film that would be titled *The Thief of Bagdad*.[9] Raoul Walsh assumed the directorial helm for *Thief* instead of the pirate picture.

One result from this flurry of pirate activity was the arrival of a gentleman named Dwight Franklin. Producers began bidding for the services of this one-man source authority whose knowledge ranged from the life of prehistoric man to the Vikings, American Indians, Eskimo, and, or course, pirates. His miniature models of pirates had invaded the sacred precincts of staid art museums and universities. In addition he had been for seven years connected with the New York Museum of Natural History as a wild-animal photographer, field collector, taxidermist, and sculptor.[10] This astonishing man would play a major part in the production of *The Black Pirate*. As will be seen, the film would depend heavily upon its art direction. Franklin was vital in this respect.

Fairbanks holds off the pirate crew in Black Pirate *(1926), a triumph of exactness in detail and art direction.*

It is surprising perhaps to realize that the history of the color film has been plagued by critical reaction against the very idea of film in natural colors. Following the release of *The Black Pirate* in 1926, *Motion Picture Magazine* released an editorial that sums up an important reason for this antagonism. "Color effects are excellent for titles, inserts, cutbacks, visions, dreams, allegories . . . but the average drama is more impressive without color. . . ." The editorial goes on to say that "color seems to cross the line between the real and the unreal and leaves too little for the imagination."[11] Writing later in 1933 Rudolph Arnheim touches upon the objections to the color film. He, too, objects to the supposed lack of flexibility that a "natural" medium of color would impose upon the black and white film:

The painter, who does not—as color film does—take colors ready-made from nature but creates them afresh on his palette, is able by suitable choice of tones, by distribution of color masses, and so forth, to get as far away from nature as is necessary to convey his artistic intention. Judging from what we have seen up to now, the colors in a color film are at best naturalistic—and if owing to imperfect technique they are not yet so, this lack of naturalness does not provide the artist with a potentially useful medium of expression.[12]

The point these two men make perhaps has an aesthetic validity. It is not applicable, however, to a film like *The Black Pirate*. *Pirate* was made in a color process far different than those known today. Its very limitations (and there were many) caused the film's producers to literally alter nature and color as a painter would subordinate a painting to his available palette. At the time of *The Black Pirate* in 1926, a successful three-color process had not as yet been devised. Technicolor at this time was a *two-color* process. Two-color processes "are a compromise of the three-color systems. One film is usually sensitive to red, orange and yellow, while the other attracts blue and green. Some other colors are absent from these two-color systems and the remaining colors are not nearly so true as in full-color films."[13] The problem was that one strip attracted more red than yellow, the other more green than blue. Cameraman Hal Mohr, who shot the two-color work for *The Wedding March* and *The King of Jazz,* recalls:

In the two-color process the blues were not true and the yellows were not true; blues were green, and the yellows were orange, but other than that, two-color Technicolor wasn't bad.[14]

Obviously objects being photographed were not registering on film in their true colors, only insofar as they contained the reds and greens of the spectrum. Arnheim has objected that perfectly naturalistic colors merely reproduce nature, that a "lack of naturalness does not provide the artist with a potentially useful medium of expression." *The Black Pirate does* represent an attempt to utilize color. Because of the limitations, the producers had to alter many things in nature and in doing so used color creatively.

First the producers and craftsmen had to determine just what the problems would be. By 1925 the picture was underway. Technicolor had two advisers on the scene, Arthur Ball and George Cave, assisting cameraman Henry Sharp. They had with them four Technicolor cameras—four out of only eleven existing at that time. Art directors included the aforementioned Dwight Franklin and the Swedish artist Carl Oscar Borg. Borg headed his own staff of artists. These men spent six months and fifty thousand feet of color film and $125,000 before actual shooting even began on the film. By contrast to the six months of research, the production schedule lasted only ten to twelve weeks. It was the six-month period that really counted, however. The problems encountered and delineated were threefold: (1.) how to restrain the color; (2.) how to work with a color scheme that was virtually exclusive of blue and weak with yellow; (3.) how to ensure that the color recorded on film was exactly the hue that had been desired.

(1.) It might be supposed that a film representing an early attempt at color would feature bright, vivid colors; that it would be in effect a showcase of rainbow hues. Fairbanks' idea behind *The Black Pirate* was quite different. He felt it was better to *subdue* the colors, to "take the color out of color."[15] This motto underlay the entire production. Photographing with the Technicolor cameras often worked against this notion. Fairbanks himself describes this rationale:

> The color camera is remarkable. You can't feed it too much color at a time, because it will always eat up more than you give it, and instead of obtaining a natural effect . . . the exact opposite results. Nature's beauties are spread over so much landscape that the impression can never be garish. But when these same beauties of light and shade are brought to the screen, they are concentrated into so small a space that, unless precautions are taken, they become overemphasized.[16]

The paintings of Rembrandt, he realized, represented complete subordination of colors toward harmonic and compositional unity. There may be reds, blues, and greens in it—but they were cloaked in neutralizing shadow and so harmonized that it was the picture and not a spot here and there that impressed itself upon the mind. Accordingly, the filmmakers worked out a "keying" color scheme that would dominate the film's palette on the whole—green and a reddish brown. For the most part, all vivid colors were banished from the set. "If, in the hurry of outfitting a mob of extras, a scarlet bandanna was allowed to reach the set, it was immediately returned and *locked up* in a closet, never to see the light of day again!"[17]

Vivid colors did have their role. It was thought that they would tend to overstress ordinary action, but would create sufficient contrast if they were reserved for special moments. These moments might be one of great charm—as seeing the parrot in a vivid green sitting on a pirate's shoulder—or of dramatic impact—as when the galleon blows up and the screen is filled with a bright red flash. A recent viewing of the two-color print verifies that the first appearance of the pirates features the most vivid palette in the film. In all of this, the art directors were not only following the model of Rembrandt's subdued color, but were bowing to the more recent work of the book illustrators of the turn of the century—Howard Pyle and N. C. Wyeth. Close examination of the paintings now included in the compilation known as *Howard Pyle's Book of Pirates* reveals a number of paintings seemingly lifted right out of *The Black Pirate* (or is it the other way around?), such as a painting of a sword duel between two pirates. The composition and, above all, the muted tones of browns, reds, and greens (no blues) are astonishingly similar to the dueling scene between Fairbanks and villain Anders Randolph early in the film. The N. C. Wyeth illustrations for *Treasure Island,* moreover, reveal a mastery of muted colors, the dramatic impact coming from the judicious (and sparing) use of vivid colors. That the film was successful in this attempt to restrain colors was acknowledged by this review:

> . . . the colors themselves are always subdued, and, in fact, made so natural and inconspicuous that one soon forgets the color and retains only the feeling that what one sees is very real and very satisfying.[18]

Wishing to restrain colors is quite a different thing than doing it. The film's art staff found that a number of locations selected for shooting displayed yellows and blues that were too "violent." Catalina Island, for instance, was regarded as "all wrong" after a series of initial color tests. Many of the sets, therefore, were recreated in the studio under the complete control of Oscar Borg and his staff. "Borg painted what he would, secure in the knowledge that it did not matter whether nature had ever thought of the combination before him."[19] In this way "skies" were toned down, either through use of backdrops or simply letting the sky register as white. The galleons were studio-built and were placed in a giant tank that occupied most of the studio space. In fact, the vast majority of the shooting was done in the studio where color could be controlled and restrained completely.

Great care was taken that highlights, reflections of light off polished surfaces, not obtrude upon the eye:

> . . . it was found necessary to dull the surfaces of the silver and brass mountings of the pistols and cannon, and all the ironwork upon the ship, so that they would not distract the eye,

Fairbanks duels with pirate leader (Anders Randolf) on a sandy beach early in Black Pirate.

nor even be noticed, until brought into use. Even the gold and jewels of the looted ships could not make these firm ascetics lose their heads![20]

Compositions of scenes were handled so that a single point of emphasis was achieved through the manipulations of color intensities. For instance, characters who were to stand out in groupings of men wore shirts keyed colors of a brighter intensity than those men standing in the background. If a light-costumed man were forced by the action to come closer to the camera, he would be dusted down with a powder of a darker hue—wig, costume, and all—to compensate for the increased emphasis his costume would entail.

(2.) Working within the two-color limitation created special problems, problems solved only with great industry and patience. What was to be done about the relative absence of blue? "We found it impossible to do anything at all with purple, and that blue cannot be satisfactorily handled, as it takes a greenish tinge," said the film's director, Albert Parker. "This latter presented quite a difficulty—for, as perhaps you know, skies are blue."[21] Yes, and the ocean water will often appear with a blue color also. The story of how the art directors worked around this problem is a fascinating one.

Sometimes photographing blue hues was inevitable and, as Parker further admits, "Toward the end there is a scene where it was necessary that the sky be blue—when you see it, I think you agree with that it is far less pleasing than the others."[22] It was decided to alter the face of nature to get around this limitation. The blue sky, for instance, appears mostly as just a white hue with just the slightest suggestion of a warm tinge of brown. The sea was literally a particular hue of dye that enabled it to "register" according to the demands of the art directors, avoiding the chancy consequences of photographing blue. When one pauses to reflect a moment on that last fact—staining the ocean . . . well, it is staggering. Hundreds of thousands of gallons of water were treated this way. It is only one of many indications of the extreme lengths Fairbanks was willing to go in shooting a color film.

(3.) In adhering to a strict color scheme of green and brown it was necessary to alter the colors of those objects appearing in front of the camera. This formidable problem has been described in this fashion:

Mr. Fairbanks soon found, as had others before him, that, excellent as this process is, it will not reproduce on the screen the exact color that was originally in front of the camera, and, even when it does, it fails of artistic effect. It always causes nature to take on strange and unexpected tints, and not always desirable ones.[23]

How, then, to insure that the color resulting on the film was the color that was desired? Much of the testing done in those first six months was taken up with this problem. At first, sets were built in all colors of the rainbow for test shots. Walls of the studios were painted in patches of blue, green, pink, lavender and orange, mauve, etc. By this means it could be determined how each color would register on film and from this construct a color chart. This chart would enable the filmmaker to know what color the object to be photographed must be if it were to register as the desired hue on film. This is further complicated by the fact that colors are not the same under artificial light as when under the sky. Consequently two systems of charts had to be made—one indicating the color "keys" for daylight exterior shooting; the other indicating the "keys" for studio interiors. The conclusions one reaches from all this are that the Technicolor artists were kinds of artists in reverse. The painter may work for his effects directly, mixing his colors on his palette, placing them on the canvas and manipulating their arrangement and intensity as he goes—even to scraping them off if the effect is not the one desired. But artists in Technicolor, reports Albert Parker,

. . . must work indirectly. They first apply their colors to fabrics, to wood, to metals, to the skin of living beings, and even to landscapes.

Then these colors must be mixed with light, gathered by the camera lens, transferred to celluloid, developed, and printed, and projected. Every step offers complications the painter does not encounter.[24]

Early in these experiments it was discovered that the same paint applied to different kinds of wood would register as different colors on film—similarly, when applied to different kinds of cloth. By means of these charts, it might be found that paint combination no. 7 on pine wood, for instance, would yield a similar color as dye no. 103 on cotton material. In this way complete harmonic unity could be achieved on the film. "Scenes which on the screen present a harmonious whole may have looked like a crazy-quilt of clashing shades. It was necessary to make the tests first and then color the scene before the camera so that the camera would record the effect desired."[25] Again, it was important to know if the scene was to be shot in artificial light or in the sunlight. These two variables would in themselves affect the Technicolor film's registration of hue.

Fairbanks as "The Black Pirate," posed with his leading lady, Billie Dove.

152

In effect the entire world presented to the camera was painted. As a result of testing and the compilation of the color charts, as a result of the dominant concern for muting and harmonizing each scene's color values, it was found that virtually *everything* had to be painted. Cutlasses and culverins, pistols and pieces-of-eight, gunpowder, costumes, sails, longboats, jewelry—everything suffered the artist's brush. This applied to makeup also. The actors had their own "facial color schemes" for interior and for exterior shooting. In order to maintain the same physical appearance, indoors and out, it was necessary to alter the makeup for each situation. The kind of makeup varied. For some individuals their skin was covered with a kind of oil so as "to give their skin the soft and velvet sheen of the ideal 'skin you love to touch'—but never find."[26] Fairbanks had a very heavy beard that tended to register on film as green. It was found that by applying a reddish powder to that area of his face the problem could be alleviated. His leading lady, Billie Dove, had to have her face toned a mellow ivory.

It is obvious that not all films shot in color would be able to take such pains as *The Black Pirate* did. It is unique. It represents a rare fusion of the filmmaking process with the art of the painter. Moreover, it represents an attempt to alter and rearrange the exterior world to match the vision of the artist. One is tempted to listen with astonishment when told stories of how Michelangelo Antonioni will paint his sets, even nature itself, for his films. It must be admitted, however, that this astonishment is tempered somewhat when faced with the awesome problems encountered and dealt with in *The Black Pirate*— made over forty years earlier!

Fairbanks himself was the dominant force in the incredible energy and effort expended on the production. Not only did he firmly believe in the possibilities of color, but he had the money and the good sense to follow through on it. Total expenses for the production amounted to a cool million dollars, no mean sum in those days. He also had the acumen to surround himself with artists/illustrators of the caliber of Carl Oscar Borg and Dwight Franklin. Their collective vision enabled the film to share in the robust vision of the N. C. Wyeth tradition. All these efforts were necessary to as complex an operation as *The Black Pirate* represented. But they alone were not enough. Fairbanks himself supplied the missing factor—he knew what he wanted. This complete trust in his own taste guided the whole film. Many times when both Borg and Franklin were satisfied

with results Fairbanks vetoed them. "Time and time again he did this," declared Ted Reed, Fairbanks' production manager. "He was determined to get the exact effect on the screen that he wanted, and he was certain from the beginning of just what that effect should be."[27]

If the film was a triumph for Fairbanks and the history of the color motion picture, it was also, in some ways, a nightmare for the Technicolor people. As was mentioned earlier, *The Black Pirate* was a two-color, subtractive, imbibition process film consisting of two strips of celluloid (one strip for the green dyes, the other for the reds) cemented together. This meant the film was twice as thick as regular film, and had emulsion on both sides. A certain amount of sharpness of focus was lost on the screen and needed constant correction by the projectionist. The presence of emulsion on both sides of the film strip tended to make it buckle more easily in either direction, throwing the image in and out of focus. Fairbanks toyed with the idea of projecting the film with an extra-strong light, due this thickness. He found that such a projector light would give more depth to the image, but detracted from the muted colors of the hues. No changes were made—the film was finally shown with regular projection apparatus. Another problem encountered was the film strips' propensity for incurring scratches. A scratch on a black-and-white film shows as a white line on the screen. A scratch on this Technicolor film, however, was something else again. It showed as a brilliant green or red flash—most distracting to the viewer. The two-color process doubled the cost of the film stock, the developing, the printing, and even doubled the light required on the set for interiors and exteriors. The imbibition process was a particularly troublesome headache. The matrix used to print the dyes onto the film was useful for only fifteen or twenty prints before it had to be discarded and another one made.[28]

TWO COLOR TECHNICOLOR—AN EVALUATION

Was it all worth it? The two-color process survived into the Thirties but was replaced by 1932 with a three-strip process that would yield better focus, more reliable registration of color, and access to the primary range of blue colors. Instead of struggling with a double-thickness film, a new method was devised to print all three color plates onto a single strip of film, making sure that there was exact registration of the three plates. That same year the process was first tried by Walt Disney for his Silly Symphony, *Flowers and Trees*. By 1935 Rouben Mamoulian had made *Becky Sharp* in the three-color process and Technicolor as it is known today was launched. But what of that other world of color, that strange, beautiful halfworld of two-color Technicolor that was banished forever when the three-color process supplanted it? There are few films in the two-color process that survive today. *The Black Pirate* has only recently been found in its original dyes. Two films do survive made in this process, and viewing them will persuade the most reluctant viewer that two-color Technicolor did have its virtues, revealing a compelling world of muted, slightly reddish hue. The films are two Warner Brothers horror vehicles, *Dr. X* and *Mystery of the Wax Museum*. The absence of strong blue and purple is hardly noticeable. Instead, the dominating tones of red and green are quite beautiful and pleasing to the eye. Certainly in the case of *The Black Pirate*, conceived as it was toward the Flemish masters and the great American illustrators, the color took on a special value in itself. The viewer today, having only seen a black-and-white print, can only be maddenly tantalized by contemporary reviews of the original film. The range of colors included greens of all the softer shades, and browns running the gamut from the lightest tint of old ivory to the deepest tone of mohogany. The effect from all this was of a mobile kind of Flemish painting the whole frame faintly flushed with a warm tone of sepia. Mordaunt Hall commented that "wonderful moonlight effects on the water, glimpses of the pirates . . . are reminiscent of old masters. . . ."[29] The modern eye, jaded by the spectacular three-color processes of today could well be pleasantly refreshed by the soft earth colors of two-color Technicolor. It would be fun indeed to sail once again—"in a painted ship on a painted ocean."

NOTES

1. Kevin Brownlow, *The Parade's Gone By . . .* (New York: Ballantine Books, 1969), p. 25.

2. James L. Limbacher, *Four Aspects of the Film* (New York: Brussel and Brussel, 1968), p. 1.

3. Raymond Spottiswoode, *Film and Its Techniques* (Berkeley and Los Angeles: University of California Press, 1952), pp. 208–209.

4. Rudy Behlmer, "Technicolor," *Films in Review*, June-July, 1964, p. 334.

5. James L. Limbacher, *Four Aspects*, p. 26.

6. Rudy Behlmer, "Technicolor," p. 340.

7. Douglas Fairbanks, "Let Me Say This About Films," *Ladies Home Journal*, September, 1922, p. 120.

8. Edwin Schallert, "Yo Ho and a Bottle of Rum," *Picture-Play Magazine*, February, 1926, p. 17.

9. Edwin Schallert, "Doug Rubs the Magic Lamp," *Picture-Play Magazine*, September 1923, p. 87.

10. Barbara Little, "The Pirates are Coming," *Picture-Play Magazine*, March 1923, p. 47.

11. Eugene V. Brewster, "Why Color Pictures and Talking Movies Can Never Be Universal," *Motion Picture Magazine*, June 1926, p. 5.

12. Rudolph Arnheim, *Film as Art* (Berkeley and Los Angeles: University of California Press, 1957), p. 66.

13. James L. Limbacher, *Four Aspects*, p. 14.

14. Leonard Maltin, *Behind the Camera* (New York: Signet, 1971), p. 112.

15. Dunham Thorp, "How Fairbanks Took the Color out of Color," *Motion Picture Classic*, May 1926, p. 29.

16. Edwin Schallert, "Yo Ho . . ." p. 108.

17. Dunham Thorp, "How Fairbanks . . ." p. 87.

18. "Doug Gets Away With It," *The Outlook*, 14 April 1926, p. 561.

19. "Swashbuckling with Doug on a Painted Ocean," *Literary Digest*, 10 April 1926, p. 42.

20. Dunham Thorp, "How Fairbanks . . ." p. 89.

21. *Ibid.*, p. 87.

22. *Ibid.*, p. 87.

23. "Doug Gets Away . . ." p. 561.

24. "Swashbuckling with Doug . . ." p. 35.

25. *Ibid.*, p. 35.

26. Dunham Thorp, "How Fairbanks . . ." p. 87.

27. Edwin Schallert, "Yo Ho . . ." p. 17.

28. Leornard Maltin, *Behind the Camera*, p. 116.

29. "Swashbuckling with Doug," p. 36.

13
The Fall from Grace in *The Gaucho:* Douglas Fairbanks and the Byronic Hero

It is an awful chaos—Light and Darkness—
And mind and dust—and passions and pure
thoughts
Mixed, and contending without end or order—
All dormant or destructive. He will perish—
And yet he must not—I will try once more,
For such are worth redemption; and my duty
Is to dare all things for a righteous end.

—Byron, *Manfred*

*S*ince *The Gaucho* premiered in 1927 it has puzzled both Fairbanks' critics and his public. The sequence of costume films from *Zorro* to *The Black Pirate* had thus far featured splendidly virtuous heroes. The thief in *The Thief of Bagdad* was a thief for only two reels or so; thereafter, he

Although the Fairbanks character was different in The Gaucho *(1927), it retained distinctive traits and trademarks. The Gaucho is prefigured by this image of Don César in* Don Q. *(1925), lighting a cigarette with the last of his whip, which he has just flicked into the fire.*

155

was charged with a Mission and for the remainder of that film abandoned his nefarious ways. The outlawry of *Zorro* and *Robin Hood* attempted to correct the injustice of the established order. The black pirate was a pirate by disguise only, his real aims being the downfall of the pirate band. But there are differences in the character presented in *The Gaucho*, differences that strongly contrast him with Fairbanks' other heroes.

So misunderstood is this film that even today all that can be said about it is typified by Richard Schickel's words: "*The Gaucho*, despite Fairbanks' tricks with the bola, was the flattest of his big-scale adventure-romances. Indeed, it is hard to determine just what he thought he was doing here."[1] Indeed, *The Gaucho* is *not* like the other costume romances and should not be judged in the same standard. In its pretentions toward a different

end it needs quite another kind of viewpoint. It is, in a word, a true swashbuckler, an interesting example of that most peculiar genre. Those qualities that link it to the swashbuckling "tradition," if you will, are those very qualities that puzzle many and that make the film seem at times a bit confusing.

Ever since the publication of Byron's *The Corsair*, the popular imagination has been inflamed by tales of proud and cynical heroes who perform daring feats and display little regard for law or authority. The so-called "Byronic hero" became the central drive for narratives of exotic locales, derring-do, and satanic implications. *The Gaucho* is one of the earliest attempts in American film to deal with the Byronic style of heroism. Whether this was done consciously or not is perhaps irrelevant. It is true that *The Gaucho* shares many

Fairbanks in costume for The Gaucho *(1927).*

156

affinities with the other costume films. The difference lies chiefly in that the exposition of the Fairbanks character sounds deeper waters. The clear-eyed atmosphere of boyish romance has been clouded somewhat; night and brimstone lower over the land.

As one title says, "It is the story of one of them who came to be known as 'The Gaucho' and of the usurper Ruiz, and how these two came together at the 'City of the Miracle.' " This city is the site of a miracle wherein a young girl had received the healing apparition of the Madonna after a fall from a cliff. A shrine was built on the spot and soon passing pilgrims had poured much gold into its coffers: At the film's beginning, the girl who had been healed by the miracle is the mistress of the shrine and is aided by a kindly Padre. Suddenly, lured by the wealth, an outlaw (The Gaucho) rides into town and captures it single-handedly from the despotic clutches of the villainous Ruiz. After a night of drunken revelry, the Gaucho attempts to seduce the virginal girl of the shrine. The Gaucho's gypsy lover intervenes and he receives a knife wound. A leper, who earlier had been banished from the town, touches the wound and the Gaucho is infected with the disease. In despair he is about to commit suicide when the girl of the shrine leads him to the healing waters. He is miraculously cured after having received the apparition of the Madonna, but then he is captured by Ruiz and thrown into prison. The tale concludes when the Gaucho escapes and with the help of his men restores order to the city by deposing Ruiz.

What emerges from this bare outline is astonishing in light of Fairbanks' other films. The Gaucho flaunts the Padre and his religion. He lives as an outlaw whose initial purpose is not to restore justice but merely to defy it. He indulges in drunken revelry. He attempts the seduction of the mistress of the shrine. He considers killing himself, and he even contracts leprosy. Excepting, perhaps, *The Private Life of Don Juan*, this film is the darkest product of Fairbanks' art. It is the one film that seems to reveal essential truths about the kind of hero that Fairbanks had been portraying all along. *The Mark of Zorro* may contain more physical acrobatics, *Robin Hood* more satisfying production values, *The Black Pirate* more boyish thrills, yet *The Gaucho* remains Fairbanks' most satisfying venture in the genre of the swashbuckler.

The Byronic hero spearheaded a philosophy of rebellion against established systems in the early nineteenth century. His actions usually placed him outside the law. A leader of men he was

himself an isolated individual, the foe of all save one, a woman, to whom he devoted his chivalrous love. Aristocratic blood ran in his veins. Byron's Conrad, the Corsair, loved but one woman, Medora. It is significant that this love was beyond Conrad's grasp. The Corsair occupies a zone detached from laws and removed from love. Consider another Byronic hero, Manfred, who invoked his lost love Astarte with the help of spirits, but was unable to communicate with her. Alienation, isolation, and outlawry—the standard ingredients of the Byronic hero. They attracted then and still attract an audience's fascination:

> As long as situations occur, private or historical, in which deliberately anti-social behavior proves worthier of regard than conventional behavior, so long will the bold brigand aspect of Byronism find expression and justification in art.[2]

Of his past we know nothing. "No one knows whence he comes, nor whither he goes. He is wrapped in mystery. His past always contains a crime which is kept dark from us."[3] This enigmatic aspect establishes a kind of open end into which our imagination is funneled. It emphasizes his existence outside a given system of laws and lovemaking. He becomes in effect a kind of universal symbol for man's unfulfilled broodings, longings and frustrations. He embodies the only resolution for these—*action*. Always the man of action the Byronic hero flings away the scabbard and, at a stroke, demonstrates the power of the individual against a hostile world.

Since the inception of the costume films, Fairbanks' heroes were beginning to reveal characteristics in common with the Byronic hero. His actions often placed him outside the law, he was a natural leader of men, he was able to resolve conflicts with the dynamism of movement and daring, and he was often a creature of mystery. It was often suggested that he was an aristocrat either directly, as in *Robin Hood,* or indirectly, as in the Gascon heritage and service to the Queen seen in D'Artagnan in *The Three Musketeers.* But there are still major differences between his style and the Byronic style. The surface (i.e., the dynamism and the political alienation) seemed to be the same, yet the interior characteristics were different. It remained for the *The Gaucho* to remedy this.

Up to *The Gaucho* the Fairbanksian hero had not displayed the inner, fatalistic drives common to the Byronic hero. He lived outside the law, yet seemed to feel neither alienation nor self-damnation as did Manfred or Conrad. His relations with women were entirely successful and he was not haunted by either the ghost of an unsuccessful love or of a past crime. But there was an even more important difference. The Byronic hero's rejection of society led him, inevitably, if not to atheism, at least to the mocking rejection of religious tenets. The hero of *The Giaour* says

I would not, if I might, be blest;
I want no Paradise, but rest. . . .

Here is the true Romantic, not responsible to established political orders or to religious ones. Donald Sutherland has described him this way:

Romanticism cannot be responsible to anything, as it cannot be justified by anything, since it will not recognize any fixed authority. But it is essentially responsive, and so all but bound to answer a challenge or put up a fight, especially in the losing game against death. . . . The game is to force death into one's own style, which the Romantics eminently do, or to rise to the style of death.[4]

This magnificent defiance touches both heaven and hell. Its heroism is transcendent yet its consequences are satanic. As Arthur Machen has said, "sin is an effort to gain the ecstasy and the knowledge that pertain alone to angels, and in making this effort man becomes a demon."[5] Part of the fascination with this kind of hero, then, is that he *does* seem somehow demonic, as if the very air around him were charged with brimstone. We think of heroes from Don Juan to Manfred and everywhere is seen this devilish aspect. Byron describes Conrad as having a "laughing Devil in his sneer" and Manfred's defiance of the priest's plea for penitence with the words

Old man! there is no power in holy men,
Nor charm in prayer—nor purifying form
Of penitence. . . .

Redemption comes for him only through the *deed,* a "daring act of revenge that condemns the corrupt society he has abjured—in a word, the Byronic hero in action is a noble outlaw."[6]

The Gaucho is the first film to bring Fairbanks within range of this kind of hero. For the first time, the Fairbanksian hero answers to no belief or dogma—other than his own. He appears at the film's beginning with the simple title: "Far in the North, an outlaw—." Nothing else is learned about him—neither why he is an outlaw, nor what misdeed drove him to this kind of life. His chief foe is Ruiz the Usurper who is the villain, apparently only because he is a greater rascal than the Gaucho.

His relations with women are typified by his relation to the gypsy girl (Lupe Valez in her film debut). Their lovemaking takes on a mocking, combative aspect. If anything, it resembles more a pugilistic encounter. The promptness and gusto with which they literally attack each other may be further indicative of the swashbuckling tradition. They are like children who, upon meeting each other for the first time, kick each other in the shins and then stand back to see what will happen. The knightly tradition of friendships beginning in combats is worked over throughout *The Gaucho.* The combative nature of their relationship is first seen when they meet in a low tavern. They approach each other in the smoky, crowded room and move into a tango. The Gaucho unslings his bola and whirls it about them, encircling both their waists, binding each to each. Then he tucks his cigarette back into his mouth, kisses her firmly, pops the cigarette back out and then blows smoke into her face. She in turn pummels him more than once. They are companions of like nature and that is that.

Like the Corsair, it develops that the Gaucho's chivalrous love is devoted to one woman only, and she is irrevocably removed from him. She is the mistress of the shrine. After a night of drink and revelry the Gaucho lurches toward her room bent, obviously, on seduction. He makes the attempt, but discovers he cannot carry it through, that he does not understand her, that her virginal innocence places her quite beyond his grasp. "You're like a beautiful sunset," he tells her later; "something I can't embrace yet I love." These words virtually echo those of Byron's Childe Harold, who

Had sighed to many though he loved but one,
And that loved one, alas! could ne'er be his.

For the first time in a Fairbanks film the hero displays a mocking defiance of God. The confrontation of the Gaucho and the Padre stands at the core of the entire film. The two figures stand etched in black against the dazzling white stone steps of the city. The Padre is dressed in simple robes, the Gaucho in an elaborate costume, the bolas and whip slung at his belt. The Gaucho had beaten one of his men for unduly abusing the Padre. The Padre now pleads mercy for the man, pointing out the law of Holy Writ on display at the

Confrontation between Fairbanks and the Padre (Nigel de Brulier) in The Gaucho *(1927).*

top of the steps. Fairbanks mocks the principle of forgiveness when he snarls at the man he has beaten: "You can go. You don't know what you do." He smiles and with a swagger puts his hands on his hips, puffing the omnipresent cigarette all the while. "You see, Padre," he continues, "I get what I want—without the help of God and his Holy Book." Later he exercises this contempt for mercy by dismissing the leper from the banquet hall with the admonition: "You poison the very air we breathe. Go find some hidden spot and kill yourself."

Throughout the film the Gaucho seems to move in an atmosphere of magic and brimstone, a black-clad rebel fallen from Grace. The film conveys this in a number of ways, the most obvious of which is the episode of the leprosy. After he contracts the dread disease, he is prevented from killing himself only by the gentle words of the mistress of the shrine. She leads him to the healing waters and he immerses his hand. He emerges cured and, significantly, tests the cure by holding a lighted match under his hand. When first afflicted he had been able to hold a lighted match under the hand without feeling any pain. He had been, in effect, impervious to the flame just as he had been to laws and to religion. But now, cured, the flame painfully scorches his hand. The immortality of his defiance has been sacrificed to the mortal pain of his acceptance of religion. He is now able to practice his redemption in the Byronic tradition by overthrowing the corrupt society he has abjured. In this case it is the army of the usurper Ruiz. His final act is another kind of rebellion—a rebellion in that he overthrows a gang of thieves and rascals not that far removed in practice from his own band of robbers.

The Byronic hero had always seemed to be allied, somehow, with dark forces. Manfred is able to invoke the ghost of his beloved Astarte, and Conrad's success with the cutlass seems to imply darker agencies at work. This kind of hero has come to possess, over the years, a singularly superhuman prowess in combat, and it should be remembered that Nietszche first used the term "superman" with reference to Byron's heroes. Fairbanks' heroes are all supermen. By virtue of Fairbanks' own extraordinary physical powers and canny manipulation of the film medium, these heroes move about the landscape and manipulate it toward their will in a manner decidedly not ordinary. This is seen in Fairbanks' growing obsession toward weapons. From *Zorro* to *The Iron Mask* the heroes relied more and more upon devices like the bow and arrow, the sword, the whip, and the bola as his extensions. These acted like a magician's magic wand. With a gesture the whip would trip up the retreating villain, the bola would whirl forward and pin the rascal to a post. All of this gave the films a marked emphasis on combat and a magical implication too.

In addition to this *The Gaucho* implies the hero's association with dark forces by the constant preoccupation with rituals. Use of the device here emphasizes the importance of *process*. As Donald Sutherland points out, ritual is a baroque device:

> since it makes of an activity originally a means to an end an end in itself, thus converting a becoming into that much of a being, or, if it reenacts or commemorates a past event or myth, it both conducts power or divinity out of absent Being into present becoming—thus making of the Being not a closed and removed thing but a vital and immediate source—and at the same time consecrates or separates the present activity from the rest of passage.[7]

Thus in a film dominated by an almost mystic black and white—the confrontation between the lawless Gaucho and the sanctity of the Church—the employment of ritualistic devices is singularly appropriate. The Gaucho's every move seems like an incantation, an invocation to invisible powers. He moves like a priest not of light but of darkness.

One of the main visual metaphors in this ritualization is the cigarette. Here, it is the *process* of smoking that the Gaucho emphasizes. The very act begins to convey of itself a kind of demonic association or invocation. In almost every shot he is smoking lustily, smoke issuing in clouds from his mouth. When he talks to the gypsy girl there is a cloud of smoke constantly between them, as if the very atmosphere suddenly had become palpable. The Mephistopelian association is enhanced by such simple devices as having a puff of smoke preceed the Gaucho's appearance into a room like a satanic calling card. Watch for that puff of smoke—it presages extraordinary events every time. The Gaucho does not just light a cigarette. He has to go through an elaborate series of steps. He lights a new cigarette from the butt of the old one, puts the butt in the toe of his shoe and then kicks it away. Sometimes

Fairbanks and the gypsy girl, Lupe Valez, with the omnipresent cloud of smoke in The Gaucho.

one of his men will stand at a distance of six feet or so and throw a cigarette at him for him to catch between his teeth. Often he will rid himself of the cigarette by looking one direction while snapping it from the corner of his mouth in another. One writer has noted this, saying that

> every time he lights up he fights a duel with the match, subdues the cigarette before putting it between his lips and then has to reach round the back of his neck when removing the cigarette to exhale and put a wrestler's lock on it.[8]

Like any kind of ritual in the eyes of the uninitiated, all this seems most strange and bizarre to the viewer. And that is the point. The smoke and the strange gestures help to convey a demonic dimension to the Gaucho, a figure who seems to mock our understanding.

This very Byronic quality is further heightened by more rituals. The ritual is the very foundation for the magician just as it is for the priest. At times the Gaucho seems very much a magician, a magician, perhaps, who has dabbled a bit in the black arts. In the seemingly deserted tavern he casually reaches over the bar and produces in his fingers the ear of the bartender, the rest of his body following, as if he were a coin he had just plucked from the air. Immediately afterward the Gaucho lifts his glass in a toast with some companions. From the camera's placement behind the Gaucho's head we see his gaze swivel from one peasant to another, each jerk of his head causing them to look up in turn, like flowers blooming, one by one, toward a dark sun. Still later in the steaming, crowded tavern the Gaucho sits above the roisterers like a god of the Saturnalia. Above him a girl dances provocatively on a balcony railing. There is more magic as the Gaucho whirls his wide-brimmed hat up to her. It spins like a saucer as it floats upward, receives the rose from her outflung hand, and descends back down to the Gaucho's waiting hand. The magic becomes even more bizarre as in the scene where the Gaucho is preparing to move his band of robbers out of the mountains. He sits in a little hut with the gypsy girl. She reproaches him for not taking her with him. He reflects. Then, presto! more magic. "Throw ropes around the floor beams," he orders his men. "Hitch on a hundred horses, we take this place with us." And sure enough, the horsemen pull the entire house down the mountain path while the Gaucho and the girl dine merrily inside.

The sense of the ritual as movement and

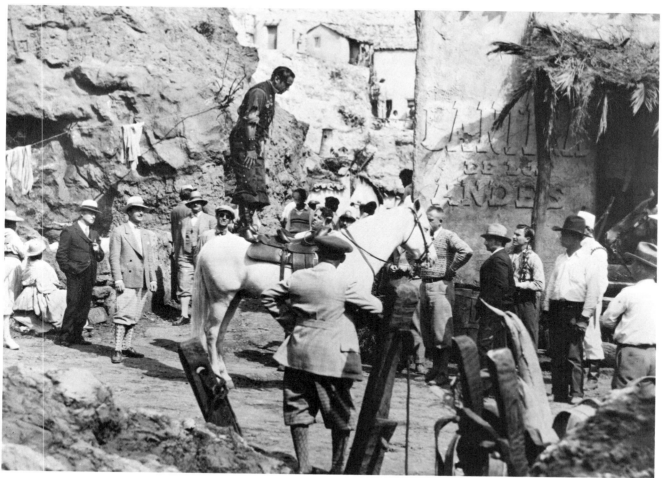

Production shot of Fairbanks rehearsing a scene from The Gaucho *(1927): Ritual as Movement.*

acrobatics is essential to the appreciation of every Fairbanks film. In *The Gaucho* it takes on a special meaning within the Byronic context of the demonic hero. In all of his films there are scenes wherein the acrobatics seem quite obligatory. We become not so much interested in where he is going, or from whence he comes, but in *how* he gets there. The straight line of movement has become embellished by the baroque curve. Suddenly it is preoccupation with process again, every movement achieving purpose and meaning of itself rather than in the larger context of dramatic function. Thus, these movements become rituals, in this case, functioning in conjunction with the use of the cigarette and the magic. One of the most beautiful scenes in the film (or in any of his films) occurs when the Gaucho has gone to outwit Ruiz and capture the city of the miracle. Up to this point the flamboyant acrobatics have functioned, more or less,

to outwit the pursuing soldiers and gain him access to Ruiz' chambers high above the street. But after this there is a scene wherein the Gaucho moves about a chamber, quite alone. He faces the camera, backs away, holsters his pistols, and jumps to the shaft of a spear where he looks over a partition. He holds himself stiffly away at arm's length from the shaft, swivels to look over the barrier. Releasing his grip he whirls into another room, transfers his pistols into his tunic, and waves his whip about him. Then he eases back onto a tabletop, lights a cigarette and flings the match away, holding the cigarette aloft for a precious, motionless second while he gazes out the window. Suddenly he picks up a nearby mug and flings it away, tossing the cigarette in the opposite direction. With an expansive flutter of his legs he twists off the table and exits from the frame. The sequence has no dramatic function whatsoever. It is, simply, beautiful to watch. Its sole justification, if it must have one, lies here. While someone else might just have walked about the room, Fairbanks transforms the simple act of getting from one place to another into a ritual, a graceful dance, utilizing the various objects at his disposal as a kind of counterpoint. Blake has said that Exuberance is Beauty. With Fairbanks, the sheer joy of movement gives this film some of its most beautiful moments.

This untrammeled sense of freedom echoes the essential lawlessness of the character. This is seen more clearly in the scenes where he seems to mock even gravity. In escaping from the jail he seems to fly up out of the ground. Seconds later he is seen moving through an aerial network of trees and vines, to all intents airborne. He runs and shinnies up a slanting palm trunk, leaps to a branch, swings out and down through space to another treetop, thence to a vine, slides down to another branch, and *runs* up another steeply inclined tree trunk. In another sequence he clambers up a series of awning railings, mounts and dismounts from a horse by turning flips over the saddle, and hops about the housetops of the city as he were treading a broad highway.

The demonic implications of the film itself are conveyed by a consistent use of the black-and-white palette. Tony Gaudio's photography ranges from the Technicolor opening sequence wherein we see the miracle of the shrine, to the black-and-white values of the world of the Gaucho himself. Fairbanks' costume is all black with spangles of ornament while his complexion and shock of hair is likewise dark. The Padre, on the other hand, displays white hair. Their confrontation on the steps seems to bring together in one cogent image the clash between black and white. The leper shrouded in black, known only as "the Black Doom," interrupts the merrymaking of the banquet and casts a pall over the bright festivities. The very atmosphere is suffused with darkness and a baroque style of shadow, as in the robber camp and the tavern. In fact, most of the film seems to occur in dark places, extending from the grotto of the shrine to the Gaucho's jail cell. In the night scenes the revelling figures throw huge, distorted shadows, while the burning torches seem to touch the very atmosphere into flame. By contrast, the city of the miracle is first seen as a dazzling, white, polished jewel of light. An intricate dolly shot slowly retreats and the city gradually expands in the frame like a blooming white flower. The abundant use of glass shots enhance the fancifulness of all the sets and backdrops, providing a painterly "feel" to the landscapes.

It is, then, because of the very things that many critics have objected to—the mocking of religion, the dark elements of leprosy and seduction and suicide, the seemingly arbitrary presence of acrobatics, even the religious conversion—that *The Gaucho* achieves a parallel with the Byronic tradition. One senses this direction in a number of other films, notable *The Mark of Zorro*, but it remained for *The Gaucho* to realize it to a fuller extent. As such, it seems a richer, more resonate film, an interesting filmic equivalent, for the most part, of a literary genre.

Finally, it must be admitted that the brooding pensiveness of a figure like Conrad is tempered in the more high-spirited Gaucho. The parallel between the Gaucho and the Byronic hero is weakest at this point. Yet it must be remembered that at one point the Gaucho suffers such a morbid turn of mood that he almost commits suicide. As for the religious conversion, one might think that Fairbanks is turning his back on the exhilarating lawlessness that marked the first three-fourths of the film. Yet as a result, movement and laughter are restored to him. We should remember Byron's words: "I am not one of your dolorous gentlemen: so now let us laugh again."

NOTES

1. Richard Schickel, *His Picture in The Papers* (New York: Charterhouse, 1973), p. 112.

2. Jacques Barzun, *The Energies of Art* (New York: Harper and Brothers, 1956), p. 53.

3. André Maurois, *Byron* (New York: D. Appleton and Co., 1930), p. 241.

4. Donald Sutherland, *On, Romanticism* (New York: New York University Press, 1971), pp. 255–256.

5. Vincent Starrett, *Buried Caesars* (Chicago: Covici-McGee Co., 1923), p. 7.

6. Jacques Barzun, *The Selected Letters of Lord Byron*, (ed.) from the Introduction, (New York: Farrar, Strauss and Cudahy, 1953), p. xi.

7. Donald Sutherland, *On, Romanticism*, p. 37.

8. Alexander Walker, *Stardom* (London: Michael Joseph, 1970), p. 115.

14

The Three Musketeers and *The Iron Mask*: Farewell to All That!

Alistair Cooke has characterized Douglas Fairbanks as a philosopher, an athlete, and a showman, and during the costume period Fairbanks continued to play all of these roles. But the image was changing as the man became older. The "Doug" that one generation had known, Cooke points out, disappeared after *The Nut,* his thirty-first film. The new image was described by the *New York Times* after the opening of *The Three Musketeers* in 1921: "It was a slightly heavier Fairbanks, with a businessman's moustache, who took the stage to express his thanks."[1] *The Three Musketeers,* the second of the costume films, was directed by Fred Niblo, who had also directed *The Mark of Zorro* the year before. In that film, it will be remembered, Fairbanks used a pasted on moustache as part of his Zorro disguise, but it was the clean-shaven Doug who satirized the foppishness of Don Diego. As we move deeper into the Twenties, Fairbanks becomes more the "swashbuckling costume-hero" (as Cooke describes him). Traces of the earlier comedian-

Doug in costume as D'Artagnan for The Three Musketeers *(1921). The mustache grown for this role Fairbanks was to retain for the rest of his life.*

satirist do linger on, however, though both the man and his times were changing.

In *The Three Musketeers*, Fairbanks again discovered the prime ingredients for popular success. Like *Zorro, Thief of Bagdad,* and *Robin Hood, Three Musketeers* was one of those popular costume vehicles that would be remade by succeeding generations, according to the taste and style of the times, but the original magic would never be quite duplicated. Ignoring the French *Trois Mousquetaires* (1953) and a British version made in 1951, one remembers at least three major American attempts to film this story. The version that was directed by George Sidney for MGM in 1948 with Gene Kelly (as D'Artagnan) and June Allyson (as Constance) was rather different in treatment and style from the 1921 film. It was

made in color and executied in a highly romantic and melodramatic style. The relationship between the lovers was idealized, their amorous rendezvous always accompanied by the romantic music of Tchaikovsky. As a corrective to this version is the radically different treatment of the recent Richard Lester film (20th-Century Fox, 1974), which amusingly attempts to blend slapstick and swashbuckling in a way that far exceeds anything that might be found in the original Fairbanks treatment.

The plot of *The Three Musketeers* is so familiar as not to require summary. Robert E. Sherwood, who was so impressed by the film that he judged Alexandre Dumas might have written the original in order "to provide a suitable story for Douglas Fairbanks to act in the movies," noted

"All for one, and one for all": Fairbanks as D'Artagnan with Athos (Leon Barry), Porthos (George Siegmann), and Aramis (Eugene Pallette) in The Three Musketeers.

It is remarkable how easily and convincingly this thirty-eight-year-old actor portrays the role of D'Artagnan, whose face fairly beams with provincial innocence and adolescent naiveté. Fairbanks' energy and exuberance certainly do not betray his age here, and even if he must share the action with a fairly large cast of interesting characters (in comparison, say, to the situation in *Zorro*), there are touches throughout the film that make it his own. For example, the "I smell a rat!" gesture of placing a finger alongside the nose is used to good comic effect here as D'Artagnan sees through the schemes of Milady de Winter late in the film. The swordplay is good from the tripartite challenge "Behind the Luxembourg" early on right through to the end. And there is some good acrobatic stunting. "Behind the Luxembourg," for example, Doug does an amazing somersault whereby he manages to stab a wounded foe by combining the stabbing thrust with his needed handspring. When he is summoned to the Cardinal's quarters just as he is about to leave for Calais with his colleagues to retrieve the Queen's diamond buckle, he makes one of his most impressive screen exits. One of the Cardinal's men has him covered from behind an arras, ready to shoot at the signal of the Cardinal's dropped handkerchief. But D'Artagnan happens to notice the pistol barrel. With a flourish of his sword, he skips out of the room, then slides down the bannister past the Cardinal's astonished guards. He is out of the Palace before they realize what has happened.

Fairbanks is the most diminutive of the four

one significant plot change—that Constance, D'Artagnan's beloved, "was no longer married to another man, was not characterized as the hero's mistress, and does not die at the end of the film as she did at the end of the book."[2] Of course, the death of Constance was later to be depicted in *The Iron Mask*. The change in her marital status was no doubt in deference to the morality of the times in which the film was made. (In Richard Lester's version, her poor, senile, cuckolded husband becomes the butt of a number of farcical gags. This degree of clowning would have been unthinkable in the Fairbanks treatment.)

The Three Musketeers is very important to the development of the Fairbanksian costume drama, because it represents the first attempt at lavish historical reenactment. The Old California presented in *The Mark of Zorro* is a small step in this direction, but a modest one, to be sure, in comparison to the Court of France. There is, then, an increased emphasis here on production values, which become increasingly more dominant as we move on toward *Robin Hood, Thief of Bagdad,* and *The Black Pirate.*

Doug dueling "Behind the Luxembourg" in The Three Musketeers.

Fairbanks, the most diminutive of the four comrades, expresses concern in Three Musketeers.

comrades, but when the four of them walk, united arm-in-arm, his gait has the most spring. Even in moments when danger cannot threaten him, his body is coiled for action. When it moves, it gives direction to his impetuous and constant restlessness. In this film, however, he succeeds as much by his wits as by his strength and agility. At Calais, for example, he easily boards the ship that carries Milady de Winter, who has by then recovered the diamond buckle the Queen so desperately needs. D'Artagnan catwalks the side of the ship and slips into her cabin as she sleeps. He cannot find the buckle, so he conceals himself and raps on a wooden cabinet. Milady, roused and thinking that someone is at her door, instinctively reaches for the buckle. Even though she attempts to keep it from him by depositing it within the safety of her cleavage (where *this*

D'Artagnan would not think of retrieving it), the wily Gascon wrenches it from her hand by *biting* it to make her release her grip! Later, in the Queen's chamber at Court, he avoids giving the buckle back to Milady de Winter when he recognizes his own teethmarks on the unidentified hand that reaches for it through the drapes. D'Artagnan, typically, makes a joke of the situation by giving Milady de Winter the empty case, then waits to deliver the buckle to the Queen in person. Not until Milady de Winter sees the Queen advancing toward the King does she realize that she has been duped.

But the pattern is a familiar one. As happens in so many of Doug's films, the bright, energetic "young" boy from the provinces quickly adapts to the machinations of a courtly and sophisticated society, then outwits the foremost politicians and

166

Doug, the young man from Gascony in Three Musketeers, *is presented with a sword.*

schemers in these high circles. In this respect, the distance from Gascony to Paris is no greater than the distance from "Mudero, Mexico" (or Denver, for that matter!) to New York.

Such films as *Zorro* and *The Three Musketeers* typify a trend that Vachel Lindsay had prophesied: "The Action Picture will be inevitable," Lindsay wrote, adding "Charlie Chaplin and Douglas Fairbanks have given complete department store examples of the method, especially Chaplin in the brilliantly constructed *Shoulder Arms,* and Fairbanks in his one great piece of acting, in *The Three Musketeers.*"[3] Acting ability, then, in conjunction with the charisma of his

Doug in action in The Three Musketeers: *"His one great piece of acting."*

screen *persona,* is still important, but despite Lindsay's judgment of Fairbanks' performance in this film, the presence of the costumed adventurer is subordinated, not only to the production values just noted, but also to the unfolding of the plot. *The Three Musketeers* is a very carefully scripted film, and much screen time is given over to the matter of court intrigue. The script is an effective one. The story is well told, and tension is created and sustained by visual metaphors, such as the chess game that emblemizes the machinations at court. But such business removes Fairbanks from the foreground, and even when he appears, he often has to share the action with his comrades-at-arms. The problem of keeping Fairbanks in the foreground is perhaps better solved in the sequel to *The Three Musketeers* made several years later, *The Iron Mask,* to which we must now turn.

The Iron Mask was begun as a silent film, but changing technology caught up with it—that is to say, sound came, and a spoken prologue and middle speaking section were to be inserted. Later, Fairbanks, Jr. rereleased the film, deleting the original titles and replacing them with a voice-over narration that had been written for him by Richard Llewellyn. The prologue is worth quoting here, for its rhyming cadences and romantic diction help to establish the atmosphere for this film:

. . . bear with me the while, your fancy to engage, to look upon another age, an age when on the human tide the plumed wave of chivalry rose to its summit, sweeping wide across a nation's mighty sea. France never showed a brighter power, than in this high, romantic hour, so come with me to France of old, to fiery days when hearts beat high, when blood was young and hate was bold, and sword crossed sword to do or die. For love and honor gloried then, and friendship reached its peak with men. Friends were friends in those brave days: Athos, Porthos, Aramis, I!—graved our hearts with the mystic phrase, bound out lives with the mystic tie! Come, stir your soul with our ringing call, of "All for One, and One for All! Come on! Come on!

As we have noted, this film, directed by Allan Dwan for United Artists in 1929, appears as the sequel to *The Three Musketeers,* to which it bears much in common, as might be expected. (The Lotta Woods scenario is based upon *The Three Musketeers, Twenty Years After,* and *The Man in the Iron Mask,* by Alexandre Dumas, *père.*) In both films the action is tied to an involved plot, and in

167

D'Artagnan slips away: Fairbanks in the foreground in Three Musketeers.

both, Fairbanks himself is not so central as one would like to see him be. Yet there is more of Fairbanks' D'Artagnan here than in *Three Musketeers*, where so much of the action is shared with Porthos, Athos, and Aremis. Even so, Fairbanks is still not so much in the spotlight as we find him in almost all of the other costume films. Perhaps it is partly a matter of age. We see him swagger, and we certainly see a fair amount of swordplay, and good swordplay at that. At the same time, we see fewer of the athletic stunts that give the figure its style in so many of the other costume adventures.

If the acrobatic stunts are generally few and far between here, one also misses the comic touches that characterize his more flamboyant days, even though there is humor now and then. But it is not so *active* as it once had been. When D'Artagnan is

summoned to rescue Constance, for example, we follow a servant into his quarters to find the four men sleeping in one huge bed, above which is described the motto "One for All, and All for One." (More cynical times are of course likely to find this perversely amusing in a way that was presumably not intended when the film was made.) Elsewhere, we see the four of them carousing at an inn, D'Artagnan skewering doughnuts on the end of his sword and, with the aid of a rather awkward and obvious cut, catching one of them in his mouth. These examples provide only hints of the old exuberance; moreover, they are not entirely consistent with the major movement of the film—a hero coming to grips with the realities of age and sorrow.

On the other hand, Fairbanks' dueling

"All for one, and one for All!" The second time around: Fairbanks with comrades Athos, (Leon Barry), Porthos (Stanley J. Sandford), and Aramis (Gino Corrado) in The Iron Mask *(1929).*

Fairbanks and friends carousing in The Iron Mask.

technique is greatly improved in this film, as is evidenced in the scene where he duels with the young king. We see him in this scene wearing a broad-belted coat with ruffled wrists and a sash from his throat—one of the few times he ever wore a costume in a movie that encircled the throat. (Fairbanks had a theory that a swashbuckling costume should leave the throat open, perhaps waived here for the sake of historical accuracy.) And, although not so frequent in this film, there are some notable athletic feats, as in the sequence where Fairbanks climbs a tree to leap out onto a balcony. Moreover, in one early scene when D'Artagnan courts Constance, we find a perfect example of Fairbanks' athletic kind of wooing, as he offers her his back to climb over a wall and carries her at arm's length to the carriage. Finally, the dueling scenes in the interior of the chateau are extremely well staged. The circular stairs divide the masses of combatants into discrete patterns of motion, and the cramped walls and ceilings serve to confine the action within the frame.

Allan Dwan earlier had directed Fairbanks in *Robin Hood* (1922), surely one of the best of the

Cardinal Richelieu (Nigel de Brulier) decides to disband the Musketeers.

costume films, despite its relatively slow pace. In *The Iron Mask* Dwan employed William Cameron Menzies (who had also worked on *Thief of Bagdad*) as Art Director, and Fairbanks himself enlisted the aid of Lawrence Irving, Henry Irving's son, to help with the set designs. So concerned was Fairbanks about the proper researching of the period for the film that he went to Paris and contracted with the Dumas illustrator Maurice Leloir to come to Hollywood for five months and do designs for the costumes and carriages.[4] Leloir had himself been a friend of Dumas *fils*, while Leloir's father had been a friend of Dumas *pére*. Much talent and expense, therefore, went into the creation of the "proper" atmosphere for this period piece.

The plot, however, creaks along with some monotony. The political background alone requires more than a little exposition. There are numerous factions at court. The villain here is DeRochefort (played by Ulrich Haupt) who seeks to play the King, Louis XIII, against Cardinal Richelieu (Nigel de Brulier). The political and structural complications derive from the birth of two sons, twins, both heirs, of course, to the throne of France. The firstborn is destined to become the Dauphin, the second Richelieu manages to smuggle out of the country. But not before De Rochefort manages to intercept Father Joseph's note to the Cardinal, which advises him of the birth of the twin heir. De Rochefort, banished, goes to Spain to groom the pretender so that he may ultimately usurp his brother. The Cardinal, sensitive to divisive factions, also breaks up the Musketeers, sending each into retirement

Fairbanks as D'Artagnan courting Constance (Marguerite de la Motte): An athletic kind of wooing.

in his home province. D'Artagnan, however, is asked to remain at court to serve as friend and tutor to the young king.

Constance (played by Marguerite de La Motte) is party to the secret. De Rochefort arranges to have her kidnapped, to be lodged at a convent under the keeping of Milady de Winter (Dorothy Revier). News of her kidnapping is brought to D'Artagnan, who, with the aid of his colleagues, goes to her rescue. To this point the plot has followed the predictable adventurous pattern, but the action then becomes very sinister. Just as D'Artagnan is about to rescue her—he is at the very gates of the convent—Constance discovers that Milady de Winter's shoulder bears the brand of a common criminal. Enraged, the lady stabs Constance and wounds her mortally just as the rescue is about to be completed. All Constance can utter of her secret is "the other one . . . ,"

these being the final words she speaks to D'Artagnan before she dies.

Thus, halfway through the film Fairbanks' D'Artagnan appears as a broken man. (One finds a similar turn of events in *Robin Hood*, but there the lady is not in fact dead.) He recovers, necessarily, to save his colleagues, who have taken the Lady de Winter to a common executioner (they, too, noticed the brand), who have since been captured by the Cardinal's men, and who now face a firing squad. D'Artagnan first rescues the Cardinal himself from a band of De Rochefort's thugs. (He holds them off as the Cardinal's carriage breaks into a gallop. As it passes him, he grabs the back of the carriage and swings aboard in a marvellous piece of stuntwork rare to this film.) Since he has saved the Cardinal, the Cardinal pardons his friends at the very last minute, but with the stipulation that they disband.

D'Artagnan and Constance in happier days in The Iron Mask.

Thus, midway through the film D'Artagnan has lost both the woman he loves (and, Romantic that he is, he cannot, of course, take another) and his brave and loyal comrades-at-arms. The emblem of an hourglass takes over at this point, as time passes and proves to be one of our hero's most formidable foes. There is a strange little prologue here to the second part of the film, in which D'Artagnan faces the camera, sword in hand, and promises the audience that the Musketeers will be reunited again. It is almost as though, having experienced already the traditional rescue-finale midway through the movie, the audience now needs assurance that more action will come as an incentive for staying.

Time defeats the Cardinal, who dies without divulging his secret of the second heir, not even to the trusted D'Artagnan. Half of a split dubloon he gives to the rightful heir, half to the tutor D'Artagnan, who himself remains at court until Louis XIV comes of age. Then he, too, goes into retirement, narrowly escaping a would-be assassin on the very night he leaves the court. For the conspiracy has begun. That night, also, De Rochefort makes the exchange, planting the evil halfwit brother in the King's bed chamber and giving the rightful, kidnapped heir a double prison sentence—seclusion in a remote tower, and the Iron Mask. But the resourceful prisoner scratches a message for help on a pewter plate and signs it with a tracing of his half of the coin. He pitches the plate from his tower window to a fisherman below, who sees it is intended for D'Artagnan and delivers it without hesitation or question.

D'Artagnan gets the message and is bewildered. He steals into the court. He finds a King whom he does not recognize—a King advised by the once-banished De Rochefort. Putting his finger to his nose, he signifies to the audience that he "smells a rat!" He immediately sends word to his comrades that France and their King once again need their swordly services. All that remains is the final rescue from the Tower and the restoration of the rightful King to his throne. But the price is dear.

From his younger days as an officer, D'Artagnan knows of a secret grotto that gives access to the guarded tower. He finds the underground passageway walled over, but, with the aid of Athos and Aramis, he breaks through the wall. They rescue the King, and Porthos arrives in time to help them hold off the tower guard. They go back to the passageway, but as they are leaving, Porthos is wounded by a pistolshot. He blows up the passageway (and himself) in order to allow his friends to escape.

On the way to Paris, they encounter De Rochefort and his men. Athos and Aramis hold them off and kill De Rochefort, but are themselves killed in the process. D'Artagnan takes the King on to the palace and arrives just in time to prevent the Queen Mother (Belle Bennett) from being poisoned by her evil son. Justice is done, and the pretender himself becomes the victim of the Iron Mask. But he manages to avenge himself on D'Artagnan. He stabs the Musketeer, wounding him mortally.

Not wanting to spoil the King's newfound happiness and knowing he will die, D'Artagnan steals away to a courtyard, falls, and dies. Then, amazingly, the jolly spectres of the Three Musketeers appear in the clouds and welcome the spirit of their fallen comrade D'Artagnan, who leaves his earthly prison and joins them in the skies. From their immortal perspective they view the shocked King and his retinue as D'Artagnan's body is discovered. They are at peace with the world, happy to be beyond the world's suffering, and secure in the knowledge that the valor of their deeds will survive them. This is one of the most eerie and moving evocations of the supernatural in the American cinema.

For a parallel to this incredible ending, one can turn to the conclusion of Chaucer's magnificent poem *Troilus and Criseyde,* when the spirit of the slain Troilus ascends to the "eighth sphere," and assumes a Boethian perspective on the pettiness of earthly things. Like Chaucer's Troilus, D'Artagnan views "this litel spot of erthe," this "wrecched world," and, like Troilus, as Chaucer has it:

D'Artagnan at court as tutor to the young King (William Bakewell) in Iron Mask.

And in hymself he lough [laughed] right at the wo[e]
Of [t]hem that wepten for his deth so faste.

Beyond this similarity, the situations are not exactly the same, to be sure (the Romantic D'Artagnan, for example, has not been so sorely disappointed in his love); but the ironic distance is created here in roughly the same way, and in either case the viewer or reader is surprisingly moved. Allan Dwan perhaps deserves credit for this successful touch, for he had handled similar elements sensitively in the earlier *Robin Hood.* But, surely, some of the credit must also go to Fairbanks himself.

This ghostly farewell is all the more affecting because it signifies an adieu to the most colorful stage of this supreme actor's cinema career. For never again are we to see him in the familiar costume roles, swashbuckling with the same vigor that had sent his star to its heights. Here was a man who had preserved his youthful image

Douglas Fairbanks as the mature D'Artagnan in The Iron Mask *(1929): Farewell to all that.*

Doug in 1921 as the young D'Artagnan, the immortal spirit that ascends to the heavens eight laters later in The Iron Mask.

longer than most could have done, and who was about to turn the corner. Technological changes in the cinema were clearly on the way, and his career, his popularity, and his personal life were soon all to be seriously altered. One doubts that he could have sensed all that was to come, but in retrospect the poignancy of his farewell here is something to behold. One might wish that the film's final title—"The Beginning"—might have held some truth. In fact, it was the beginning of the end.

Even so, audiences unaware of what was to happen are left with this romantic evocation that is voiced over the departure of D'Artagnan and his slain comrades:

Only remember us. Only open a little book and we shall always be with you, to ride a fine horse, or to cross a sharp blade, or carouse with a barrel, or dally with a maid. Come one, come all . . . Only think, and we live again, we live forever, for with us now is ever, one for all and all for one. Thus it was in France of old.

These words provide an extremely effective conclusion for the film.

NOTES

1. As quoted by Cooke, *Douglas Fairbanks: The Making of a Screen Character* (New York: Museum of Modern Art, 1940), p. 25.

2. As quoted by Richard Schickel, *His Picture in the Papers* (New York: Charterhouse, 1974), p. 74.

3. *The Art of the Moving Picture* (New York: Liveright, 1970), p. 44.

4. Leloir wrote a book about his experiences in Hollywood entitled *Mois cinq mois a Hollywood* (Paris: J. Peyronnet and Co., 1929). See also Bogdanovich, *Allan Dwan,* p. 82.

15
Love and Marriage: *The Taming of the Shrew*

In an Industry notorious for its superlatives, what may be said to constitute a "great" movie? The question is of course partly absurd, but it may nonetheless have some bearing upon the task currently at hand. We would like to suggest that Sam Taylor's adaptation of William Shakespeare's *The Taming of the Shrew* is, indeed, a "great" movie. It is not, let us hasten to add, a great adaptation of the play from which it derives. Yet, as an adaptation it is interesting, entertaining, and even useful, though it certainly changes the structure and meaning of the play and therefore is not very faithful to its original. Even so, much of the spirit of the original is successfully captured, to a degree that one need not conjure up the rather macabre image of the Bard revolving in his grave. A playwright who himself recognized the comic value of farcical action and who designed his own plays at least partly to accomodate the talents of the actors in his Company could reasonably be expected to understand the way in which this early talkie

Mary Pickford and Douglas Fairbanks together as Kate and Petruchio in The Taming of the Shrew *(1929). The spirit of Shakespeare was captured.*

transformed his perennially popular comedy into a dramatic vehicle for its two stellar principals.

Moreover, we are not suggesting that Sam Taylor's *Shrew* is great because of the quality of its acting (as least as one defines acting in the theatrical sense). No, the greatness of this film derives from its considerable charm—a rather vague quality, to be sure, and one in this case perhaps touched with nostalgia—and from the appealing vitality of the Hollywood personalities for whose talents the play has been molded. This statement may appear to be contradictory, but it is the astonishing screen presence of Mary Pickford and Douglas Fairbanks—who gloriously maintain their identities in spite of the exigencies of the text—that makes the movie an entertaining, if not always a critical, success. This is obviously not the only time a man-and-wife team of screen personalities has exploited Shakespeare's play. It is very important, however, in the precedent it established.

At first blush it would seem that Mary Pickford, "America's Sweetheart," was probably miscast as the shrewish Kate. In fact, she was to bring to the

Mary Pickford, "America's Sweetheart," as Shakespeare's Shrew, as we first see her in Sam Taylor's The Taming of the Shrew.

role a maturity of talent and inventiveness that had developed over years of experience. Miss Pickford has been considered the first great star of motion pictures. She recognized the potential of the cinema at a time when other "legitimate" actors were unwilling to do so. She started her screen career in 1909—before the movies had discovered either Charlie Chaplin or Lillian Gish, or *vice versa*[1]—working at the Biograph Studios, there to serve her apprenticeship under the Master, David Wark Griffith. By the time she was twenty, she had made nearly 150 films. By 1916 her popularity was established to the degree that Paramount Studios formed its Artcraft division, solely for the distribution of Pickford films.[2] Then, in 1919 (as we have seen), Miss Pickford, in conjunction with Douglas Fairbanks, Charlie Chaplin, and D. W. Griffith, set an historical precedent by joining together as the United Artists Corporation, giving them autonomy to an extent hitherto unknown over the mechanics of studio production and distribution. Her performance in *The Taming of the Shrew* therefore comes at the further end of her career. Four of her last five pictures were directed by Sam Taylor—*My Best Girl* (1927, with Buddy Rogers, "America's Boyfriend," who was later to become her husband, after she and Douglas Fairbanks had separated), *Coquette* and *The Taming of the Shrew* (both made in 1929), and *Kiki* (1931). The last motion picture she made before retiring to Pickfair was entitled *Secrets* and was directed by Frank Borzage in 1933.

In 1920 Mary Pickford and Douglas Fairbanks were married. According to Richard Griffith and Arthur Mayer, "The union of Doug, the all-American male, with Little Mary, America's Sweetheart, had a sentimental logic which thrilled the fans of both, which was nearly everybody."[3] Fairbanks as Petruchio is perfectly consistent with the flamboyant and swashbuckling image he so carefully cultivated during the Twenties, the great period of his costume films. As Petruchio, Fairbanks is a familiar character, the swashbuckling idol immediately recognizable to his fans. When we first see him, it is as though he has just stepped out of *The Black Pirate* (1926) or *The Thief of Bagdad* (1924)—his talents with the whip he had already demonstrated in *The Mark of Zorro* (1920) and in *Don Q.* (the "Son of Zorro," 1925). Yet, as is sometimes forgotten, Fairbanks was more than simply the swashbuckler *par excellence*. He was also a talented comedian in his own right, and the quality of his humor was often incongruously at odds with his heroic stance, ironically undercutting it. His Petruchio may at

Douglas Fairbanks as a swashbuckling Petruchio, here with Edwin Maxwell as Baptista in The Taming of the Shrew.

times seem highly stylized and perhaps a little peculiar, but he embraces the role with refreshing gusto, and plays it out with force and vitality. What the part lacks in terms of gymnastic opportunity, Fairbanks compensates by drawing upon his inner reserve of charm and humor.

Likewise, Mrs. Fairbanks also brought a store of comic talent to her interpretation of the **Shrew**. In typically laudatory terms, Kevin Brownlow has noted that:

Her films were almost always comedies. . . . The character of Mary Pickford was an endearing little spitfire. She was delightful; she projected warmth and charm, but she had the uncontrollable fire of the Irish. Whenever a situation got out of hand, she would not submit to self-pity. She would storm off and do some-

thing about it, often with hilariously disastrous results.[4]

And these general comments would seem to be consistent with her performance as Kate, particularly after the newly married couple arrives at Petruchio's country house. They may, as well, help to explain why the film situationally alters the play in order to give Kate the upper hand in a way that distorts Shakespeare's original design. Certainly she is spirited enough to meet the formidable task of coping with Petruchio, who outstrips her in brute strength, and whose whip is obviously longer. Her Kate is proud, arrogant, disdainful, incapable of giving in to self-pity, even when she is thrust into the mire with the swine. Significantly, therefore, she is not entirely intimidated by the Petruchio whom her husband represents.

Clearly, this movie is a tour-de-*farce,* but, even so, the farcical elements are well handled. This is, without question, an extremely competent studio film, impressively cinematic in its camera movement. At times the camera appears to be constantly on the move, to the point that its wandering seems imitative of the German Expressionist directors, and overdone in that it calls attention to itself. On further consideration, however, that movement proves to be functional, some of the long tracking shots serving, for example, to break the film up into sequences that roughly correspond to the traditional act-scene divisions.

Camera movement is also used for emphasis. Mary Pickford's first appearance in the film, dressed, as she is, in a dark gown trimmed with feathers, is unforgettable, but here, as frequently in the film, the effect is mainly the result of good timing and impressive camerawork. We have not yet seen her, but we sense her fiendish presence behind that door at the top of the staircase. Servants traverse the stairs, enter the room, and, after a horrendous bumping and crashing, come tumbling out of the door and down the stairs, landing in a jumbled heap. Then the camera moves up the stairs and through the door, surveying the disordered room before it slowly pans left to present a proud and angry Kate. She speaks no lines at this moment, nor does she need to. Her defiant attitude and the combination track and pan, slowed down for measured dramatic effect, provide sufficient commentary, with a visual eloquence that is typical of the silent cinema.

This rendering of Shakespeare brings together an impressive array of screen talent. The fluid and nearly flawless camerawork of Karl Struss has already been mentioned. The sets designed by William Cameron Menzies and Lawrence Irving are also impressive, as are the other accomplishments of their designers. Art director William Cameron Menzies is known especially for his work on a number of memorable films, including *The Thief of Bagdad* (1924, in which, it will be remembered, Fairbanks also starred), *The Eagle* (1925, Valentino's penultimate film), *Things to Come* (which he codirected for the Korda Studios in 1936), and, perhaps most significantly, *Gone With The Wind* (1939). Lawrence Irving had come to Hollywood in 1928 to work on another Sam Taylor/Douglas Fairbanks production, *The Man in the Iron Mask.* Consequently, the principal actors, the director, the art director, and the scene designer had all at one time previously worked together on films.

Before the "taming" and after the wedding. The sets were designed by William Cameron Menzies and Lawrence Irving.

Besides directing the film, Sam Taylor is credited with the screen adaptation of the play. The man's background is of more than passing interest here. Just as Frank Capra began his directing career as a gag writer at the Mack Sennett Studios, so Sam Taylor worked in Harold Lloyd's gag room before going on to direct one of Lloyd's best-remembered films, *The Freshman,* in 1925. He was Lloyd's favorite director, as the following testimony gives witness:

Of all the directors, Sam Taylor was the most valuable man I ever had. He was a tremendous help to me. He had a brilliant mind. He parted from me, amicably, because I had stopped producing for a while, and he went off and directed Pickford, Fairbanks, Bea Lillie, John Barrymore.[5]

A man so trained in the slapstick tradition of silent comedy would necessarily be expected to utilize that training and talent in his treatment of Shakespeare. One studio functionary is quoted as having admitted that they were making *The Taming of the Shrew,* but that they "were turning it into a comedy." Lawrence Irving, who tells that story, goes on to discuss the quality of Sam Taylor's comic inventiveness and "unsophisticated zeal" in rather disparaging terms:

> Day and night he was attended by two gagmen—rude, nonsensicals after the Bard's own heart—with faces like battered bantamweights an an inexhaustible fund of practical comicalities in the Mack Sennett tradition. Whenever dialogue that could not be cut tended to lag, or was reckoned incomprehensible to the ninepennies, they were called upon for a diversion. And here and there Sam, who was a secret dramatist, interpolated a line or two in the vernacular.[6]

Now this is all rather engaging and critical, to be sure, but, regardless of Irving's ironic reservations, the slapstick elements still seem to work well with audiences. There is nothing wrong in attempting to make a comedy as enjoyable as possible. Some of the gags are "classic" and archetypal, others rather vulgar and imitative. Gremio's dilemma as to what to do with an apple core in church, for example, and the comic repercussions of his solution, is very much like a gag that Buster Keaton used in one of his shorts, *Cops,* in 1922. In the Keaton situation, Buster is at a loss as to what to do with a set of false teeth. He pockets them and forgets them, only later to be reminded of what he has done when he sits on them and is bitten. The point here is, however, that *most* of Sam Taylor's gags are effectively funny.

Nevertheless, this kind of foolishness is added at the expense of Shakespearian material that is often altered, deleted, excised, and here the purist may find reason to protest. The Bianca subplot is present, for example, but compressed and diminished in importance, as is Bianca herself. The rival suitors Lucentio and Hortensio are compressed into a single character, Hortensio (played by Geoffrey Wardell), who poses as a combination tutor and music teacher, Litio, and who, accordingly, wins Bianca's heart. This secondary wooing, however, in the film takes on a decidedly ancillary importance. After the lute has been broken over his head, we quickly forget Hortensio. The romantic and sentimental dimensions of the subplot are subordinated to the farcical thrust of the main plot. Some may regret the absence of Shakespeare's Lucentio, but he is, after all, one of Shakespeare's glib and rather dull young lovers in the original, and one not quite so interesting as either Demetrius or Lysander, those all but interchangeable beaux in *Midsummer Night's Dream.* And since Hortensio is able to win

Bianca, the business with the rich widow is of course conveniently eliminated.

Because the original Hortensio and his lusty widow are removed, the last act of the play has to be compressed and redesigned for the film. Gremio (played by Joseph Cawthorn in the movie) is present, but his role is no longer exactly that of a comic rival suitor for Bianca's hand. Since we also see very little of Dorothy Jordan's Bianca, the relationship between Kate and her sister as a further means of explaining Kate's shrewishness in the Shakespearian original is all but gone in this adaptation.

Sam Taylor's *Shrew* is rich in visual humor. Petruchio's arrival at the wedding—reported action in the original text—and the wedding itself become central scenes in the film. Fairbanks in tatters on his swayback nag, a jackboot perched jauntily on his head, recalls his earlier portrayal of D'Artagnan in *The Three Musketeers* (1921). But the essence of the brazen character of Petruchio is perhaps best captured in the church when, while the marriage ceremony is being read, Fairbanks nonchalantly munches an apple, thwarting decorum and visibly shaking the priest as well as his bride-to-be, whose foot needs to be stomped in

Petruchio (Fairbanks) arrives, finally, for the wedding: A Shrew *that is rich in visual humor.*

Grumio (Clyde Cook) is spared a beating as Mary Pickford intercedes with his irascible master, Douglas Fairbanks, in The Taming of the Shrew.

order to prompt, almost involuntarily, her reluctant and painful "I do." Edwin Maxwell's Baptista Minola here, as elsewhere in the film, effectively conveys his sense of comic incredulity.

More reported action is translated into visual terms when we see Petruchio and Kate arriving at Petruchio's country estate. In the play Grumio tells Curtis (IV.i.) "how her horse fell, and under her horse . . . in how miry a place; how she was bemoiled . . . and how she waded through the dirt. . . ." In the film the action is slightly changed. Grumio is spared his beating (at that point), and the horse does not run away. Rather, as Petruchio attempts to tether his horse in his courtyard, he gives the bridle a tug, causing the horse to bold forward as Kate slides off its

hindquarters, landing upon her hindquarters in the mud, there to be nuzzled affectionately by a pig. Such horsing around and pratfalling may at first seem too physical, vulgar, and farcical, but the play itself invites this sort of treatment. The purist will no doubt object to the considerable loss of verbal humor; but few would argue that the knockabout additions which the film provides to compensate for this loss are not entertaining.

The poetry of this play, and the rather mechanical Bianca subplot, after all, hardly constitute the apotheosis of Shakespeare's comic art. Quite the contrary, Shakespeare's critics were once so embarrassed by the perfunctory nature of this subplot that they attempted to explain it away as the work of a presumed collaborator.

*Fairbanks as Petruchio announces to the wedding guests that
the newly married couple cannot stay for the wedding feast.*

Though specialists may now tend to give Shakespeare himself the credit (or the blame) for the entire play, the subplot may still be considered imitative, unduly complicated, and less than compellingly interesting. A longer film might have attempted to capture it (as Zeffirelli's does), but Taylor's abbreviated version does not appear to be extraordinarily flawed by its absence.

Still, there are other substantial alterations. Petruchio's lines at the end of IV.i. (spoken presumably in soliloquy) are so treated in the film as to change the design of the original. At this point in the play Petruchio tells the audience exactly what he plans to do in order to "curb her mad and headstrong humor." Sam Taylor "corrects" the awkwardness of this soliloquy in the film by having Petruchio return to the dining hall after he has taken Kate to her bridal chamber, in order to satisfy his own appetite. While at the

table he speaks the latter part of the soliloquy to his dog Troilus. The most significant change that occurs here is that Taylor has Kate leave her chamber and appear on the balcony above, so that she overhears Petruchio's lines and understands from that point forward exactly what he is up to. This eventual understanding, of course, is hinted in the play, but the whole thrust of this film is to render obvious that which is more subtly suggested in the original. The perceptive powers of the popular audience for whom this adaptation was designed were most certainly not taken for granted.

The action that follows IV.i. in the play is considerably shortened in the film. The treatment here is typical of Sam Taylor's approach. The verbal interplay and situational involvement of Shakespeare's comedy is simplified, replaced by physical and farcical action. The film, because

An ill-tempered Petruchio refuses to allow a hungry Kate to eat, as part of his design in The Taming of the Shrew.

of its earlier transformations, cannot present Kate and Petruchio's return trip to Padua when we find them encountering Vincentio in the play. The argument over whether the sun or moon is shining takes place in the bridal chamber and not on the road, hence, this show of submission can be presented without resorting to a separate sequence in the film.

Because Mary Pickford's shrew has overheard Petruchio outlining his plan to tame her, the whole idea of her "taming" is brought into question in a Taylor-made way that is much more obvious than Shakespeare ever suggested. Moreover, this movie version strongly implies the idea of equality in marriage. The interpolation of this contemporary attitude as Sam Taylor presents it would seem to be alien to the spirit of Shakespeare's play. Act V is redesigned out of necessity, since the film has eliminated many of the characters who are involved in the contest/ wager. Hence, the film moves rapidly to its conclusion after Kate has well nigh brained Petruchio with a stool that she flings at his head. After they are reconciled, there is a fadeout that moves us from the bridal chamber to Baptista's banquet, where Kate delivers most of her final speech on obedience, winking knowingly, however, at Bianca. And there the film ends, with a jovial drinking song that, obviously, is non-Shakespearian.

Some will perhaps have noticed that we have so far avoided the often-cited canard that has more or less permanently come to be associated with this film. We refer, of course, to the supposed

initial credit that presumably appeared when the sound version of the Fairbanks/Pickford *Shrew* was first released: "Written by William Shakespeare with additional dialogue by Sam Taylor." How presumptuous, how idiotic, how typical of the Hollywood booboisie mentality that stands behind this commercial product!—so goes the condescending attitude of the bemused intellectuals who may have heard of the film and consequently passed judgment upon it without having seen it. The latest authority to perpetuate this story is Roger Manvell in the third chapter of his recent book, *Shakespeare and the Film.* Dr. Manvell here depends upon the memory of Lawrence Irving, the codesigner for the film and Sir Henry Irving's grandson. "Lawrence Irving," he writes, "did his best to persuade Sam Taylor not to make himself a laughing-stock by insisting on his credit for 'additional dialogue,' but in vain."[7] And, without doubt, it *does* make a good story: "Well, I did write the stuff, didn't I?" was reputedly Sam Taylor's defense for taking the questionable "credit."

It will be noticed, however, that the print of Taylor's film now available from the Mary Pickford Corporation[8] tells us nothing about Sam Taylor's "additional dialogue," and presumably for good reason. According to *The Reader's Encyclopedia of Shakespeare*, "The story that the credits for this picture include the line 'Additional dialogue by Sam Taylor' is apocryphal; it began as a joke."[9] In an attempt to clarify these contradictory statements, we have consulted Robert Hamilton Ball, who is now himself doing research on Shakespeare films of the sound era, and is soon to publish the companion volume to his monumental *Shakespeare on Silent Film.* Professor Ball responded in the following words:

> As to the "Additional dialogue" story, I stick to my sentence in the *Reader's Encyclopedia of Shakespeare*. I knew Sam Taylor. He denied to me how it got started. Lawrence Irving refers to a period *before* the film was released, and I strongly suspect Taylor was pulling his leg. It is just possible that the credit appeared in early advertizing which Taylor did not see (nor have I), but I find no evidence whatever that it was on the film, and a good deal to confute the assumption that it was.[10]

Yet the story lives on, as legends are prone to do, and would seem to have influenced the later Zeffirelli version of the play. In the later film the scriptwriters admit that they would be "at a loss" without Shakespeare's lines,[11] indicating that they have not shared Sam Taylor's supposed temerity, and furthering the tradition of crediting jocularity.

An additional word needs to be said about the print of the 1929 *Taming of the Shrew* that is available from the Pickford Corporation. This print is a completely revised version. The revision, undertaken by Mr. Matty Kemp, involved first restoring the image to some semblance of its original quality, then attempting to bring the sound up to theater standards, wiping out all of the old music and sound effects and separating it from the dialogue. Mr. Kemp, whose description we have been paraphrasing, writes of the particular problems of sound restoration as follows:

> Fortunately, in the old days of sound, because of the few mixing channels they had to work with, music was used only for bridging. They seldom had music over dialogue—as in the case of the "Shrew." Therefore, I had a separate track made from the dialogue, which was transferred many times to get the maximum quality. Then I made an entire new musical score and built new sound effects, many of which augmented, or embellished the original. Then the picture was re-dubbed with the new tracks.[12]

Consequently, we are unable to see and hear *exactly* what audiences saw and heard in, say, December of 1929. Yet the sound quality of the dialogue is surely better than it was, thanks to Mr. Kemp's labors. Even so, the *quantity* of the dialogue is something of a disappointment, as one contemporary reviewer noted: "As it stands, Mr. Fairbanks's adaptation is merely a silent picture of the conventional pattern with the sub-titles spoken by the actors instead of being read by the audience."[13]

By comparison, Franco Zeffirelli's 1966 version demonstrates a much higher degree of verbal fidelity. In that film Zeffirelli himself coauthored the script with the aid of two experienced writers, Paul Dehn, a published British poet, whose original story for the film *Seven Days to Noon* won an Academy Award in 1952, and whose screenplay for *Orders to Kill* won a British Academy Award in 1958, and Suso Cecchi D'Amico, who wrote with Cesare Zavattini the scenario for the Academy Award winning neorealist masterpiece, *Bicycle Thief,* directed by Vittorio DeSica in 1948. Miss D'Amico at the time was considered Italy's foremost scenarist. Mr. Dehn, earlier in the decade, had scripted two very popular films—*Goldfinger,* and *The Spy Who Came in From the Cold.*

Yet, both adaptations take liberties with the text from the very beginning of the play by excising the Christopher Sly "Induction." Sam Taylor begins instead with a Punch-and-Judy show on the streets of Padua, while Zeffirelli begins by establishing an atmosphere of carnival madness, presenting images of mischief and misrule that seem to foreshadow his conception of Petruchio. And Zeffirelli, no less than Sam Taylor, allows additional comic business for cinematic effect—that chase scene across the rooftops, for example, that concludes with Richard Burton and Elizabeth Taylor's falling through the roof and landing in the woolstack below consumes seven minutes of screen time.

It is rather difficult to compare the central players of these two films. Needless to say, the play itself demands star talent. (Zeffirelli is said to have first envisioned Marcello Mastroianni and Sophia Loren in the feature roles.) The Douglas Fairbanks' Petruchio is far different from Richard Burton's. Fairbanks is certainly energetic enough, and delivers his lines credibly, though not quite with Burton's facility. But while the Fairbanks Petruchio is gentlemanly and more or less considerate (given the situation!), Burton's Petruchio is rough and churlish. His temperament is that of a drunken and mercenary boor. His country house is a shambles (in comparison to the *art nouveau* elegance of the country estate in the 1929 version), but of the two, Burton's Petruchio would seem the more likely to tame his Kate.

On the other hand, who would attempt to determine which is the prettiest Kate in Christendom? Yet even though the comic determination and stubbornness of Mary Pickford's performance is amusing in its own right, one is forced to conclude that Elizabeth Taylor probably gives us a more spiteful and convincing shrew.

In conclusion, we cannot say that this earlier *Shrew* is necessarily better or worse than the later Zeffirelli rendering, though the latter is certainly more complete. Neither is entirely successful as an adaptation, but, as movies, each has its strengths and weaknesses. As an entertaining vehicle, however, the Fairbanks/Pickford version can hardly be considered much inferior. Film critic and historian Paul Rotha wrote in 1930:

> Both Mr. and Mrs. Douglas Fairbanks are extremely serious about this film business. They realise their responsibility. They are both of extreme importance to the cinema. With Chaplin, Stroheim, and, to a lesser extent, Griffith, they are the outstanding figures of the American cinema. It would be wise not to

Mary Pickford as Kate and Douglas Fairbanks as Petruchio, with the longer whip. "They turned it into comedy."

underestimate the value of their work. They have separately and jointly given much that is good to the film.[14]

Taking Rotha seriously, we judge that their joint contribution to this film indeed provides "much that is good," and we certainly are not about to underestimate "the value of their work."

NOTES

1. Robert B. Cushman, *Tribute to Mary Pickford* (Washington: American Film Institute, 1970), p. 1.

2. *Ibid.*, p. 4.

3. *The Movies*, rev. edn. (New York: Simon & Schuster, 1970), p. 61.

4. *The Parade's Gone By* (New York: Alfred A. Knopf, 1969), p. 120.

5. As quoted by Kevin Brownlow, *The Parade's Gone By*, p. 468.

6. As quoted by Roger Manvell, *Shakespeare and the Film* (New York: Praeger, 1971), pp. 24–25.

7. *Ibid.*, p. 25.

8. Inquiries about the film should be addressed to Mr. Matty Kemp, Executive Director, Mary Pickford Corporation, 9350 Wilshire Boulevard, Beverly Hills, Calif., 90212.

9. O. J. Campbell and E. G. Quinn (eds.), (New York: Thomas Y. Crowell, 1966), p. 227.

10. Quoted with permission from a letter dated 25 May 1972.

11. Carey Harrison, "The Taming of the Shrew," *Sight and Sound,* 36 (Spring 1967), 97; reprinted in Charles W. Eckert, ed., *Focus on Shakespearean Films* (Englewood Cliffs: Prentice-Hall, 1972), pp. 159–160.

12. Quoted from a letter written from Mr. Matty Kemp to Mr. John C. Tibbetts, 18 February 1970.

13. Alexander Bakshy, "Films: Mostly 'For the Family,'" *The Nation,* 129, 25 December 1929, 784.

14. As quoted by David Robinson, *Hollywood in the Twenties* (New York: Zwemmer-Barnes, 1968), p. 145.

16
Turning the Corner: The Final Bow

*A*fter *The Taming of the Shrew,* Fairbanks' career takes another quirky turn, one, finally, that proves not to be so propitious. In fact, the star's greatest films are behind him by 1930, as he turns away from the costume dramas and attempts for awhile to rework some of the simpler formulas of his earlier years in Hollywood. Unfortunately, however, the times had changed, and the man had too. *Mr. Robinson Crusoe* provides a convenient example of what has gone wrong. This film is marked by an unbelievable posturing cuteness, as it depicts modern man coping with the wilderness, amazing savages with his inventiveness and technical know-how. There is much fluff and little substance here. The jokes are frequently hackneyed and overdone—unfunny business, for the most part, and, although Fairbanks' escape at the conclusion recalls the old Fairbanksian trajectories and is interesting in itself to watch, there is no escaping the fact that it is a long time coming. One may reasonably question whether or not it is worth the wait. Some of the failings of this film, moreover, are even more exaggerated in *Around the World in 80 Minutes.*

At the very end of his career we find *The Private Life of Don Juan,* which proved a more apt vehicle for the star whose light was fading, whose life had gone beyond the fantastic proportions of his

The final phase: Fairbanks as erstwhile swashbuckling hero and lover in The Private Life of Don Juan *(1934).*

Doug seated on a railing with the cast of Reaching for the Moon *(1931): His restlessness brought forth an urge to travel.*

screen image. But to understand the final phase of the screen career of Douglas Fairbanks, to watch him turn the corner before taking that final bow in *Don Juan*, we must consider some of these last films in detail.

REACHING FOR THE MOON

From December of 1930 to January of 1936, Fairbanks' life pursues a swiftly careering trajectory marked by one constant—travel. This is the single factor that unites his last films before *Private Life of Don Juan*. Fairbanks, Jr. named travel as the most important thing in Sr.'s life besides his work and home. His first sound film with dialogue, *Taming of the Shrew*, behind him, he left for Scotland and the Walker Cup golf tour-

nament, leaving Mary back at Pickfair. This move raised a good many eyebrows but it was only the first of several transcontinental jaunts to come. After making *Reaching for the Moon* (released on 21 February 1931), he set sail in January for big game hunting in Indochina, Siam, and India. He was in England by May for a reunion with Mary. This was the trip that provided most of the footage for *Around the World in Eighty Minutes*. In November 1931, he left for Europe, Africa, and Asia to make another travel picture, but changed his mind while in Paris and returned to Pickfair by Christmas. By January of 1932 he was abroad again, this time in the South Sea Islands where much of *Mr. Robinson Crusoe* was shot. He returned in May of that year, but turned right around and left in August on the S.S. *Chichibu Maru* to hunt long-haired tigers in Manchuria.

Doug hunting big game in Around the World in 80 Minutes *(1931).*

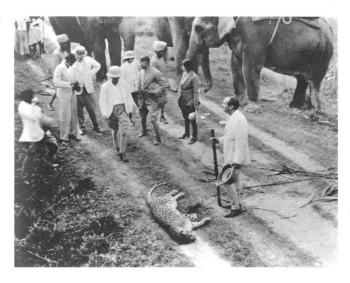

Another scene from Around the World. *Plans for a screenplay about China never materialized.*

The party was forbidden entry to Tibet to hunt the giant panda but managed to safari through Indochina. Plans for a screen play about China never materialized. He returned to Pickfair by Christmas, 1932. By February he was off to Europe with his son. Between this time and 1936 he spent much of his time in England and France.

In the light of all this it is perhaps no surprise that *Reaching for the Moon* has much of its action in the ocean liner *l'Amerique* bound for Europe. Mr. Larry Dacy's (Douglas Fairbanks) reason for taking the trip is solely in order to pursue a female, a motive apparent in subsequent events with Fairbanks' relationship with Lady Sylvia Ashley in England. It also marks Fairbanks' severing of the ties that bound him to the costume spectacles of the Twenties. It was the first film he made in modern dress since *The Nut* in 1921.

The public's expectations of the Fairbanks' persona as they had known it in the Twenties doubtless suffered something of a shock. Here is a fortyish (Fairbanks was forty-seven at this time) Wall Street business man, described as a "modern financial wizard," in pursuit of a conniving Vivian Benton (Bebe Daniels in blonde wig). The original conception was for the film to have been a musical, but all the numbers, save the "Lowdown" routine with Bing Crosby were cut out. Even Irving Berlin's theme music, "Reaching for the Moon," is heard only in the background. At the end we see Dacy suffering total financial losses in the Stock Market crash, only to discover that his feminine quarry is now only too willing to marry him. When we remember that she is a successful businesswoman, a sort of feminine Busby Berke-

ley, the marriage coming at this particular point seems especially propitious.

It is indeed an awkward film. Today, like most of Fairbanks last films, it is totally neglected. The main interest in it would seem to be the peculiar kind of tension the Fairbanksian persona generates in conflict with the plot and trappings of the film. His own style of free-swinging, all-American gusto grates harshly throughout. A Wall Street tycoon, our first meeting with him is when a dolly shot follows his swinging stride into a conference room. He is surrounded by associates and telephones, all the apparatus of big business. He shouts, "Bring me some cornflakes and milk—warm," and crunches away, talking about a variety of business and patriotic topics at a breathless pace. "One must impede this explosive urge," mutters an associate, who leaves because he is unable to get a word in edgewise. True, this explosive, testimonial side of Fairbanks' screen character is most discordant here. The youthful charm of the go-getter in the earlier Fairbanks "business" films, like *When the Clouds Roll By,* has been lost. Not only is the character now too old, but the whole attitude toward the working world is changed. He now looks as if he could really be a tycoon, whereas in some of the earlier films, he more than likely would have laughed at the whole prospect, perhaps climbing a tree instead. Indeed, *Reaching for the Moon* is more like a sequel to the 1917 version, or many of the little social comedies that usually ended with our hero settling down with the girl or being accepted into the business. One can see what has happened here. He has become part of "big business" now, and his business success belies the casual iconoclasm seen in the earlier films. When we realize that this is the same man fifteen years later, the prospect is not very attractive. We are willing to watch Fairbanks thumb his nose at the world and even jokingly settle down to business at the picture's end, but we are not willing to see the consequences, as we see them here.

Another major problem is the characterization of Fairbanks' butler Roger (Edward Everett Horton). Fairbanks always had butlers in his films. It rankled somewhat to see an idle gentleman with a servant at his behest. In this case, the relationship is even more awkward. Roger is apparently something of an elderly snoop or peeping Tom who habitually employs binoculars in his activities. He smirkingly informs his master that love might make his life "go boom." He then asks, "Do you ever dream of girls?"—to which Fairbanks replies, "Whenever I dream, it's about horses." (Apparently Larry has been so obsessed

Doug as Wall Street businessman, the swashbuckler as "financial wizard" in Reaching for the Moon *(1931).*

Holding a good man down: under the influence of "Angel's Breath," Doug displays "free-swinging, all-American gusto" in Reaching for the Moon.

Doug with Bebe Daniels in Reaching for the Moon, *looking like a real tycoon.*

Doug responds to the charms of Bebe Daniels in Reaching for the Moon.

with piling up millions, he has had no time for women.) To observe mature people indulging in such dialogue is to squirm at the spectacle of grown men behaving like little boys. In another scene Fairbanks has been smitten by the charms of Bebe Daniels and asks her to dine with him. We are to believe that he needs the advice of his faithful Roger in order to successfully make love. Roger demonstrates the proper techniques of hand-holding, and it is difficult to understand how anyone might find humor in that. His endeavors to help Larry's wooing are, as the *New York Times* pointed out (11 January 1931) "sometimes quite silly, and at other times reprehensible." Roger mixes a drink he calls "Angel's Breath." Although it only causes Vivian to be ill-tempered, its effects on Larry are spectacular. In short, the usually reliable Horton is much too cute here.

A major source of the awkward tension in this film is the utilization of the expected Fairbanksian acrobatics. Some of the fascinations of the early films were in the way he could turn a city into a gymnasium. At times it required a certain amount of ingenuity to allow Fairbanks his elbow room, but we realize that *Reaching for the Moon* has left no room for this sort of thing. Whereas the athletics shaped the early films, this film governs the athletics and the result is odd to say the least. The most obvious example has Fairbanks drinking down the "Angel's Breath" mixed by his butler and then going berserk. Apparently a completely arbitrary sequence, it seems to have been inserted merely to give Fairbanks an opportunity to dash about. He races about making inarticulate sounds, leaps up the stateroom wall and hangs from a ledge, dangling in simian style. He attacks the fiancé of Bebe Daniels in a

Another shot of Fairbanks and Bebe Daniels in Reaching for the Moon.

In Around the World in 80 Minutes *(1931) Doug wanted to couple his love of travel with moviemaking.*

series of jarring flying tackles. The ship's stewards try to restrain him but he climbs up the wall again and launches full upon them. The problem with all this is the gratuitous nature of the sequence. In addition we feel cheated to know that Larry has to take a drink to become airborne. The essence of the Fairbanksian character is its natural inclination toward flight. This athletic insertion here, while impressive—particularly for a man of forty-seven—denies this basic point.

With the possible exception of *Around the World in Eighty Minutes, Reaching for the Moon* survives today the most difficult of Fairbanks' films for modern audiences. The old gusto seems sadly out of joint with the context, the dialogue is weak and awkward, and even the athletics fail to satisfy due to their gratuitous use. Fairbanks in modern dress after an absence of eight years was a disappointing sequel.

AROUND THE WORLD IN EIGHTY MINUTES

"Except perhaps from a sociological point of view, it is a film of no importance," says Eileen Bowser in the Museum of Modern Art film notes of Fairbanks' next film, *Around the World in Eighty Minutes.* This is typical of the reaction accorded to Fairbanks' last films. This film, originally called just *Around the World with Douglas Fairbanks,* has, for its flaws, a great deal of interest—particularly for its revelation of the later years in Fairbanks' life.

Fairbanks had always been intrigued by the idea of coupling his love of travel with moviemaking. As early as 1916, he had plans for around-the-world filmmaking. By 1917 he reportedly was planning a tour of South America to do a few pictures in each of the big cities, then travel to Europe with a film company.[1] These plans never materialized. The pressures of his career with Artcraft, the demands upon him for the Liberty Bond drives during World War I, and the later formation of United Artists, left him no time save for pleasure trips to Russia, Paris, and England.

By the time sound came in, his friends, Osa and Martin Johnson had made several filmic records of their African safaris, notably the 1929 *Simba.* Equipment like longer lenses and the continuous zoom lens were employed by them for a new freedom in exterior and wildlife photography. Perhaps Fairbanks was impressed by efforts like this, perhaps he was only realizing a longstanding ambition, perhaps he was only bored with life in Hollywood and saw an opportunity of travelling and filmmaking at the same time—perhaps because of all of these reasons he decided to do a travelogue, a filmic record of one of his globe-trotting jaunts.

We have seen that his last years were restless, that he led a mobile life. The sense of movement that pervades his best films seemed to be now dominating his own life. In January of 1931 he set

191

In Around the World, *Doug, bored with Hollywood, films an African Safari.*

If he had remembered those words, the resulting *Around the World* would have been considerably better than it is. It was made at a modest cost of only $80,000 and could have led the way for others of its kind. Its failure seemed to spell doom for further efforts. The main complaint about it is the same one that can be directed against the Martin and Osa Johnson efforts, such as *Congorilla*. There is too much cuteness, both in the sound track and with the principal players. The wisecrack, the somewhat patronizing "great white father visiting the native" tone manages to deflate an otherwise arresting film. In the Fairbanks case the constant, sometimes insensitive narrative, supplied by Robert E. Sherwood, does little credit to the American abroad.

The film itself is a highly self-conscious kind of "day book," interspacing a weird blend of trick photography, location footage, and even at the end, a film-within-a-film kind of machinery.

He presents himself at the beginning by stepping out of a photograph. He is wearing business clothes and announces the following:

> I'd like to emphasize two things: First, that the world is essentially funny; it's a great place for laughs; it's also the dwelling place for magic; absolutely anything can happen. . . . Being a travelogue lecturer I must have a pointer . . . ."

He gestures with one hand and a golf club suddenly appears in his fist. He introduces his cameramen, Victor Fleming and Henry Sharp (who filmed many of his earlier features) and their equipage of luggage pops into the frame. The cruise is off and we have been prepared for nothing so much as a view of the world as a great playground.

As in *Reaching for the Moon*, Fairbanks loses no time in utilizing his ocean liner as a gymnasium. "Now I'm going to show you a few exercises by which you can get rid of all your ailments," he says. What follows is the first of several extended athletic trajectories to come in the film. Doug cavorts all about the ship, his voice-narration commenting as he flies along. He runs down corridors, up ladders and smokestacks, swings around poles ("now this is good for warts"), slides on his hands down stair railings (as he did in the opening of *Don Q.*), up ladders, over railings. It is one of his most successful trajectories, a clean line of movement that is beautiful to watch—quite gratuitous—but beautiful nonetheless. Immediately thereafter, he appears dressed only in a towel, and describes the isometric style of exercise. He reaches and pulls at invisible objects,

sail on a big-game hunting expedition to Cambodia, Siam, French Indochina and India. The trip reads like a picaresque *Innocents' Abroad.* Following the newspaper headlines, we are informed that on 27 March 1931, he killed a huge panther in India and was a guest of Her Highness, Maharanee Sahiba, Regent of the State of Cooch Pehar. On 3 April 1931, he was the guest of Manarajah of Patiala, one of the delegates of the London Round Table Conference. On 7 April he was the guest of the Viceroy, Lord Irwin, in Bombay, India, and so on.[2] Back from the Orient to London he finally returned to New York on 29 April 1931. By September he was off on a 15,000 mile air venture into the wilds of South America and the headwaters of the Amazon for new travelogue material.

Shortly before the release of the *Around the World* he was quoted as saying:

> I'm not a serious artist at all. In a world such as this to-day, the new fiction is reality. No imaginary story about China is as exciting as China itself. If I can get away with it, I am going to travel.[3]

Location footage from Around the World.

Doug and his camera as world travellers in Around the World.

Fairbanks in the South Seas. His next project was Mr.
Robinson Crusoe.

commenting, "You pull down the Woolworth Building like this . . . and you lean way over and lift up social conditions like this." It is almost like a reference to his athletic way of righting social conditions in the 1916 *Habit of Happiness*.

The first stop is Honolulu. As was his custom in real life he immediately sought out the reigning champion of a sport—in this case, surf boarding—and challenged him. It is "like riding Niagara rapids on a match," he says. Some stunning shots of divers off the ship's rail are interspersed with the action. We get an idea of the type of wisecrack that mars so much of the film as they cross the dateline. He drives golf balls off the ship and quips that some shark's going to catch that and think it is a codfish ball.

There is an extended sequence in Yokahama, where he describes Mt. Fujiama as "the world's largest bald spot." Doug pursues the thematic line

of golfing his way around the world: "One thing that appeals to me about the world is that you can play around it with a mashy—good courses everywhere." Later in a Geisha house we see a Geisha waking up, going through her morning toilette, including a tedious hair dressing: "No underclothes are worn," Doug comments, adding, "—I'm told." He says that after the maid has finished dressing, all she needs to complete her regalia is a license and a taillight. "Clever people, Japanese—they play it safe—they always make a bow *before* they do anything." A young girl runs after him to sign her autograph book. "Isn't she marvelous," he glows, at which point Fleming off screen threatens to "tell Mary."

It is clear by now what is happening, and this picture of the wisecracking American tourist is an uncomfortable one. Doug does not take anything seriously, commenting on the Chinese civil war:

"One day I wanted to play golf and was told that the course was being used for a battle." The world is seen only as a playground, and the patronizing tone rankles.

There follows in rapid succession a visit to Hongkong Harbor where there an interesting montage of the harbor, the beggars, the boats, and the clogged street traffic. Next is a visit to China's greatest actor, Dr. Me Long Fang and his family. In the Phillipines he visits General Aguinaldo who resisted the U.S. Army under Dewey. Then Fairbanks with his golf club appears standing on a giant floor map of the Orient. He demonstrates a chip shot that lands in Angkor and the film fades to the ruins of an old wall there with the comment: "These ruins are in a perfect state of preservation—like the Republican party;" at which point he begins a strenuous climb to the top. Later at the palace of the King of Siam, he dances the fox trot to a Siamese dance rhythm. Off to India and Calcutta where a swift montage follows of harbor shots, the Ganges, the cremation of Hindus, the custom of "well-jumping" down ninety foot shafts, and finally a big-game shoot with a Manarani after leopards. Fairbanks comments on this last in a satiric note:

Funny isn't it? We apparently assembled the entire population of Kush-Baha; we had the help of the Queen herself; she called in scientists, statesmen, generals; we set forth with innumerable followers of a battery of guns; and what did we get? Something to put on the floor for people to stumble over.

This last visit has a peculiar footnote. Fleming shoots a leopard that has broken from cover. The injured animal heads for a village and scatters the inhabitants. A dream sequence follows. The big cat drags off a man and Doug is off in hot pursuit. His rifle fails and, gritting his teeth, he chases it in another long trajectory sequence, an exhilarating series of leaps and vaults through the jungle, including a particularly spectacular torso twist from a tree limb up and over a large boulder. This is the closest the film comes to the kind of aerial wonders we have seen earlier in films like *The Gaucho* and, later, in *Mr. Robinson Crusoe*. The dream is interrupted when Fleming wakes him and he comments, "I dreamt I was Trader Horn."

Quoting McCauley's remark that history is a compound of fact and fancy the scene changes to the bazaars where they watch an Indian fakir putting a boy into a basket which he spears with knives. A magic rope appears which the boy

Fairbanks and His Girl Saturday (Maria Alba) in Mr. Robinson Crusoe.

climbs, gathering the length from beneath him as he climbs. The boy disappears. "How did you do it?" Doug asks. The response is, "The same way you did it in *The Thief of Bagdad!*" Then, Doug and Fleming climb aboard a carpet and are whisked away to complete their trip around the world, the trick device used in *The Thief*. The trip ends in this fashion with quick aerial shots of the world below them.

Probably the most interesting part of the film is the last sequence after the party has arrived back at Hollywood. The camera pulls back and we realize we are in a studio at United Artists, the boom mike, camera and rear screen behind the carpet very much in evidence. Doug and Fleming climb off the carpet setup and men swarm over the set. Fleming offers to end the picture and pulls the power switch. In the darkness a match flares and there is Doug illumined solely by the match. In offering farewell, he says he will explain the rope and carpet trick—but the match burns out.

On all counts it is an extraordinary film. Its detractors will point to the jarring, wisecracking tone, the image of the American traveller, the loose structure—with justification. On the other hand, the film pretends to be nothing more than it is—a kind of filmic diary, a home movie, actually. There is probably no more an accurate filmic record of the man than here. If that image itself is an uncomfortable one, we should remember that this was the twilight of his film career and the man was in the grip of a restlessness that would plague him until his death in 1939. Consequently, the film, considered as a

195

Douglas Fairbanks in Mr. Robinson Crusoe.

whole, is extremely fragmented. Its fleet course—touching a country here and a country there—is very much like the record of his travels during these years. Just about the only thematic unity in the film—of golf—suggests an accurate picture of the kinds of priorities in this man's life, a man who has lived long enough to see his ideals embraced by a public larger than that of any other star, save perhaps Pickford and Chaplin.

MR. ROBINSON CRUSOE

Mr. Robinson Crusoe might have been a good Fairbanks vehicle had it been made fifteen years earlier, for the formula at work here resembles the early precostume comedies. The idea is to take an American go-getter and drop into an exotic setting wherein he can prove his mettle and conquer the wilderness. We are asked to believe that Doug, on a bet, can bounce onto a South Sea island and, through his energy and inventiveness, transform that island into a sort of mechanical paradise, coping with the natives as necessary. This rather foolish updating of the Crusoe idea proves to be little more than an absurd paradigm of the American myth of success and initiative.

This movie, obviously intended as a one-man show, is feebly plotted. There is very little that can be established in the way of dramatic interest. The very situation that pits the intruding white man against the threatening dangers of a primitive society is itself clichéd. In *The Navigator*, made eight years earlier, Buster Keaton used a comparable idea at the end, saving himself and his girl from an army of cannibals. In Keaton's film, however, the contrived ending is even more absurd, but it occurs in a more cohesive context of absurdity.

Much of the first part of *Mr. Robinson Crusoe* concerns Doug's taming of the wilderness, turning the jungle into something approximating a suburban environment with street signs and an elaborate treehouse. Fully aware that his audience would expect a Crusoe to have his man Friday, Fairbanks gives us instead his girl Saturday, played by Maria Alba, whom he discovered during his travels. He then has to tinker and invent machines in order to impress her and, presumably, the audience as well. One of the central events of this film, for example, is the building of a radio, and this in itself demonstrates the script's paucity of ideas.

In *His Picture in the Papers* Richard Schickel supposes that Fairbanks may have made this film in order "to prove to his brother, who was

Production shot showing the tree-house set for Mr. Robinson Crusoe.

complaining about its drain on his finances, that his huge yacht should be regarded as a necessity, not a luxury." One hopes that a better rationale might explain the film, that it might have been

Fairbanks and "Saturday" (Maria Alba) ponder the radio in Crusoe.

made for other and better reasons. On the other hand, the reason that it attracted so little critical attention is fairly obvious. The genuine charm and exuberance that a younger Fairbanks might have brought to this task could have been sufficient to sustain the picture, perhaps, despite the weaknesses of its script. But as it stands, *Mr. Robinson Crusoe* appears to be little more than a curiosity, made during a disturbing and curious phase in Fairbanks' career.

THE PRIVATE LIFE OF DON JUAN

In the spring of 1933 Douglas Fairbanks and Doug, Jr. sailed for Europe amid a storm of controversy. Fairbanks, Sr. had in the opinion of the press "abdicated" his Hollywood throne. Rumors flew about a "divorce" in the offing with Mary Pickford. Fairbanks was reported to have remarked:

> Why don't I stay in Hollywood? Well, it probably wouldn't look well in print, but it bores me. That is the truth. Why should I spend my life in a narrow little village when there's a whole world to amuse myself in?[4]

He and Doug, Jr. were pictured as believing that they could get along without Hollywood and that Sr. would be happier working in England. The purpose for the trip was seen at first to be an attempt to form a British film company that would produce pictures rivalling American films. English newspapers and magazines openly rejoiced at having acquired his services and hinted that he would become a British citizen.[5] They announced plans for three pictures—one about

Douglas Fairbanks intimidates a native in Mr. Robinson Crusoe.

Fairbanks in costume again for The Private Life of Don Juan *(1934). He thought he would be happier working in England.*

Czar Peter III and Catherine of Russia, starring Doug, Jr.; one called *Exit Don Juan,* starring Doug, Sr.; and a third, a Zorro story, costarring them. Other rumors linked Sr.'s name with Lady Sylvia Ashley. She was the former Sylvia Hawks, a chorus girl who married Lord Anthony Ashley, son and heir of the Earl of Shaftsbury.

Events bore out at least some of these rumors. Doug, Jr. made *Catherine the Great* for Alexander Korda. Sr.'s business plans with Korda included discussing a partnership for him in United Artists. Korda wanted to secure American distribution for his films. United Artists had a large and costly distribution section but could not provide a sufficient number of pictures to cover the overhead. Korda and his London Films company might supply those needed pictures. It was Sr.'s idea to sponsor Korda's entrance into UA as a partner. Then on 1 January 1934, it was announced that Fairbanks had joined the board of London Films. From then until 1944 Korda and Sam Goldwyn attempted to buy out Fairbanks and his associates at UA, a move that was never consummated. *Exit Don Juan* was made at Elstree,

retitled *The Private Life of Don Juan,* and released on 30 November 1934. Plans for the projected Zorro collaboration never materialized, but there are some hints that Fairbanks considered producing a film called *The Californian* starring his son. This, too, never came about. As for the involvement between Fairbanks, Sr. and Lady Ashley, Mary Pickford filed suit for divorce on 8 December 1934, and the following February, Lord Ashley obtained a divorce from his wife. Fairbanks and Sylvia were married on 7 March 1936.

The Private Life of Don Juan was Fairbanks' last film. Alexander Korda had early displayed a penchant for the period film. His *Private Life of Henry VIII* had put his London Films company on its feet in 1933. In addition to the "Catherine" biography with Fairbanks, Jr., he also made in the Thirties, films like *The Scarlet Pimpernal, Rembrandt,* and *Four Feathers.* Perhaps it seemed natural, then, with Fairbanks at his service to make a film about Spain's fabulous and legendary Don Juan. The script was adapted from the play of a popular French author, Henri Bataille, by two writers long associated with Korda, Lajos Biro and Frederic Lonsdale. Biro had known Korda from his early days in Hungary. In the early Twenties he had left for America and Broadway and by 1926 he was under optional contract with Paramount and. later for First National. He scripted the first two Emil Jannings films, *The Way of All Flesh* and *The Last Command. Don Juan* was augmented with music by Ernst Toch and lyrics by Arthur Wimperis.

Fairbanks was eminently suitable for the production. The script called for a figure of middle age with a fabulous reputation of swashbuckling exploits already behind him. By the end of the film the Don was to tire of his strenuous and notorious activities and decide to go back as a faithful husband to his wife Dolores. The parallels between the movie role and Fairbanks are striking. Fairbanks was fifty at this time, his best years behind him. Despite a neatly trimmed beard and still athletic figure, he looks his age. His reputation as a swashbuckling character was well established and, as has been seen, mixed in later years with rumors of extramarital affairs. His efforts at reconciliation, like the Don's, had been a sometime thing, but, unlike the Don's, were to end in failure. Like the Don, his life was constantly echoed both in films and in the press until the public image threatened to overshadow the private one. Don Juan comes out of retirement and makes a return to Seville seeking his legendary self. Fairbanks came out of retirement to go

Douglas Fairbanks and his new bride, the former Lady Sylvia Ashley, as they arrive in New York on the Bremen, *14 January 1937.*

The script of Don Juan *called for a middle-aged man with a fabulous reputation of swashbuckling behind him. Douglas Fairbanks was perfect.*

to England to once again portray a romantic character.

The film opens in a flurry of fans, lace, and window lattices. It is night and Don Juan's cloaked shadow overspreads the balconies of Seville. Expectant, breathless women's faces yearn toward it. The shadow figure tosses a rose in a graceful gesture. But who casts that shadow? It seems the Don is being challenged by a rival, a younger man who by his own admission is after "the last trick—the mastery of women." The rival, a bumbler after all, is killed by an outraged husband. The news goes out—Don Juan is dead. The real Don Juan, meanwhile, hears the news and decides to attend his own funeral. He and Leporello sardonically observe the ceremonies while the women mourn The Great Lover's passing and the men celebrate. . . . Glad to seize this opportunity to go into retirement at last, the Don leaves for the country and in the guise of "Captain Mariano" strides down the morning stair of a little village inn, content to live the life of an anonymous bachelor. It is not long before restlessness sets in. When a book is published purporting to be the "Private Life of Don Juan" he scoffs at its excesses and at its popularity. Spurred on to resume his former activities, he attempts a series of seductions but no one pays much attention to him. He's too old, they say, to be Don Juan. Stung, he decides to return to Seville, home of his greatest triumphs and explode the myth of Don Juan's death. He has a much more difficult myth to contend with, however—Don Juan's life.

Back in Seville no one recognizes him. The only Don Juan anybody acknowledges is the hero of a dramatic piece, "The Love and Life of Don Juan," being rehearsed at the theater. Outraged, the Don interrupts an evening performance. He leaps onto the stage, shoulders the actors aside and proclaims to the astonished audience, "You're under the delusion Don Juan is dead. I'm the *real* Don Juan." But he is only arrested for disrupting the peace. Later, summoned before his wife he admits that at last he realizes he wants nothing more than to be her husband.

About the bare bones of this plot a broad cloak of fact and fancy is wrapped. There are a lot of "Don Juans" here, but perhaps the real one is seen only in the opening scenes—nothing but an enticing shadow upon a lady's balcony that tosses a rose. Everyone else is an imposter. Fairbanks' rival is a bumbling young man who can not even woo a young lady without falling off her trellis. Fairbanks himself is introduced as a character no longer young being admonished by

"You're under the delusion Don Juan is dead," Fairbanks explains to a startled audience.

his physician to cut down on his amorous pursuits. He prescribes a decreasing number of balconies to be climbed each week. Fairbanks soliloquizes on the virtues of rest and peace in his life and wants to retire to the country. The death of his rival gives him his chance to slip out of Seville, but it also marks the birth of the Don Juan legend. Nothing so enhances the Don's reputation as his death, and the amorous feats the people celebrate belong now to the more enduring realms of fantasy.

In self-exile as Captain Mariano, he seems to acknowledge for the first time that the shadow of his reputation is now something quite apart from the real man. As Mariano he is not recognized by the barmaid. He learns that she suffers his advances only because she wants some earrings Mariano can get her. Later a beautiful lady in a coach summons Mariano to visit her that night in her turret room. Ah! this is more like it! he thinks, only to learn that she looks upon him as a father figure and wants him to deliver a message to her lover. Even the aging proprietress of the inn sees in him only someone to share her old age with and help run the business.

Captain Mariano painfully realizes the real Don Juan is lost somewhere back in Seville and so he decides to return there and look for him. First he visits the last girl he kissed in Seville. *She'll* recognize him. He finds Antonia (Merle Oberon) grown more attractive to her many suitors because of her association with the late Don. "No," she says, confronting Mariano, "Don Juan is much taller and younger . . ." and pushes him out the door.

All of the imposter Don Juans finally meet in the center of the theater stage. Captain Mariano leaps onto the stage and yells, "Stop this foolery! Ladies and Gentlemen, the performance is over! I bid you a good night!" He pushes the performers, including the Don Juan character, off stage and strides about arguing with an audience that does not recognize him as Don Juan. The Don of the play retorts scornfully, "Yes, of course! This is the theater." The audience screams "We want to see the end of the play!" while Mariano wheels about toward the play's author and says, "You lied about my life."

The author in turn faces the audience, asking, "Do you care that much about Don Juan's real life and real character?"

"No!" they scream.

But, Mariano protests, the author has the Don Juan in the play make love to two women at once. That is impossible.

The author shrugs: "For you it is impossible, but to Don Juan . . ."

"Yes!" finishes the audience, a great open throat. One shout rises above the chorus and derides Mariano: "He couldn't even manage *one*;" at which point the author delivers the final stinging blow to Mariano: "That's how much *you* know about being Don Juan."

The gulf is clearly impassable now between Mariano and his former identity of Don Juan. Even he is an imposter. The separation is made final when he is dragged away from the stage set, his own wife's rebuking words ringing in his ears: "No, there is a likeness . . . but my poor husband was so much bigger, and broader, and better looking . . ."

Smiling wryly and a bit sadly, Mariano is dragged away. This confrontation between man and legend is the central setpiece of this film and one of the key scenes in all of his films. Many critics have seen the moving climax to the 1928 *The Iron Mask* as Fairbanks' farewell to the kind of role that had made him famous. When the ghostly figures of Athos, Porthos, and Aramis, reach down from the clouds to lift up the fallen D'Artagnan, it is as if this world were no longer suitable for the larger-than-life Fairbanksian persona. But, as D'Artagnan, he joyfully rejoins his comrades for greater adventure beyond. In *Don Juan* he is forcibly removed from the stage to a prosaic existence of meek husband. His visit to his wife in the final scenes is a travesty of the classic Don Juan wooing style. Rather than surmounting his balcony with agile leaps and handholds, he merely climbs a rope ladder. Instead of seducing a maiden he is seducing his own wife. In other

Fairbanks in Don Juan *portrays a man undone by his legend. Here he is asked merely to be an emissary.*

words the Don, after being forcibly ejected from the theatrical conventions of the stage set, is reduced to a common life.

Don Juan's legend has in effect destroyed the young imposter and Captain Mariano. The legend, once created, took on an independent life and turned about and destroyed the creator, with whom all resemblance had been lost. It is the tragedy of Fairbanks' own life, too. Fairbanks' career had been founded upon the precepts of movement and youth. It was Samuel Johnson who said that men and dogs grew worse as they grew older. And age was rapidly corroding the man who had raised such a monument to youth. If, like Don Juan, Fairbanks could be said to have left a legend behind him—in this case his films— then it began to haunt his last years with their persistent reminders of a youth that was gone forever. It is possible that no one would have identified the aging Fairbanks with the dashing figure in his vintage films, just as no one related Captain Mariano to the Don Juan legend. It is a situation that the film celebrity was acutely aware of. His was the unique fate of having his youth preserved for posterity's eyes while his last years were haunted by it.

202

Paul Tabori, in his book on Alexander Korda, says that the main flaw in *The Private Life of Don Juan* is its casting of Fairbanks as Don Juan:

> Douglas Fairbanks, Sr. had triumphed in many a swashbuckling action-packed picture. But here he had to do a great deal more than vault over balustrades, climb balconies or fight duels. His rasping voice with the strong American accent was incongruous and unsuitable for the suave Spanish lover.[6]

Tabori obviously has not noted the many parallels under discussion that make Fairbanks the ideal choice for the role. He also seems to forget that this is not really a picture of Don Juan at all, but of his imposters. It is a *modern* account, rendering Fairbanks' accent a useful asset after all. But strongest in Fairbanks' favor is the powerful visual impact that he makes, particularly in the frustrated seduction scene by the castle tower midway in the picture, and in the unforgettable confrontation and farewell of the stage scene near the end.

In the first scene, Captain Mariano has been mysteriously summoned to the tower room of a lovely girl. Sure that his Don Juanish aspect is still intact he confidently repairs to the tower wall. It is a beautiful scene. His expectations are high and he happily strides through the night, a rope slung over one shoulder. Soft music attends on the soundtrack. He lithely unslings the rope from his torso and casts up one end over the tower parapet. Nimbly in the hushed stillness he climbs the rope, hand over hand, to the lady's bower. What follows is an effective counterbalance to this romanticized imagery. The lady merely needs his services as a messenger and frankly regards him solely as a father figure. His indignant return home is further attended by a soaking downpour that gives him a sneezing cold. The disparity between legend and cold reality that drives the entire film is seen here in just a few minutes.

In the stage confrontation Fairbanks appears dressed in black with a broad-brimmed hat. He swirls through the lace and finery of the stage actors like a dark wind upsetting a shelf of china. He stamps his boots at the lace-bound actors and they give way. He whirls his broad-brimmed hat about, scattering them. It is the sort of thing that Fairbanks did best—present a kind of disruption, scattering proprieties and finery right and left. One review at the time particularly noted this:

> . . . for whatever you think of his calisthenics, the man has a certain rank swagger and grace: with a cape and go-to-hell hat and a clear hip line, he is fine costume material. Here he fits nicely into a picture that suggests a phenomenon peculiar to the medium, namely that of a background's coming to life, coming to mean something, getting its own mood into the audience.[7]

This scene leaves a strong impression and even catches overtones that harken back to the Don Juan legend of works like *Don Giovanni*, as when the prompter from his box below Fairbanks scowls noisily at him, providing the impression of the Devil calling to the Don from Hell.

The third sequence is easily the visual highlight of the film—Don Juan's funeral. Don Juan and Leporello attend the funeral of the slain rival and wander about collecting impressions of the proceedings. The whole sequence seems bathed in an unearthly white light. The rough stones, walls, and equestrian statues heave dark shapes against the dazzling sky. Juan and Leporello stride about, wrapped in dark cloaks, their images burning themselves into the white walls. There is a strange buoyancy to all of this. The people move in dark masses up the stone steps, the women wailing in bereavement, the men chuckling in relief. The bells toll, a choir of voices moans, and a strong wind whips the Don's cloak about his shoulders. Altogether, it is a chilling, beautiful sequence, deriving much of its strength from the clean designs of blacks cutting into vivid whites, and the strength and grace of Fairbanks as he makes his way through the funeral procession.

Taken altogether *The Private Life of Don Juan* functions more as an inquiry into the modern status of Don Juan. His imposters include the young bumbler killed in the duel, the figure on the theatrical stage, Captain Mariano, and even Fairbanks himself. The classic figure seen in the Tirso de Molino play, the Mozart/Da Ponte opera, *Don Giovanni*, the Moliére play has shrunk here to the dimensions of a man smaller than the shadow he casts. The classic Juan was a rebel who defied Hell and damnation, whose pursuit of women flaunted the tradition of courtly love. His attitude toward women was neatly expressed by Da Ponte in these words:

> It's all for love . . .
> The man who's faithful to one alone
> Is cruel to all the others;
> I, who experience
> A sentiment so extensive,
> Love all and sundry.
> However, women, who don't know
> How to estimate my good disposition,
> Call it deceit.

Fairbanks in costume for Don Juan, *fifty years old at the time.*

The modern figure as seen in this film and Shaw's *Man and Superman,* is instead subjugated to conventions and women. Jack Tanner is conquered by Miss Anne Whitefield and Fairbanks is captured by his marriage to Dolores. As Henry Grunwald has pointed out, the Don today is in a predicament of psychology. We understand him now as we might approach a case history. The psychoanalyst would try to limit the riot of Juan's libido to reasonable proportions, condemning the Don not to damnation or even defiance, but merely to mediocrity. The Don's plight today, as we can infer from the film, is due to:

> . . . the decline of aristocracy, the new status of women, the weakening both of convention and of religion that leaves a rebel so much less to rebel against, the fading of the supernatural, and the cult of psychology, which makes excess no longer a sin but merely a disease.[8]

Another modern look at the Don should be mentioned, Max Frisch's *Don Juan And The Love of Geometry,* which shows the weary Don staging his own death and retiring to the countryside with his wife. The implication is that a modern version of the Don's private hell is marriage, the Don's acceptance of the woman in his life, or, more importantly, his subjugation to a convention in society, in this case the exclusivity of marriage.

All these modern bathetic elements are seen in the film. Don Juan is an aging and weary man, unrecognizable in the giant shadow of his legend, condemned to saying to Dolores, "Don Juan is dead. I don't want to be anything but your husband." The woman he speaks to is stronger than he. He admits this to her, saying it is because of her intelligence—an intelligence that strips a man of his power until he becomes "just a husband." Where are the ringing words of Moliére's Don who can say in the face of damnation, "Nothing can frighten me . . . come what

may, it shall never be said that I am the repenting sort." No, this Don Juan is in a world that demands repentance. His origins, the birth of his legend, are commented on succinctly by Captain Mariano when he speaks of the author of a book circulating in Spain called *The Private Life of Don Juan*: "If he couldn't make me a hero he wouldn't write it; if he didn't make a cad he couldn't sell it." Don Juan is now a mercantile product wherein his heroism is equated with his villainy. During a rehearsal of the stage play about Don Juan the lady sighs dreamily about "inhaling his breath," and is interrupted by the comment, "indeed, shouldn't he gargle at breakfast?"

The film is capped by the final scene wherein Captain Mariano is accepted back into his wife's arms. He makes a stab at saying all the words and phrases that won him so many embraces over the years. But they are empty now. Dolores merely answers, "Every woman wants more than just a husband, every woman wants Don Juan, all to herself." This presages Max Frisch's ironic picture of Don Juan in Hell. We cannot help but wince at this domestication. Our only consolation is the memory of the graceful shadow of the Don seen in the film's opening scene, a shadow cast by a figure that, after all, is never seen in the frame.

NOTES

1. *Picture Play Magazine* (September 1916), p. 123.
2. "The Headline Career of Mary and Doug," *Motion Picture Classic* (March 1933), p. 68.
3. *Ibid.*
4. "How Can Doug Stay Away from Hollywood?" *Motion Picture Magazine* (February 1934), p. 82.
5. *Ibid.*
6. Paul Tabori, *Alexander Korda* (New York: Living Books, 1966), p. 156.
7. *The New Republic* (9 January 1935), p. 246.
8. Henry Anatole Grunwald, "The Disappearance of Don Juan," *Horizon* (January 1962), Vol. IV, No. 3.

The Swashbuckler-Adventurer.

Epilogue

After 1934 and The Private Life of Don Juan, Douglas Fairbanks seemed to stumble and falter, both in his career and in his private life. From that point forward until his death in 1939, his life traced an increasingly restless and erratic trajectory. His marriage to Mary Pickford was clearly failing. His restlessness, her own fading career were both factors in the final breakup. It was apparent that he was seeking romantic involvements outside the marriage, and in 1934 he was named co-respondent in a divorce suit filed in London by Lord Ashley. By the time Fairbanks' own divorce with Mary Pickford was finalized and by the time he took Lady Ashley for his third wife, his film career was finished.

The outlet of motion picture production no longer seemed feasible for this restless, ageing man. At best he could concentrate only on projects for Douglas, Jr., and in only one or two of them could he envision appearing himself. Although these projects were all abortive, they are interesting indicators of the direction of his mind. They were all to be historical subjects concerning men of action. The kind of film that Fairbanks had done better than anyone else was to be passed on to the next generation. These projects included the story of Lord Byron in Venice and another spectacular venture dealing with the life of Alexander the Great and his father, Philip of Macedon.

Two of his projects came close to realization. One of these was the filming of *Marco Polo.* Plans to make it with Samuel Goldwyn fell through, however, when the title role went to Gary Cooper instead of Douglas, Jr. The other was a project called *The Californian.* As Fairbanks, Jr. recalls:

My father commissioned some draft synopses to be written and these are still sitting on the shelf or in files. No complete shooting script was ever made. It was a story based upon a true episode in the life of a well-known 19th century outlaw who had a brief romance with Lola Montez. It was an original idea of my father's augmented by ideas of other friends and associates and, I dare say, I contributed one or two thoughts to it myself at the time.*

One of the collaborators must have been Johnston McCulley, who had been associated with Fairbanks since the days of *The Mark of Zorro.* In 1936, shortly before Fairbanks began actively pursuing the idea of *The Californian,* McCulley wrote a book called *The Caballero* which bears some similarities to the sort of idea Sr. was considering. At any rate, the idea of Sr. as producer and Jr. as star never came to pass.

Fairbanks said on several occasions that he could not stand the idea of his becoming an invalid. When he died in 1939, he was fifty-six years old, having suffered only minor discomforts from circulatory ailments. It was a merci-

---

* Recalled in a letter from Douglas Fairbanks, Jr. to John Tibbetts, 19 August 1974.

fully quick conclusion to a lifetime that had founded itself upon the transience of youth and health. Many words have been written describing the, at times, almost pathetic circumstances of his last few years—the declining health, the desperate attempts to maintain travel and social schedules, the inability to find satisfaction and fulfillment any more in his work. And it is true enough that Fairbanks lived long enough to feel many regrets and to sense that a life founded upon the precepts of youth was behind him. In his case, the final irony, bordering upon tragedy, was that his vanished youth was not allowed to pass gracefully away, but mocked him continually on the motion picture screen, where it was recorded forever on celluloid—glimpses of cosmetic immortality.

Yet, there is in Fairbanks' life something poignantly reminiscent of the Peter Pan. When in motion, when doing the thing he did best, Fairbanks achieved a timeless quality in his work. The true nature of the man is not seen in these last years, nor should it be sought for there. The real man is somewhere else, captured in a kind of flight that informs so many of his finest films. Like another Peter Pan character, Tommy Sandys in James Barrie's novel *Tommy and Grizel,* who laments his faults and his reluctance to grow up, Fairbanks could say at the end: "I believe I am a rather fine fellow when I am flying!"

Douglas Fairbanks as his fans may wish to remember him, as legendary swashbuckler and lover in his last film, The Private Life of Don Juan *(1934).*

Appendix:
A Fairbanks Filmography

The information that follows was collated from many sources, but De Witt Bodeen's "Douglas Fairbanks Filmography" was frequently used, especially for the early works, as was, of course, Kenneth W. Munden's *American Film Institute Catalog of Motion Pictures Produced in the United States: Feature Films, 1921–1930*. Also consulted were the "Chronology" in Alistair Cooke's *Douglas Fairbanks: The Making of a Screen Character*, Denis Gifford's *The British Film Catalogue, 1895–1970* (especially useful for acting credits in *The Private Life of Don Juan*), and "Dwan's Career Filmography" in Peter Bogdanovich's *Allan Dwan: The Last Pioneer*. Cameo appearances, such as the one Fairbanks makes in King Vidor's *Show People* (1928), are not listed here. Some selected reviews are cited for the early films. An "F2" entry number indicates that the film is listed in *The AFI Catalog*.

The Lamb

Directed by W. Christy Cabanne (Supv. D. W. Griffith). Released 23 September 1915, Triangle/Fine Arts, Five reels. Photography Wm. E. Fildew (Supv. G. W. Bitzer). Scenario: W. Christy Cabanne, from a D. W. Griffith story, "The Man and the Test."
Cast: D. Fairbanks (Gerald); Seena Owen (Mary); Lillian Langdon; Monroe Salisbury; Kate Toncray; Alfred Paget. Reviewed: *Variety* (24 Sept. 1915).

Double Trouble

Directed by W. Christy Cabanne (Supv. D. W. Griffith). Released 5 December 1915, Triangle/Fine Arts, Five reels. Photography: Wm. E. Fildew.

Scenario: D. W. Griffith, from W. Christy Cabanne's adaptation of a novel by Herbert Quick.
Cast: D. Fairbanks (Mr. Amidon/Mr. Brassfield); Margery Wilson (Fiancee); Tom Kennedy (Judge Blodgett); Gladys Brockwell; Olga Grey; Kate Toncray; Monroe Salisbury. Reviewed: *Motography* (13 Dec. 1915), p. 1030.

His Picture in the Papers

Directed by John Emerson (Supv. D. W. Griffith). Released 10 Feb. 1916, Triangle/Fine Arts, Five reels. Scenario by John Emerson and Anita Loos.
Cast: D. Fairbanks (Pete Prindle); Loretta Blake (Christine Cadwalader); Clarence Handyside (Proteus Prindle). Reviewed: *The Theater* (Feb. 1916), p. 62.

The Habit of Happiness

Directed by Allan Dwan (Supv. D. W. Griffith). Released 13 March 1916, Triangle/Fine Arts, Five reels. Scenario by Shannon Fife and Allan Dwan (from an idea by D. W. Griffith).
Cast: D. Fairbanks ("Sunny" Wiggins); Dorothy West (Elsie Pepper); George Fawcett (Jonathan Pepper); George Backus (Mr. Wiggins); Grace Rankin (Clarice Wiggins); Macey Harlan (Foster); William Jefferson (Jones).

The Good Bad Man

Directed by Allan Dwan (Supv. D. W. Griffith). Released 13 April 1916, Triangle/Mutual, Five reels.

Scenario by Douglas Fairbanks. Photography: Victor Fleming.

Cast: D. Fairbanks ("Passin' Thru"); Bessie Love (Amy); Sam de Grasse (Bud Frazer); Joe Singleton (Amy's father); Mary Alden ("Passin's" mother); Geo. Baranger; Pomeroy Cannon; Fred Burns. Reviewed: *Variety* (14 April 1916), p. 25.

Reggie Mixes In

Directed by W. Christy Cabanne (Supv. D. W. Griffith). Released 28 May 1916, Triangle/Fine Arts, Five reels. Photography: Wm. E. Fildew. Scenario by Roy Somerville.

Cast: D. Fairbanks (Reginald Morton); Bessie Love (Agnes Shannon); Frank Bennett (cafe proprietor's assistant); Joseph Singleton (Reggie's valet); W. E. Lowery (Tony Bernard). Reviewed: *New York Times* (29 May 1916), p. 9; *Variety* (2 June 1916), p. 16.

Flirting with Fate

Directed by W. Christy Cabanne (Supv. D. W. Griffith). Released 25 June 1916, Triangle/Fine Arts, Five reels. Photography: Wm. E. Fildew. Scenario by W. Christy Cabanne (based on a story by Robert M. Baker).

Cast: D. Fairbanks ("Augy" Holliday); Jewel Carmen (Gladys Kingsley); Howard Gaye (Roland Dabney); Lillian Langdon (Mrs. Kingsley); W. E. Lawrence (Augy's friend). Reviewed: *Variety* (30 June 1916), p. 20.

The Mystery of the Leaping Fish

Directed by John Emerson (Supv. D. W. Griffith). Released June, 1916, Triangle/Keystone, Two reels. Scenario by Granville Warwick [D. W. Griffith].

Cast: D. Fairbanks (Coke Anneyday); Bessie Love (Little Fish Blower); A. D. Sears (Gent Rolling in Wealth); Alma Rubens (His Female Accomplice).

The Half Breed

Directed by Allan Dwan (Supv. D. W. Griffith). Released 9 July 1916, Triangle/Fine Arts, Five reels. Scenario by Anita Loos (from a Bret Harte story, "In the Carquinez Woods"). Abridged and reissued under the title *Flames of '49*.

Cast: D. Fairbanks (Lo Dorman); Alma Rubens (Teresa); Jewel Carmen (Nellie Wynn); Tom Wilkinson (Curson); Jack Brownlee (Winslow Wynn); Geo. Beranger (Jack Brace). Sam de Grasse (Sheriff Dunn). Reviewed: *New York Times* (10 July 1916), p. 9; *Variety* (14 July 1916), p. 19.

Manhattan Madness

Directed by Allan Dwan (Supv. D. W. Griffith). Released 10 September 1916, Triangle/Fine Arts, Five reels. Scenario by Charles T. Dazey from a story by E. V. Durling. (Possible writing credit also to Anita Loos—see Chapter 6 of Part One.)

Cast: D. Fairbanks (Steve O'Dare); Jewel Carmen (The Girl); George Beranger (The Butler); Warner P. Richmond (Jack Osborne); Ruth Darling; Eugene Ormonde; Albert MacQuarrie; Macey Harlan. Reviewed: *Variety* (22 Sept. 1916), p. 41.

American Aristocracy

Directed by Lloyd Ingraham (Supv. D. W. Griffith). Released 5 November 1916, Triangle/Fine Arts, Five reels. Scenario by Anita Loos.

Cast: D. Fairbanks (Cassius Lee); Jewel Carmen (Miss Geraldine Hicks); Albert Parker. Reviewed: *New York Times* (6 Nov. 1916), p. 9; *Variety* (27 Oct. 1916), p. 27.

The Matrimaniac

Directed by Paul Powell (Supv. D. W. Griffith). Released 3 December 1916, Triangle/Fine Arts, Five reels. Scenario based on a story by Octavus Roy Cohen and J. V. Giesy.

Cast: D. Fairbanks (Jimmy Conroy); Constance Talmadge (Marna Lewis); Winifred Westover (The Maid); Fred Warren (Rev. Tobias Tubbs). Reviewed: *New York Times* (4 Dec. 1916), p. 11.

The Americano

Directed by John Emerson (Supv. D. W. Griffith). Released 24 December 1916, Triangle/Fine Arts, Five reels. Photography: Victor Fleming. Scenario by John Emerson and Anita Loos (based upon a novel, *Blaze Derringer*, by Eugene P. Lyle, Jr.).

Cast: D. Fairbanks (The Americano); Alma Rubens (The President's Daughter); Spottiswoode Aitken; Lillian Langdon; Carl Stockdale; Tom Wilson. Reviewed: *Variety* (29 Dec. 1916), p. 22; *Photoplay* (March 1917), pp. 116–117.

In Again, Out Again

Directed by John Emerson. Released 23 April 1917, Fairbanks/Artcraft-Paramount, Five reels. Art Direction: Erich von Stroheim. Scenario by Anita Loos.

Cast: D. Fairbanks (Teddy Rutherford); Arline Pretty (The Sheriff's Daughter); Bull Montana (Quentin Auburn); Albert Parker (Jerry).

Wild and Woolly

Directed by John Emerson. Released 5 July 1917, Fairbanks/Artcraft-Paramount, Five reels. Photography: Victor Fleming. Scenario by Anita Loos (based on a story by Horace B. Carpenter).

Cast: D. Fairbanks (Jeff Hillington); Eileen Percy (Nell); Sam de Grasse (Steve). Reviewed: *Variety* (2 June 1916), p. 23.

Down to Earth

Directed by John Emerson. Released 16 August 1917, Fairbanks/Artcraft-Paramount, Five reels. Photography: Victor Fleming. Scenario by Anita Loos, based on a story invented by Douglas Fairbanks.

Cast: D. Fairbanks (Bill Gaynor); Eileen Percy (Ethel Forsythe); Gustav von Seyffertitz (Dr. Jollyem); Charles Gerrard (Society Fop); Bull Montana. Reviewed: *Variety* (10 August 1917), p. 23.

The Man from Painted Post

Directed by Joseph Henabery. Released 1 October 1917, Fairbanks/Artcraft-Paramount, Five reels. Photography: Victor Fleming. Scenario by Douglas Fairbanks (from a story by Jackson Gregory).

Cast: D. Fairbanks (Fancy Jim Sherwood); Eileen Percy (Schoolteacher); Frank Campeau (Bull Madden); Herbert Standing (Mr. Brandon); Monte Blue. Reviewed: *New York Times* (1 Oct. 1917), p. 14; *Variety* (5 Oct. 1917), p. 41.

Reaching for the Moon

Directed by John Emerson. Released 19 November 1917, Fairbanks/Artcraft-Paramount, Five reels. Photography: Harry Thorpe. Scenario by Anita Loos and John Emerson.

Cast: D. Fairbanks (Alexis Caesar Napoleon Brown); Eileen Percy (Elsie); Eugene Ormonde (Minister of Vulgaria); Richard Cummings (Old Bingham, owner of the buttom factory); Frank Campeau (Black Boris). Reviewed: *Variety* (23 Nov. 1917), p. 45.

A Modern Musketeer

Directed by Allan Dwan. Released 3 January 1918, Fairbanks/Artcraft-Paramount, Five reels. Photography: Hugh C. McClung and Harry Thorpe. Scenario by Allan Dwan (based upon a story by F. R. Lyle, Jr., "D'Artagnan of Kansas").

Cast: D. Fairbanks (Ned Thacker); Marjorie Daw (Dorothy Moran); Kathleen Kirkham (Mrs. Moran); Tully Marshall (Phillip Marden); Frank Campeau (Indian Guide); Zasu Pitts; Eugene Ormonde.

Headin' South

Directed by Arthur Rosson (Supv. Allan Dwan). Released 21 March 1918, Fairbanks/Artcraft-Paramount, Five reels. Photography: Hugh C. McClung and Harry Thorp. Scenario: Allan Dwan.

Cast: D. Fairbanks ("Headin' South"); Katherine MacDonald (Lady); Frank Campeau. (Spanish Joe); James Mason. Reviewed: *Variety* (1 March 1918), p. 43.

Mr. Fix-It

Directed by Allan Dwan. Released 22 April 1918, Fairbanks/Artcraft-Paramount, Five reels. Photography: Hugh C. McClung. Scenario: Allan Dwan (story suggested by Ernest Butterworth).

Cast: D. Fairbanks (Mr. Fix-It); Wanda Hawley (Mary); Marjorie Daw (Olive); Katherine MacDonald (Georgina Burroughs); Frank Campeau (Uncle "Hen"); Leslie Stuart; Ida Waterman; Alice Smith; Mrs. H. R. Hancock; Mr. Russell; Fred Goodwin; Margaret Landis.

Say! Young Fellow

Directed by Joseph Henabery. Released 17 June 1918, Fairbanks/Artcraft-Paramount, Five reels. Photography: Hugh C. McClung.

Cast: D. Fairbanks (The "Young Fellow," a Manhattan Newsreporter); Marjorie Daw (The Girl); Frank Campeau (The Villain); Edythe Chapman; James Neill.

Bound in Morocco

Directed by Allan Dwan. Released 29 July 1918, Fairbanks/Artcraft-Paramount, Five reels. Photography: Hugh C. McClung. Scenario: Allan Dwan.

Cast: D. Fairbanks (The Boy); Pauline Curley (The Girl); Edythe Chapman (Her Mother); Frank Campeau (Basha El Harib); Tully Marshall; Jay Dwiggins; Marjorie Daw.

He Comes Up Smiling

Directed by Allan Dwan. Released 9 September 1918, Fairbanks/Artcraft-Paramount, Five reels. Photography: Hugh C. McClung. Scenario by Frances Marion, after a novel by Charles Sherman and the play by Byron Ongley and Emil Mytray.

Cast: D. Fairbanks (Jerry Martin); Marjorie Daw (Betty); Herbert Standing (Mike); Bull Montana (Baron Bean); Albert MacQuarrie (Batchelor); Frank Campeau (John Bartlett, Betty's father); Jay Dwiggins; Kathleen Kirkham.

Arizona

Directed by Douglas Fairbanks (and, possibly, Albert Parker). Released 8 December 1918, Fairbanks/Artcraft-Paramount, Five reels. Photography: Hugh C. McClung, Hugh Carlyle, Glen MacWilliams, Scenario by Douglas Fairbanks, after the play by Augustus Thomas [possible assistance by Allan Dwan].

Cast: D. Fairbanks (Lt. Danton); Marjorie Daw (Bonita); Marguerite de la Motte (Lena); Theodore Roberts (Canby); Kate Price (Mrs. Canby); Frank Campeau (Kellar); Raymond Hatton (Tom); Kathleen Kirkham (Estrella).

The Knickerbocker Buckaroo

Directed by Albert Parker. Released 26 May 1919, Fairbanks/Artcraft-Paramount, Five reels. Photography: Hugh C. McClung and Glen MacWilliams. Scenario: Douglas Fairbanks.

Cast: D. Fairbanks (Teddy Drake); Marjorie Daw (Mercedes); William Wellman (Her Brother); Edythe Chapman (Her Mother); Frank Campeau (Crooked Sheriff); Albert MacQuarrie (Manuel Lopez, the Bandit). Reviewed: *New York Times* (26 May 1919), p. 17.

His Majesty, the American

Directed by Joseph Henabery. Released 28 September 1919, United Artists, Eight reels. Photography: Victor Fleming. Scenario: Jos. Henabery and Elton Banks [Douglas Fairbanks]. (This was the initial UA release.)

Cast: D. Fairbanks (William Brooks); Marjorie Daw (Felice, Countess of Montenac); Lillian Langdon (Marguerita); Frank Campeau (Grand Duke). Reviewed: *Variety* (31 Oct. 1919), p. 57.

When the Clouds Roll By

Directed by Victor Fleming. Released 29 December 1919, Fairbanks/United Artists, Six reels. Photography: Harry Thorpe and William C. McGann. Scenario: Douglas Fairbanks, Lewis Weadon, Tom Geraghty.

Cast: D. Fairbanks (Daniel Boone Brown); Kathleen Clifford (Lucette Bancroft); Frank Campeau (Mark Drake); Ralph Lewis (Curtis Brown); Daisy Robinson (Bobbie De Vere).

The Mollycoddle

Directed by Victor Fleming. Released 14 June 1920, Fairbanks/United Artists, Six reels. Photography: William C. McGann. Scenario by Tom Garaghty and Douglas Fairbanks, after a story by Harold McGrath.

Cast: D. Fairbanks (Richard Marshall); Ruth Renick (Virginia Hale); Betty Boulton (Molly Warren); Wallace Berry (Henry Von Holkar); George Stewart (Ole Olsen); Albert MacQuarrie (Driver of "Desert Yacht"); Charles Stevens (Yellow Horse). Reviewed: *New York Times* (14 June 1920), p. 13; *Variety* (18 June 1920), p. 33.

The Mark of Zorro

Directed by Fred Niblo. Released 29 November 1920, Fairbanks/United Artists, Seven reels. Photography: Wm. C. McGann and Harry Thorpe. Scenario by Elton Thomas [Douglas Fairbanks], based on Johnston McCulley's "The Curse of Capistrano."

Cast: D. Fairbanks (Don Diego/Zorro); Marguerite de la Motte (Lolita); Noah Beery (Sgt. Gonzalez); Charles Hill Mailes (Don Carlos Pulido); Clair McDowell (Dona Catalina, his wife); Robert McKim (Capt. Juan Ramon); George Periolat (Gov. Alvarado).

The Nut

Directed by Ted Reed. Released 19 March 1921, Fairbanks/United Artists, Six reels. Photography: Harry Thorpe and Wm. C. McGann. Scenario by Wm. Parker, Lotta Woods, and Elton Thomas [Douglas Fairbanks], based on a story by Kenneth Davenport. [F2.3904]

Cast: D. Fairbanks (Charlie Jackson); Margeurite de la Motte (Estrell Wynn); Barbara La Marr (Claudine Dupree); Charles Chaplin (as himself); Gerald Pring (Gentleman George); Morris Hughes (Pernelius Vanderbrook, Jr.).

The Three Musketeers

Directed by Fred Niblo. Released 28 August 1921, Fairbanks/United Artists, Ten reels. Photography: Arthur Edeson. Scenario: Edward Knoblock and Elton Thomas [Douglas Fairbanks], after the novel by Alexandre Dumas. Script Editor: Lotta Woods. Art Direction: Edward M. Langley. Costume Design: Edward Knoblock. Master of Costumes: Paul Burns. Tech. Director: Frank England. Film Editor: Nellie Mason. Ass't. Director: Doran Cox.

Cast: D. Fairbanks (D'Artagnan); Marguerite de la Motte (Constance); Barbara La Marr (Milady de Winter); Adolphe Menjou (Louis XIII); Leon Barry (Athos); George Siegmann (Porthos); Eugene Pallette (Aramis); Mary MacLaren (Queen of France); Nigel de Brulier (Cardinal Richelieu); Lon Poff (Father Joseph); Boyd Irwin (De Rochefort); Thomas Holding (George Villiers, Duke of Buckingham); Sidney Franklin (Bonacieux); Charles Stevens (Planchet, D'Artagnan's lackey); Willis Robards (Captain de Treville); Walt Whitman (D'Artagnan's father); Charles Belcher (Bernajoux). [F2.5665]

Robin Hood

Directed by Allan Dwan. Released 18 October 1922,

Fairbanks/United Artists, Eleven reels. Photography: Arthur Edeson. Trick Photography: Paul Eagler. Scenario by Elton Thomas [Douglas Fairbanks]. Scenario Editor: Lotta Woods. Literary Consultant: Edward Knoblock. Supv. Art Director: Wilfred Buckland. Art Directors: Irvin J. Martin and Edward M. Langley. Tech. Director: Wilfred Buckland. Art Directors: Irvin J. Martin and Edward M. Langley. Tech. Director: Robert Fairbanks. Research Director: Arthur Woods. Film Editor: William Nolan. Costumes: Michell Leisen. [F2.4663]

Cast: D. Fairbanks (The Earl of Huntingdon/Robin Hood); Wallace Beery (Richard the Lion-Hearted); Sam de Grasse (Prince John); Enid Bennett (Lady Marian Fitzwalter); Paul Dickey (Sir Guy of Gisbourne); William Lowery (The High Sheriff of Nottingham); Roy Coulson (King's Jester); Billie Bennett (Lady Marian's Servant); Merrill McCormick and Wilson Benge (Henchmen to Prince John); Willard Louis (Friar Tuck); Alan Hale (Little John); Maine Geary (Will Scarlett); Lloyd Talman (Alan-a-Dale). Kid McCoy, Bull Montana, Mary Pickford (Townspeople).

Thief of Bagdad

Directed by Raoul Walsh. Released 18 March 1924, Fairbanks/United Artists, Fourteen reels, released as Twelve reels. Photography: Arthur Edeson. Scenario by Elton Thomas [Douglas Fairbanks] after a story by Edward Knoblock; Script Editor: Lotta Woods. Art Direction: William Cameron Menzies. Costumes: Mitchell Leisen. Ass't Photographers: P. H. Whitman and Kenneth MacLean. Technical Direction: Robert Fairbanks. Research Director: Dr. Arthur Woods. Film Editor: William Nolan. Ass't Director: James T. O'Donohoe. Director of Mechanical Effects: Hampton Del Ruth. [F2.5623]

Cast: D. Fairbanks (The Thief); Julanne Johnston (The Princess); Anna May Wong (The Mongol Slave); Snitz Edwards (Evil Associate of the Thief); Charles Belcher (The Holy Man); Sojin (The Mongol Prince); K. Nambu (His Counselor); Sadakichi Hartmann (His Court Magician); Winter-Blossom (Slave of the Lute); Etta Lee (Slave of the Sand Board); Brandon Hurst (The Caliph); Tote Du Crow (The Soothsayer); Noble Johnson (Indian Prince); Mathilde Comont (Persian Prince); Charles Stevens (His Awaker); Sam Baker (The Sworder); Jess Weldon, Scotty Mattraw, and Charles Sylvester (eunuchs).

Don Q, Son of Zorro

Directed by Donald Crisp. Released 20 September 1925, Elton Corp/United Artists, Eleven reels. Photography: Henry Sharp. Additional Photography: E. J. Vallejo. Scenario by Jack Cunningham, adapted from Hesketh Prichard and Kate Prichard's *Don Q's Love Story* (New York, 1925). Scenario Editor: Lotta Woods. Supv. Art Director: Edward M. Langley. Ass't Art Directors: Francesc Cugat, Anton Grot, and Harold Miles. Consulting Artist: Harry Oliver. Research Director: **Arthur Woods**. Film Editor: **William Nolan**. Lighting Effects: William S. Johnson. Technical Effects: Ned Mann. Master of Props: Howard MacChesney. Wardrobe: Paul Burns. Production Manager: Theodore Reed. Ass't Director: Frank Richardson.

General Manager: Robert Fairbanks. [F2.1396]

Cast: D. Fairbanks (Don César de Vega/Zorro); Mary Astor (Dolores de Muro); Jack McDonald (General de Muro); Donald Crisp (Don Sebastian); Stella de Lanti (The Queen); Warner Oland (Archduke Paul of Austria); Jean Hersholt (Don Fabrique); Albert MacQuarrie (Colonel Matsado); Lottie Pickford Forrest (Lola); Charles Stevens (Robledo); Tote du Crow (Bernardo); Martha Franklin (The Duenna); Juliette Belanger (Dancer); Roy Coulson (Her Admirer); Enrique Acosta (Ramón).

The Black Pirate

Directed by Albert Parker. Released 8 March 1926, Elton Corp./United Artists, Nine reels (88 minutes). Photography: Henry Sharp. Technicolor Staff: Arthur Ball and George Cove. Scenario and adaptation: Jack Cunningham, with titles by Robert Nicholls. Script Editor: Lotta Woods. Art Direction: Dwight Franklin and Carl Oscar Borg. Assoc. Artists: Edward M. Langley and Jack Holden. Marine Technician: P. H. L. Wilson. Film Editor: William Nolan. Research Director: Arthur Woods. Production Manager: Theodore Reed. General Manager: Robert Fairbanks. Story: Elton Thomas (and Johnston McCulley?).

Cast: D. Fairbanks (Michel, the Black Pirate); Billie Dove (The Princess); Anders Randolf (Pirate Leader); Donald Crisp (McTavish); Tempe Pigott (Duenna); Sam de Grasse (Lieutenant); Charles Stevens (Powder Man); Charles Belcher (Chief Passenger); Fred Becker; John Wallace; E. J. Ratcliffe. [According to Fairbanks, Jr., Mary Pickford put in a cameo appearance at the very end, replacing Billie Dove for the final (and only) kiss.]

The Gaucho

Directed by F. Richard Jones. Elton Corp./United Artists Released 1 January 1928, Ten reels. (One source lists release date as early as 4 Nov. 1927.) Photography: Antonio Gaudio. Assoc. Photographer: Abe Scholtz. (Shot in black-and-white, with Technicolor sequence.) Scenario by Elton Thomas [Douglas Fairbanks]. Scenario Editor: Lotta Woods. Art Director: Carl Oscar Borg. Film Editor: William Nolan. Ass't Director: Lewis R. Foster. Research Director: Arthur Woods. [F2.2025]

Cast: D. Fairbanks (The Gaucho); Lupe Velez (The Mountain Girl); Geraine Greear (Girl of the Shrine); Eve Southern (Girl of the Shrine as a Child); Gustav con Seyfferititz (Ruiz, the Usurper); Michael Vavitch (Ruiz's First Lieutenant); Charles Stevens (The Gaucho's First Lieutenant); Nigel de Brulier (The Padre); Albert MacQuarrie (Victim of the Black Doom); Mary Pickford (Our Lady of the Shrine).

The Iron Mask

Directed by Allan Dwan. Released 21 February 1929, Fairbanks/United Artists, Eleven reels. Photography: Henry Sharp and Warren Lynch. Scenario: Elton Thomas [Douglas Fairbanks], after *The Three Musketeers* and *The Iron Mask,* by Alexandre Dumas, and the Memoirs of D'Artagnan, Richelieu, and de Rochefort. Script Editor: Lotta Woods. Interior Decorator: Burgess Beall. Costume and Production Design: Maurice Leloir. Master of Costumes and Props: Paul Burns. Research Director: Dr. Arthur Woods. Film Editor: William Nolan. Musical Score: Dr. Hugo Reisenfeld. Song "One for All, All for One," by Ray Klages and Louis Alter. Ass't Directors: Bruce Humberstone, Vinton Vernon, and Sherry Shourds. Production Manager: Robert Fairbanks. Production Ass't: Charles Lewis. Wardrobe: Maurice Leloir. Technical Director: Willard M. Reineck. Sound: Western Electric on discs (prologue to both parts spoken by Douglas Fairbanks, Sr., in the original released version). [F2.2737]

Cast: D. Fairbanks (D'Artagnan); Marguerite de la Motte (Constance); Belle Bennett (Queen Mother); Dorothy Revier (Milady de Winter); Vera Lewis (Madame Peronne); Rolfe Sedan (Louis XIII); William Bakewell (Young Prince and his Twin); Nigel de Brulier (Cardinal Richelieu); Ulrich Haupt (De Rochefort); Lon Poff (Father Joseph); Charles Stevens (Planchet, D'Artagnan's servant); Henry Otto (The King's Valet); Leon Barry (Athos); Stanley J. Sandford (Porthos); Gino Corrado (Aramis). Robert Parrish (Page); Florence Turner (Abbess); Fred Cavens; Madame Chalif; Princess Galitzine.

The Taming of the Shrew

Directed by Sam Taylor. Released 26 October 1929, Pickford Corp./Elton Corp./United Artists, Eight reels (68 minutes). Photography: Karl Struss. Scripted from Shakespeare's comedy, with or without "additional dialogue" by Sam Taylor. Art Direction: William Cameron Menzies and Laurence Irving. Set Direction: David Forrest. Film Editor: Allan McNeil. Sound: John Craig. Rereleased in 1966 with new music and rerecorded sound.

Cast: D. Fairbanks (Petruchio); Mary Pickford (Katherine); Edwin Maxwell (Baptista); Joseph Cawthorn (Gremio); Clyde Cook (Grumio); Geoffrey Wardwell (Hortensio); Dorothy Jordan (Bianca). [F2.5526]

Reaching for the Moon

Directed by Edmund Goulding. Released 21 February 1931, Fairbanks/United Artists, 90 minutes. Photography: Ray June and Robert Planck. Scenario: Edmund Goulding (from a story by Irving Berlin), with additional dialogue by Elsie Janis. Settings: William Cameron Menzies. Fashions: David Cox. Edited by Lloyd Nosler and Hal C. Kern. Music by Irving Berlin, directed by Alfred Newman.

Cast: D. Fairbanks (Larry Dacy); Bebe Daniels (Vivian Benton); Edward Everett Horton (Roger); June MacCloy (Kitty); Bing Crosby (Bing); Claud Allister (Sir Horace Partington Chelmsford); Jack Mulhall (Carrington); Heler Jerome Eddy (Secretary).

Around the World in 80 Minutes

Directed by Victor Fleming. Released 12 December 1931, Fairbanks/United Artists, 80 minutes. Photography: Henry Sharp and Chuck Lewis, with Victor Fleming and crew playing themselves in the film.

Scenario by Douglas Fairbanks, with dialogue by Robert E. Sherwood. Fairbanks plays himself. The film is intended as a comic travelogue, and attempts to do exactly what the title promises.

Mr. Robinson Crusoe

Directed by Edward Sutherland. Released 19 August 1932, Fairbanks/United Artists, 72 minutes. Photography: Max Dupont. Scenario: Tom Geraghty, from a story by Elton Thomas [Douglas Fairbanks]. Editor: Robert Kern. Music: Alfred Newman.

Cast: D. Fairbanks (Steve Drexel); Maria Alba (Saturday); William Farnum (Wm. Belmont); Earle Browne.

The Private Life of Don Juan

Directed by Alexander Korda, and shot in London. Released 30 November 1934, London Films, 80 minutes. Photography: Georges Perinal. Scenario by Lajos Biro and Frederick Lonsdale, adapted from the comic play of Henri Bataille. Settings: Vincent Korda. Costumes: Oliver Messel. Editing: Stephen Harrison. Lyrics: Arthur Wimperis. Music: Ernst Toch.

Cast: D. Fairbanks (Don Juan); Merle Oberon (Antonia); Benita Hume (Dolores); Binnie Barnes (Rosita); Joan Gardner (Carmen); Melville Cooper (Leporello); Athene Seyler (Theresa); Owen Nares (Actor in the Role of Don Juan); Patricia Hilliard (Girl in Castle); Gina Malo (Pepita); Heather Thatcher (Actress); Claud Allister (Duke); Barry Mackay (Roderigo); Lawrence Grossmith (Guardian); Edmund Breon (Author); Clifford Heatherley (Pedro); Diana Napier (Would-Be-Wife); Gibson Gowland (Don Ascanio); Hay Petrie (Manager); Natalie Paley (Wife).

Postscript on Available Prints of the Fairbanks Films

Virtually all of the feature films of the costume period and beyond are available for rental in 16mm. The best source for the costume films is The Killiam Collection (6 East 39th Street, New York, N.Y. 10016). Killiam rentals tend to be slightly higher than prices charged by other distributors, but, considering the quality of their prints—which are tinted and enhanced with appropriate music tracks—the higher price is more than justified. The full spectacular effect of such a film as *The Thief of Bagdad* cannot be appreciated, for example, unless seen in the color-tinted Killiam print, even though, obviously, the performance of Douglas Fairbanks can be enjoyed by viewing *any* print of the film that preserves a relatively clean image. The following titles are listed in The Killiam Collection: *The Mark of Zorro* (1920), *The Thief of Bagdad* (1924), *The Black Pirate* (1926), *The Iron Mask* (1929), and *Mr. Robinson Crusoe* (1932).

One of the largest collections in 16mm is held by Macmillan Audio Brandon (34 MacQuesten Parkway So., Mount Vernon, N.Y. 10550), which offers a good balance of late and early films: *The Lamb* (1915), *Down to Earth* (1917), *In Again, Out Again* (1917), *Wild and Woolly* (1917), *A Modern Musketeer* (1918), *His Majesty, the American* (1919), *When the Clouds Roll By* (1919), *The Mollycoddle* and *Zorro* (1920), *The Nut* and *The Three Musketeers* (1921), *Robin Hood* (1922), *Thief of Bagdad* (1924), *Black Pirate* (1926), *The Gaucho* (1927), *The Iron Mask* (1929), and *The Private Life of Don Juan* (1934). *Don Juan* is of course a sound film; *Iron Mask* has music and narration; the rest are silent. Print quality is generally good, and prices are fairly reasonable.

The Museum of Modern Art's Department of Film (11 West 53rd Street, New York, N.Y. 10019) has good quality 16mm prints of *The Mystery of the Leaping Fish* (1916), *Wild and Woolly* and *Reaching for the Moon* (1917), *A Modern Musketeer* (1918), *When the Clouds Roll By* (1919), *Mollycoddle* and *Zorro* (1920), *Three Musketeers* (1921), *Robin Hool* (1922), *Thief of Bagdad* (1924), *Don Q., Son of Zorro* (1925), *Black Pirate* (1926), *The Gaucho* (1927), *Iron Mask* (1929), *Around the World in 80 Minutes* (1931), and *Mr. Robinson Crusoe* (1932). The Museum is the only source for some of these films—*Don Q.* in particular. Their print of *Crusoe* has sound effects and music, but titles rather than spoken dialogue (the film being originally released both in sound and silent versions). The Museum print of *Iron Mask* is silent, but running time is listed as twenty-seven minutes longer than the narrated version that Audio Brandon has (some of this time, of course, being reserved for subtitles). Museum prints cannot be exhibited where admission is charged, but are available for educational use by film societies and for classroom purposes.

The Taming of the Shrew (1929) is only available from the Mary Pickford Company (9350 Wilshire Boulevard, Beverly Hills, Calif. 90212). Inquiries should be addressed to Mr. Matty Kemp, Executive Director. Images Motion Picture Rental Library (2 Purdy Avenue, Rye, N.Y. 10580) has recently advertised the following Fairbanks titles: *Black Pirate* (1926), *Zorro* (1920), *Thief of Bagdad* (1924), *Iron Mask* (1929), *Reaching For the Moon* (1931). Swank Motion Pictures (201 So. Jefferson, St. Louis, Mo. 63166) rents *Black Pirate* (1926) and *Reaching for the Moon* (1931). Films, Inc. (4420 Oakton Street, Skokie, Illinois 60076) has *Black Pirate* (1926) and King Vidor's *Show People* (1928), a delightful Marion Davies picture in which Fairbanks contributes a cameo appearance.

Finally, Em Gee Film Library (16024 Ventura Blvd., Suite 211, Encino, Calif. 91436) has a sizeable collection of Fairbanks titles. A complete listing is available from Mr. Murray Glass.

Bibliography

Allen, Frederic Lewis. *The Big Change: America Transforms Itself, 1900–1950,* New York: Harper, 1952.

Amory, Cleveland. *Who Killed Society?* New York: Harper, 1960.

Arnheim, Rudolph. *Film as Art,* Berkeley: University of California Press, 1957.

Bakshy, Alexander. "Films: Mostly For The Family," *The Nation,* 129 (25 December 1929), 784.

Barzun, Jacques. *The Energies of Art,* New York: Harper, 1956.

Barzun, Jacques, ed. *The Selected Letters of Lord Byron,* New York: Farrar, Straus and Cudahy, 1953.

Behlmer, Rudy. "Technicolor," *Films in Review,* (June/July, 1964), pp. 333–351.

Bentley, Eric. *The Life of the Drama,* New York: Atheneam, 1967.

Bergson, Henri. "Laughter," in *Comedy,* New York: Doubleday/Anchor, 1956.

Bodeen, DeWitt, "Douglas Fairbanks Filmography," *Focus on Film,* No. 5 (Winter 1970), pp. 26–30.

Bogdanovich, Peter. *Allan Dwan: The Last Pioneer,* New York: Praeger, 1971.

Branch, Douglas. *The Cowboy and His Interpretors,* New York: Cooper Square Publishers, Inc. 1926.

Brewster, Eugene V. "Why Color Pictures and Talking Movies Can Never Be Universal," *Motion Picture Magazine* (June 1926), p. 5.

Brownlow, Kevin. *The Parade's Gone By . . .* New York: Ballantine Books, 1969.

Campbell, O. J., and E. G. Quinn, eds. *The Reader's Encyclopedia of Shakespeare,* New York: Thomas Y. Crowell, 1966.

Carey, Gary. "Written on the Screen," *Film Comment* (Winter 1970–71).

Chesterton, G. K. *The Defendant,* London: J. M. Dent and Sons, 1901.

Cooke, Alistair. *Douglas Fairbanks: The Making of a Screen Character,* Museum of Modern Art Film Library Series, No. 2. New York: Museum of Modern Art, 1940.

Cushman, Robert B. *Tribute to Mary Pickford,* Washington: American Film Institute, 1970.

Eckert, Charles W. ed. *Focus on Shakespearean Films,* Englewood Cliffs: Prentice-Hall, 1972.

Ellis, William T. *Billy Sunday: The Man and His Message,* New York: F. W. Mead Publishing Co., 1936.

Emerson, John, and Anita Loos. *How To Write Photoplays,* Philadelphia: George W. Jacobs and Co., 1923.

Fadiman, Clifton. *Any Number Can Play,* Cleveland: World Publishing Co., 1957.

Fairbanks, Douglas. "How I Keep Running On High," *American Magazine* (August 1922), pp. 36-9.

Fairbanks, Douglas. *Laugh and Live,* New York: Britton Publishing Co., 1917.

Fairbanks, Douglas. "Let Me Say This for the Films," *Ladies' Home Journal* (September 1922), pp. 13, 117, 120.

Fairbanks, Douglas. *Making Life Worthwhile,* New York: Britton Publishing Co., 1918.

Feinberg, Leonard. *Introduction to Satire,* Ames: Iowa State University Press, 1967.

Fielding, Henry. *The History of the Adventures of Joseph Andrews,* New York: Modern Library, 1950.

Frantz, Joe, and Julian Choate, *The American Cowboy, The Myth and the Reality,* Norman: University of Oklahoma Press, 1955.

Fussell, Edwin. *Frontier: American Literature and the American West,* Princeton: Princeton University Press, 1965.

Gifford, Denis. *The British Film Catalogue, 1895–1970: A Reference Guide,* New York: McGraw-Hill Book Co., 1973.

Grant, Paul. "John, Anita, and the Giftie," *Photoplay*, (December 1917).

Green, Abel, and Joe Laurie, Jr. *Variety, from Vaude to Video*, New York: Henry Holt, 1951.

Griffith, Richard, and Arthur Mayer. *The Movies*, Rev. Edn. New York: Simon and Schuster, 1970.

Grunwald, Henry Anatole. "The Disappearance of Don Juan," *Horizon*, IV:3 (January 1962).

Hampton, Benjamin B. *History of the American Film Industry, from Its Beginnings to 1931*, New York: Dover Publications, 1970.

Hancock, Ralph, and Letitia Fairbanks. *Douglas Fairbanks: The Fourth Musketeer*, New York: Henry Holt, 1953.

Hawthorne, Nathaniel. *The Complete Short Stories of Nathaniel Hawthorne*, New York: Hanover House, 1959.

James, Henry. *Hawthorne*, New York: St. Martin's Press, 1967.

Kracauer, Siegfried. *From Caligari to Hitler*, Princeton: Princeton University Press, 1969.

Lindsay, Vachel. *The Art of the Moving Picture*, New York: Liveright Publishing Corp., 1970.

Lewis, R. W. B. *The American Adam*, Chicago: University of Chicago Press, 1955.

Lewis, Sinclair. *Elmer Gantry*, New York: Harcourt, Brace, and Co., 1927.

Limbacher, James L. *Four Aspects of the Film*, New York: Brussel and Brussel, 1968.

Little, Barbara. "The Pirates are Coming," *Picture-Play Magazine*, (March 1923), p. 47.

Loos, Anita. *A Girl Like I*, New York: Viking Press, 1966.

McCulley, Johnston. "The Curse of Capistrano," *All-Story Weekly* (9 August 1919).

McCulley, Johnston. "The Further Adventures of Zorro," *Argosy All-Story Weekly*, (6 May 1922).

McLoughlin, William Gerald. *Billy Sunday Was His Real Name*, Chicago: University of Chicago Press, 1955.

Maltin, Leonard. *Behind the Camera*, New York: Signet, 1971.

Manvell, Roger. *Shakespeare and the Film*, New York: Praeger, 1971.

Marx, Leo. *The Machine in the Garden*, New York: Oxford University Press, 1964.

Maurois, André. *Byron*, New York: D. Appleton and Co., 1930.

May, Henry F. *The End of American Innocence*, Chicago: Quadrangle Books, 1964.

Mayer, Arthur. *Merely Colossal*, New York: Simon & Schuster, 1953.

Mencken, H. L. "The American Language," in *The American Scene*, ed. Huntington Cairns. New York: Alfred A. Knopf, 1965.

Mencken, H. L. *Prejudices* (First Series), New York: Knopf, 1920.

Morris, Peter. *Shakespeare on Film*. Ottawa: Canadian Film Institute, 1972.

Munden, Kenneth W. *The American Film Institute Catalogue of Motion Pictures Produced in the United States: Feature Films, 1921–1930*, New York and London: R. R. Bowker, 1971.

Nathan, George Jean. *Testament of a Critic*, New York and London: Alfred A. Knopf, 1931.

Parkman, Francis. *Letters of Francis Parkman*, Ed. Wilbur R. Jacobs. Norman: University of Oklahoma Press, 1960.

Pickford, Mary. *Sunshine and Shadow*, Garden City: Doubleday & Co., 1955.

Pratt, George C. *Spellbound in Darkness: A History of the Silent Film*, Greenwich: New York Graphic Society, Ltd., 1973.

Pringle, Henry F. *Theodore Roosevelt, A Biography*, New York: Harcourt, Brace and Co., 1931.

Ramsaye, Terry. *A Million and One Nights*, New York: Simon & Schuster, 1964.

Richardson, Robert. *Literature and Film*, Bloomington: Indiana University Press, 1969.

Robinson, David. *Hollywood in the 'Twenties*, New York and London: Zwemmer/Barnes, 1968.

Rotha, Paul. *The Film Till Now*, London: Spring Books, 1949.

Sanford, Charles L. *The Quest for Paradise*, Urbana: University of Illinois, 1961.

Schallert, Edwin, "Doug Rubs the Magic Lamp," *Picture-Play Magazine* (September, 1923), p. 87.

Schallert, Edwin, "Yo Ho and a Bottle of Rum," *Picture-Play Magazine* (February, 1926), pp. 17, 108.

Schickel, Richard. *His Picture in the Papers: A Speculation on Celebrity in America Based on the Life of Douglas Fairbanks, Sr.*, New York: Charterhouse, 1973.

Smith, Henry Nash. *Virgin Land*, New York: Vintage Books, 1950.

Spottiswoode, Raymond. *Film and Its Techniques*, Berkeley: University of California, 1952.

Starrett, Vincent. *Buried Caesars*, Chicago: Covici-McGee, 1923.

Sutherland, Donald. *On, Romanticism*, New York: New York University Press, 1971.

Tabori, Paul. *Alexander Korda*, New York: Living Books, 1966.

Taylor, Charles K. "Doug Gets Away With It," *Outlook* (14 April 1926), pp. 560–562.

Thorp, Dunham. "How Fairbanks Took the Color Out of Color," *Motion Picture Classics* (May, 1926), pp. 28–29, 87–90.

Walker, Alexander. *Stardom*, London: Michael Joseph, 1970.

Walsh, Raoul. *Each Man In His Time: The Life Story of a Director*, New York: Farrar, Straus, Giroux, 1974.

White, G. Edward. *The Eastern Establishment and the Western Experience*, New Haven and London: Yale University Press, 1968.

Wilson, Douglas L., ed. *The Genteel Tradition*, Cambridge: Harvard University Press, 1967.

Index

Abraham Lincoln, 108
Abrams, Hiram, 104–105, 107–108
Adams, Andy, 80
Adams, John, 54
Adams, Henry, 61
Aitken, Harry E., 21, 23
Alba, Maria, 195, 197
Allen, Fredric Lewis, 41
All Star Film Corp., 20
Allyson, June, 164
American Aristocracy, 53–54, 59–62, 84, 95–96, 100
Americano, The, 59–60, 84–85
Andere, Der, 35
Antonioni, Michelangelo, 153
Arbuckle, Roscoe ("Fatty"), 104–105, 107
Arizona, 78
Arnheim, Rudolph, 149
Around the World in 80 Minutes, 22, 49, 185–187, 191–195
Artcraft, 25, 27, 71, 75, 93, 103, 176, 191
Ashley, Lord Anthony, 199, 207
Ashley, Sylvia Hawks, 188, 199–200, 207
Astaire, Fred, 113
Astor, Mary, 127, 130
Audubon, John James, 57
Autry, Gene, 68

Bakewell, William, 172
Ball, Joseph A., 147, 149
Ball, Robert Hamilton, 182
Baltzell, E. Digby, 59
Balzac, Honoré de, 85
Banzhaf, Albert H.T., 105
Barrie, James M., 208
Barriscale, Bessie, 34
Barry, Leon, 165, 169
Barrymore, Ethel, 20
Barrymore, John, 19, 34, 178
Barrymore, Lionel, 87
Barry, Thomas, 70

Bataille, Henri, 199
Bauman, Charlie, 19, 21
Beadle, Erastus, 67–68
Becky Sharp, 154
Beery, Noah, 120
Beery, Wallace, 78, 120, 134–135
Belasco, David, 103
Bennett, Belle, 172
Bennett, Enid, 134
Bentley, Eric, 84
Beranger, Clara, 88
Beranger, George, 75
Bergere, Ouida, 88
Bergson, Henri, 84, 93–94, 96–98
Berkeley, Busby, 188
Berlin, Irving, 188
Betty of Grey Stone, 39
Bicycle Thief, 183
Bierce, Ambrose, 50
Bingham, William, 55
Biograph Co., 87, 108, 176
Biro, Lajos, 199
Birth of a Nation, 21
Bitzer, G.W., 25
Black Pirate, The, 9, 34, 108, 124, 142, 145–155, 157, 165, 176
Black, William, 58
Bodeen, De Witt, 84
Boone, Daniel, 63–67, 69, 76–77, 81
Booth, Edwin, 13
Borg, Carl Oscar, 149–150, 153
Borzage, Frank, 176
Bound in Morocco, 10, 58
Bowser, Eileen, 74, 191
Brady, James, 105
Brady, Nicholas, 105
Branch, Douglas, 78
Brent, Evelyn, 148
Briscoe, Lottie, 20
Broken Blossoms, 104, 108

Broun, Heywood, 48
Brownlow, Kevin, 88, 108, 177
Bryan, William Jennings, 44, 92
Burke, Billie, 22
Burke, Thomas, 108
Burroughs, Edgar Rice, 59, 121
Burton, Richard, 183
Bushman, Francis X., 20
Byron, Lord (George Gordon), 66, 95, 155–158, 207

Cabanne, Christy, 32, 35
Cahan, Sam, 124
Campeau, Frank, 38, 48, 66, 97
Canby, Henry Seidel, 57
Capra, Frank, 178
Captain Jinks of the Horse Marines, 20
Carey, Gary, 84, 90
Carmen, Jewel, 53–54, 62, 75
Case, Frank, 21, 143
Catherine the Great, 199
Cave, George, 149
Cawthorn, Joseph, 179
Chaplin, Charlie, 9, 11, 34, 86, 94, 102–105, 107–109, 111, 167, 176, 183, 197
Chase, Charlie, 86
Chaucer, 172
Chesterfield, Lord, 58
Chesterton, G.K., 93, 96
Choate, Julian, Jr. 67
Clair, René, 11, 132, 136
Clara Kimball Young Pictures Co., 102
Clemens, Samuel Langhorne (Mark Twain), 57, 60
Clifton, George, 105
Cocteau, Jean, 110
Cody, William Frederick (Buffalo Bill), 67–68, 70, 81
Cohan, George M., 48
Cohen, Octavus Roy, 84
Collier, John, 112
Columbia Film Co., 48
Comstock, Daniel F., 147
Congorilla, 192
Connell, Brian, 11
Cook, Clyde, 180
Cooke, Alistair, 11, 25, 40, 84, 93, 110, 163
Cool Hand Luke, 99
Coolidge, William H., 147
Cooper, Gary, 207
Cooper, James Fenimore, 66–67
Cops, 179
Coquette, 176
Coriell, Vernell, 131
Corrado, Gino, 169
Countess from Hong Kong, 109
Courtship of Miles Standish, 148
Crane, W.H., 21, 28
Crèvecoeur, Michel Guillaume Jean de, 55, 65
Crisp, Donald, 124–125, 127, 129
Crosby, Bing, 188
Curley, Pauline, 58
Cytherea, 147

D'Amico, Suso Cecchi, 183
Daniels, Bebe, 188–191
Da Ponte, Lorenzo (Emanuele Conegliano), 50, 203
D'Arrast, Harry, 96
Daumier, H., 86
Davies, Marion, 83
Davis, Richard Harding, 85

Daw, Marjorie, 30
de Brulier, Nigel, 159, 170
De Forest, Lee, 108
Dehn, Paul, 183
de La Motte, Marguerite, 122–124, 170–171
De Mille, C.B., 147
De Sica, Vittorio, 183
Desmond, William, 22
de Vega, Lope, 66
Dickens, Charles, 53, 86, 93
Dickey, Paul, 132
Disney, Walt, 154
Doctor X, 154
Don Juan, 50, 198–205
Don Q., 34, 121, 125–131, 155, 176, 192
Dorothy Vernon of Haddon Hall, 108
Double Trouble, 24, 34–36
Douglas Fairbanks Pictures Corp., 22, 27, 104
Dove, Billie, 152–153
Down to Earth, 40, 49, 53, 75, 84–85, 91, 93, 95–96, 98–99
Dream Street, 108
Dressler, Marie, 22
Dumas, Alexandre, 164, 167
Durling E.V., 75, 84
Dwan, Allan, 24, 38–40, 48, 51, 75–76, 94, 102, 132, 135, 167, 170, 173

Eagle, The, 178
Easy Street, 94
Edeson, Arthur, 108
Eisenstein, Sergei, 56
Electric House, The, 111
Eliot, George, 86
Ellis, Charles, 73
Emerson, John, 27, 38, 60, 61, 71, 84, 87–88, 91
Emerson, Ralph Waldo, 42, 55–56
Epstein, Jean, 11, 16
Essanay Film Co., 38–39, 103
Etaix, Pierre, 111
Evangelist, The, 48
Everson, William K., 7, 9

Fairbanks, Douglas, Jr., 7, 9, 11, 14, 24, 28, 167, 198–199, 207
Fairbanks, Douglas, Sr. (Douglas Elton Thomas Ulman): birth and childhood, 13; Broadway career, 13–14, 19, 28–29; transition to Hollywood, 19–27; first marriage, 13, 61; Pickford marriage, 108, 176, 186, 188, 198, 199; last marriage, 199–200, 207; business sense, 61, 104–105; restless urge to travel, 186–188, 191–192, 195; final projects, 198–199, 207
Fairbanks, Jack, 13, 22, 26–27
Fairbanks, John, 13
Fairbanks, Robert, 13
Famous Players Co., 19, 38, 103–104, 148
Farnum, Dustin, 22
Feinberg, Leonard, 96
Fellini, Federico, 114
Ferrer, Mel, 50
Fiedler, Leslie, 66, 70
Fielding, Henry, 85–86, 92, 95, 97
Fine Arts, 22, 24–27, 39, 88
Finney, Charles, 44
First National, 103–108, 199
Fiske, Minnie Maddern, 87
Fitzmaurice, George, 147
Fleming, Victor, 71, 83, 192, 194–195
Forbes, James, 19
Ford, Henry, 105

Foundling, The, 38
Four Feathers, 199
Fox Film Corp., 102
Franklin, Dwight, 148–149, 153
Frantz, Joe, 67
Freshman, The, 178
Frisch, Max, 205
Frohman, Charles, 20, 87
Frohman, Daniel, 19
Fussell, Edwin, 65

Garfield, James, 70
Gaucho, The, 50, 127, 155–162, 195
Gaudio, Tony, 162
Gentlemen Prefer Blondes, 90, 93
German of Prague, 35
Girl of Yesterday, 38
Gish, Lillian, 176
Glesy, J.V., 84
Godsol, Joseph, 105
Golden Claw, The, 34
Goldfinger, 183
Goldwyn, Samuel, 199, 207
Gone With The Wind, 178
Good Bad Man, The, 78, 81, 123
Grey, Zane, 67, 148
Griffith, David Wark, 21–25, 27, 30, 56, 69, 83, 87–88, 90, 94, 102–105, 107–109, 147, 176, 183
Griffith, Richard, 176
Grunwald, Henry Anatole, 205
Guinan, Texas, 22
Gulf Between, The, 147

Habit of Happiness, The, 37–41, 48–51, 94, 194
Hadley, Reed, 121
Hagedorn, Hermann, 72
Half-Breed, The, 76, 78, 84
Hall, Mordaunt, 154
Hamilton, Alexander, 55, 59
Hampton, Benjamin, 21, 104
Hancock, Ralph, 11, 21, 23, 28, 74
Hardy, Oliver, 87
Harte, Bret, 84
Hart, William S., 22, 74, 104–106
Haupt, Ulrich, 170
Hawthorne, Nathaniel, 41, 56, 58, 66
Hays, Will H., 104
Headin' South, 66, 79
Hearts of the World, 94, 104
He Comes Up Smiling, 13, 19, 29, 40
Henabery, Joseph, 81
Henrietta; The, 28
Henry, O. (William S. Porter), 99
His Majesty the American, 57, 59, 77, 107
His Picture in the Papers, 25, 34, 36, 38, 75–76, 84–85, 87–91, 96
Hitchcock, Raymond, 22
Hodkinson, William, 102
Holmes, Oliver Wendell, 58
Hopper, De Wolf, 22
Horton, Edward Everett, 188, 190
Howard, Bronson, 28
Howells, William Dean, 58

In Again, Out Again, 75, 84–85, 91–93, 96, 99–100
Ince, Thomas H., 22, 34
Ingraham, Lloyd, 53
Ingraham, Prentiss, 68

Ingram, Rex, 147
Intolerance, 104, 107
Iron Mask, The, 131, 159, 165, 167–173, 178, 202
Irving, Henry, 170, 182
Irving, Lawrence, 170, 178–179, 182
Italian Straw Hat, The, 11

James, Henry, 23, 56, 58–59, 64
Janis, Elsie, 20
Jannings, Emil, 199
Jazz Singer, The, 108
Jefferson, Thomas, 42
Jerome, William Travers, 147
Johnson, Arthur V., 48
Johnson, Martin, 191–192
Johnson, Osa, 191–192
Johnson, Samuel, 202
Johnstone, Julanne, 140, 142
Jordan, Dorothy, 179
Jordan Is a Hard Road, 38, 48
Joyce, Helen, 51

Kalmus, Herbert, 147
Keaton, Buster, 28, 33–34, 111, 179, 197
Keller, Louis, 59
Kelly, Gene, 164
Kelly, Luther ("Yellowstone"), 70
Kemp, Matty, 7, 183
Kessel, Adam, 19, 21
Keystone, 23–24, 87, 103
Kid Brother, The, 86
Kid, The, 103
Kiki, 176
King of Jazz, The, 149
Kingsley, Charles, 132
Kleiner, Arthur, 9
Knickerbocker Buckaroo, 78, 81
Knoblock, Edward, 148
Korda, Alexander, 199, 203
Kubrick, Stanley, 113

Laemmle, Carl, 102
Lamb, The, 24, 28–34, 73, 77, 91
Lasky Co., 102
Last Command, The, 199
Laugh and Live, 26
Laurel, Stan, 87
Lee, Richard Henry, 55
Leisen, Mitchell, 142
Leloir, Maurice, 170
Lennig, Arthur, 77
Lester, Richard, 164–165
Lewis, R.W.B., 55, 69, 72, 76
Lewis, Sinclair, 37, 45
Lillie, Bea, 178
Linder, Max, 96
Lindsay, Vachel, 11, 56, 94, 142, 144, 167
Little Lord Fauntleroy, 108
Llewellyn, Richard, 167
Lloyd, Harold, 86, 178
London Films, Co., 199
Lonsdale, Frederic, 199
Loos, Anita, 25, 33, 38, 46, 53, 83–100
Loren, Sophia, 183
Love, Bessie, 47
Love Light, 108
Lubin, Siegmund, 48, 87

Lubitsch, Ernst, 96, 108

MacDonald, Katherine, 79
Machen, Arthur, 158
Madison, James, 55
Making Life Worthwhile, 26
Mamoulian, Rouben, 154
Man from Painted Post, 81
Manhattan Madness, 71, 74–78, 84
Manvell, Roger, 182
Mapes, Victor, 28
Marion, Frances, 88
Mark of Zorro, The, 33–34, 48, 107–108, 119–131, 155–157, 159, 162–165, 176, 207
Mastroianni, Marcello, 183
Mathis, June, 88
Matrimoniac, The, 29, 84, 95, 99
Maude, Cyril, 20
Maugham, William Somerset, 57
Maxwell, Clark, 146
Maxwell, Edwin, 177, 180
Mayer, Arthur, 104, 176
May, Henry F., 42, 94
McAdoo, William Gibbs, 105, 107
McCulley, Johnston, 121–124, 131, 207
McKean, Thomas, 55
McKim, Robert, 122, 124
McLoughlin, William G., 43, 46
Mencken, H.L., 43, 83, 90, 94, 98, 100
Menzies, William Cameron, 142, 170, 178
Meredyth, Bess, 88
Merry Widow, The, 148
Metro-Goldwyn-Mayer, 102
Mix, Tom, 68, 74, 78
Mizner, Wilson, 90
Modern Musketeer, A, 29–30, 34, 74, 107
Mohr, Hal, 149
Molière (Jean Baptiste Poquelin), 50, 203, 205
Mollycoddle, The, 30, 32, 47, 59, 61, 69–70, 72, 77–78, 81
Monahan, J.P., 124
Moody, Dwight L., 44
Mozart, Wolfgang Amadeus, 203
Mr. Fix-It, 40
Mr. Robinson Crusoe, 185–186, 194–198
Mutual Film Corp., 87, 103
My Best Girl, 176
Mystery of the Leaping Fish, The, 23, 94
Mystery of the Wax Museum, 154

Nathan, George Jean, 95
Navigator, The, 111, 197
Neilan, Marshall, 83
New Henrietta, The, 19, 21, 28
New York Hat, The, 87
Niblo, Fred, 48, 125, 148, 163
Nietszche, F., 159
Nimmo, Joseph, 67
Nut, The, 33, 40, 108, 110–115, 119, 163, 188

Oberon, Merle, 201
O'Brien, Dennis F., 25–27, 105
Oland, Warner, 129–130
Oldfield, Barney, 61
Old Swimmin' Hole, The, 91
Orders to Kill, 183
Ormond, Eugene, 33, 97
Owen, Seena, 30

Paget, Alfred, 30
Pallette, Eugene, 165
Paramount Pictures Corp., 102–108, 176, 199
Parker, Albert, 9, 53, 78, 151–152
Parkman, Francis, 64–65, 69–70, 72–73, 81
Phantom of the Opera, 148
Pickfair, 23, 59, 70, 176, 186, 188
Pickford, Charlotte, 104
Pickford, Mary, 20, 26, 34, 38, 50, 87, 94, 102–109, 143, 175–178, 180, 182–184, 186, 194, 197–199, 207
Poe, Edgar Allen, 114
Pollyanna, 108
Power, Tyrone, 121
Price, Oscar, 105, 107
Prichard, Hesketh, 125
Prichard, Kate, 125
Private Life of Don Juan, The, 157, 185–186, 198–205
Private Life of Henry VIII, 199
Pyle, Howard, 150

Quetelet, Adolphe, 93
Quick, Herbert, 35

Ramsaye, Terry, 105–106
Randolf, Anders, 150–151
Ray, Charles, 91, 148
Reaching for the Moon (1917), 33–34, 43, 54, 59, 84–85, 91–92, 96–97, 99–100
Reaching for the Moon (1931), 13, 22, 186, 188–192
Reed, Ted, 153
Reggie Mixes In, 46–47
Rembrandt, 199
Revier, Dorothy, 171
Richardson, Robert, 96
Richmond, Warner P., 75
Road to Plaindale, The, 87
Robin Hood, 34, 107, 132–138, 142, 144, 148, 156–157, 164–165, 170–171, 173
Rogers, Charles ("Buddy"), 176
Romance of Happy Valley, 69
Roosevelt, Theodore, 38, 41–42, 44–46, 49–51, 67, 69–73
Rosher, Charles, 108
Rosita, 108
Rotha, Paul, 29, 109
Rowlands, Richard, 109
Royal Wedding, The, 113
Russell, Edwin, 64–65

Salisbury, Monroe, 30
Sandford, Stanley, J., 169
Sanford, Charles, 56, 69
San Francisco, 90
Santayana, George, 66, 90, 92, 94, 99–100
Saphead, The, 28
Sartov, Hendrik, 108
Say! Young Fellow, 20, 29
Scarlet Empress, 135
Scarlet Pimpernal, The, 199
Schickel, Richard, 11, 156, 197
Schulberg, B.P., 104
Secrets, 176
Selznick, Lewis J., 102
Sennett, Mack, 178–179
Seven Days to Noon, 183
Shakespeare, William, 91, 175–182
Sharp, Henry, 149, 192
Shaw, G.B., 205

Sherwood, Robert E., 144, 164, 192
Shoulder Arms, 103, 167
Show Shop, The, 13, 19
Sidney, George, 164
Siegmann, George, 165
Simba, 191
Smathers, E.E., 105
Smith, Adam, 55
Smith, Henry Nash, 65, 67–68, 79
Smith, Winchell, 28
Soldiers of Fortune, 38
Spencer, Herbert, 42, 44
Spirits of the Dead, 114
Spy Who Came in from the Cold, The, 183
Steamboat Bill, Jr., 33
Steffens, Lincoln, 41
Stella Maris, 34, 94
Sternberg, Josef von, 135
Stroheim, Erich von, 183
Struss, Karl, 178
Suds, 108
Sully, Beth, 13, 24, 27, 61
Sully, Daniel J., 13, 61
Sunday, Billy, 38–39, 42–51, 58, 70
Sutherland, Donald, 158–159

Tabori, Paul, 203
Talmadge, Constance, 83
Talmadge, Richard, 9
Taming of the Shrew, The, 175–184, 186
Tarbell, Ida M., 41
Tarkington, Booth, 34, 39, 49
Taylor, Buck, 67–68, 70, 81
Taylor, Elizabeth, 183
Taylor, Sam, 175–176, 178–179, 181–183
Tchaikovsky, Peter Ilich, 164
Ten Commandments, The, 147
Thief of Bagdad, 49, 108, 111, 113, 139–144, 148, 155, 164–165, 170, 176, 178, 195
Things to Come, 178
Thoreau, Henry David, 56
Three Musketeers, The, 48, 108, 157, 163–168, 179
Through the Back Door, 108
Thurber, James, 86
Tillie's Punctured Romance, 103
Tirso de Molina (Gabriel Téllez), 50, 203
Toch, Ernst, 199
Toll of the Sea, 147–148
Toncray, Kate, 30
Tourneur, Maurice, 102
Traitor, The, 94
Tree, Sir Herbert Beerbohm, 21, 22
Triangle Film Corp., 19, 21–22, 24–27, 33, 35, 38–39, 75, 87–88, 102, 106

Trois Mousquetaires, 164
True Heart Susie, 69, 87
Turner, Frederick Jackson, 65
Two Tars, 87
2001: A Space Odyssey, 113

Ulman, Ella Fairbanks, 13
Ulman, H. Charles, 13
United Artists Corp., 25, 102–109, 119, 176, 191, 195, 199
Universal Picture Corp., 102–103

Valentino, R., 129, 178
Valez, Lupe, 158, 160
Veblen, Thorsten, 94
Vitagraph, Inc., 102

Walker, Alexander, 59
Wall, E.J., 147
Walsh, Raoul, 141–142, 148
Wanderers of the Wasteland, 148
Warde, Frederick, 13, 74
Wardell, Geoffrey, 179
Warren, Edward, 30
Washington, George, 55
Way Down East, 23, 69, 108
Way of All Flesh, The, 199
Wedding March, The, 149
Westcott, W. Burton, 147
West, Dorothy, 38
West, Nathanael, 56
When the Clouds Roll By, 33–34, 40, 87, 107, 110–115, 188
Whistler, James McNeill, 145
White, G. Edward, 58, 64, 72
Whitman, Walt, 55, 66
Wild and Woolly, 65, 70–72, 74–78, 81, 84, 98
Wilde, Oscar, 109
Williams, Guy, 121
Wilson, Woodrow, 105
Wimperis, Arthur, 199
Wister, Owen, 63, 80
Woman of Paris, 107–109
Women, The, 90
Wood, Leonard, 70
Woods, Frank, 23, 87
Woods, Lotta, 167
Wright, Arthur, 105
Wyeth, N.C., 150, 153

Yo Yo, 111

Zavattini, Cesare, 183
Zeffirelli, Franco, 181–183
Zukor, Adolph, 103–105, 107